The Universal Journalist

The Universal Journalist

David Randall

Pluto Press

LONDON · CHICAGO, IL.

First published 1996 by Pluto Press
345 Archway Road, London N6 5AA
and 1436 West Randolph,
Chicago, Illinois 60607, USA

British Library Cataloguing in Publication Data
A catalogue record for this book is available from the British Library

ISBN 0 7453 1108 3 hbk

Library of Congress Cataloging in Publication Data
Randall, David, 1951 Apr. 10-
    The universal journalist/David Randall.
        p.   cm.
    Includes index.
    ISBN 0–7453–1108–3 (hbk.)
    1. Journalists. 2. Reporters and reporting. I. Title.
PN4775.R365   1996
070.4'3—dc20   96–8113
                                                             CIP

Impression: 02 01 00 99 98 97 96 5 4 3 2 1

Designed and produced for Pluto Press by
Chase Production Services, Chipping Norton, OX7 5QR
Typeset from disk by Stanford DTP Services, Milton Keynes
Printed in the EC by J W Arrowsmith, Bristol

To the memory of John Merritt,
the best reporter I ever met.

Contents

The Universal Journalist

The first duty of the press is to obtain the earliest and most correct intelligence of events of the time and instantly, by disclosing them, to make them the common property of the nation.

Editor of *The Times*, London 1852

In 1992 I was invited to spend a month in Moscow lecturing on Western journalism to young Russian journalists. I had not been there much more than about three days when an uneasy feeling began to creep over me. After a week I had worked out what it was: the subject I was asked to speak on did not exist. There is no such thing as Western journalism.

Nor, for that matter, is there any such thing as Russian journalism, Polish journalism, Bulgarian journalism, or French, Nigerian, British, Dutch, Thai, Finnish, Icelandic, Burmese, Saudi Arabian or Latvian journalism. There is only good and bad journalism.

And there can be no Liberal journalism, Republican journalism, or Nationalist, Reformist, Socialist, Separatist, Federalist, Atheist, Feminist or Materialist journalism. For the extent to which journalists are producing work which serves these, or any other causes, they are not journalists at all, but propagandists. There is only good and bad journalism.

Neither are there any such things as quality journalism and popular journalism; broadsheet journalism or tabloid journalism. Nor is there commercial journalism or underground journalism; establishment or anti-establishment journalism. There is only good and bad journalism.

Both know no borders and can speak any language. For every American honestly investigating, there is another riddled with the hypocrisy of objectivity; for every African spewing out the government's lies, there is another risking death to report the truth; for every Russian probing corruption, there is another earning tainted money for writing hidden advertising; and for every Briton using brute simplicities in distorted headlines, there is another penetrating the smug secrecies of government. There is only good and bad journalism.

And the two are universal. Each culture may have its own traditions, each language a different voice. But among good journalists the world over, what joins them is more significant than what separates them. Some may work where state control of the press is a daily reality, a recent memory, or a quirk of distant history. Some may operate where information floods from every organis-ation and official; others where hard facts have to be searched for like specks of gold in the gravel of a stream. Some write where papers are but a dozen pages long; others where they are so thick with sections a grown man has trouble lifting one. But good journalists wherever they are will all be attempting the same thing: intelligent fact-based journalism, honest in intent and effect, serving no cause but the discernible truth, and written clearly for its readers whoever they may be.

This common aim gives them a fraternity stronger than any they may have with journalists whom the accidents of birth or geography have placed in the same city or country. For excluded from it are many they work alongside: those who rush faster to judgement than they do to find out, indulge themselves rather than the reader, write between the lines rather than on them, regard accuracy as a bonus and exaggeration as a tool; and prefer vagueness to precision, comment to information and cynicism to ideals. In other words, those who opt for spoon-feeding and the facile, rather than the hard, painstaking, often-exposed job of getting it as right as they can.

Good journalists, universally, agree on their role. This is, above all things, to question; and, by so doing, then to:

- Discover and publish information that takes the place of rumour and speculation.
- Resist or evade government controls.
- Inform voters.
- Scrutinise the action and inaction of governments, elected rep-resentatives and public services.
- Scrutinise businesses, their treatment of workers and customers and quality of products.
- Comfort the afflicted and afflict the comfortable, providing a voice for those who cannot normally be heard in public.
- Hold up a mirror to society, reflecting its virtues and vices and also debunking its cherished myths.
- Ensure that justice is done, is seen to be done and investiga-tions carried out where this is not so.
- Promote the free exchange of ideas, especially by providing a platform for those with philosophies alternative to the prevailing ones.

In reaching for these objectives, good journalists may be better servants of their societies than the most assiduous public officials; for their loyalty is not to states but to those who live in them. They empower people with information. That is why governments and the high and mighty try to impede them, silence them and label them subversives. They are subversives. Their work subverts those whose authority relies on a lack of public information.

That is why every year thousands are arrested, hundreds imprisoned and dozens killed. It is what Peruvian journalist Sonia Goldenburg has called 'censorship by death'. And it is increasing. In 1982 nine journalists were killed around the world. A year later the number was 14; and by 1990 it was 32. The following year no fewer than 65 journalists died for getting too close to the truth.[1] Nearly all of them were reporters, for it is by reporting that, universally, journalists have corrected abuses and shone a torch on neglect. The common ownership of information has forced new laws, reformed rotten ones and brought down governments. It is the reporter who has found things out, and the editor with the courage to publish them who are the heroes of journalism – not the soft-bottomed analysts, columnists or commentators. In the history of the press, a handful of classified advertisements have done more to change the course of events than all the editorials, comments, opinion pieces and analyses ever written.

Good journalists challenge the conventional inside their offices as well as outside them. They have ideas, they ask questions of traditional methods and want to try new ones, they say: 'Why don't we do this? Or that?', they hanker after subjects that newspapers normally do not touch, and new ways of tackling ones that they do. Whenever they hear the phrase, 'This is how we always do things', they grow restless. They do not accept the time-honoured divisions between news and features. They hate stories written to a formula. They reject the assumption that certain subjects and ideas are 'beyond' their readers. They believe that good journalism is universal in every sense.

And that must include their skills. Universal journalists are not narrow specialists. They should be able to report in all circumstances, to know how to write all kinds of pieces, to be able to entertain as well as inform; to edit, layout, understand pictures, manage staff, use new technologies, and create and sell new papers. They recognise that the best story is only theoretical raw material until it has been combined with headlines, pictures, and other material and made into a newspaper; and that a paper will merely be talking to itself until it has reached readers. They recognise that the best journalists do not just subscribe to universal objectives and try to meet them in their work, but they also have a range of skills to operate universally anywhere on their paper. And operate in an industry where the ownership, technology and information is increasingly universal. This is what this book is about: setting the standards and describing the skills of the true universal journalist.

A lot of what is here quarrels with conventional approaches to journalism and does so in a forthright way. This is born of conviction, and of 20 years spent as a writer and editor mostly in Britain, but also for periods in Africa, Russia and Europe. I have also lectured and visited papers in many other countries. It is in these places – sitting in an editor's conference in Nairobi hearing the executives discussing the chances of them being jailed for running a certain story, working with Russian journalists on stories, listening to them tell me how they do their job, and visiting the offices of the *Cameroon Post*, stripped bare of equipment by the bailiffs while its publisher languished in jail for 'libel' – that I learnt not just that each country's journalists have something to teach another's but that there is such a thing as universal journalism.

It is needed now more than ever. Technology and the political upheavals of the late 1980s have made news universal – and its impact universal. Television news film (and programmes and advertisements) are increasingly exchanged between one country and another. More and more newspapers rely on fewer and larger international news agencies to cover the world for them. Individual papers on opposite sides of the earth are asking each other to cover assignments for each other. And the new generation of communications like the Internet are accelerating those changes by the minute.

In setting out what I believe to be the right attitudes, procedures and techniques which are often at variance with accepted ones, I have no desire to try and set new orthodoxies. The aim of this book is to challenge the old ones where they are cynical and sloppy. The aim is to show that there is a way, often lots of ways, to produce honest and thoughtful journalism. The aim is to ignite a few enthusiasms, to restore a little faith in a business beset from without by the enemies of free expression and from within by traitors to its best standards.

If that sounds like romantic idealism, that is because I have never met a good journalist who was not both a romantic and an idealist. All of them were excited every day of their lives by the thought that every issue of every paper starts life as blank pages. The message of this book is that the best way to fill them is by thinking all the time about what we do, how we do it – and then asking if there's a better way.

A journalist is a grumbler, a censurer, a giver of advice, a regent of sovereigns, a tutor of nations. Four hostile newspapers are more to be feared than a thousand bayonets.

Napoleon

2

The Limitations of Journalism

Newspapers are owned by individuals and corporations, but freedom of the press belongs to the people.

Anon

Every daily newspaper ought to print a disclaimer in each issue. It would read something like this:

> This paper, and the hundreds of thousands of words it contains, has been produced in about 15 hours by a group of fallible human beings, working out of cramped offices while trying to find out what happened in the world from people who are sometimes reluctant to tell us, and, at others, positively obstructive.

There are limits to the process of journalism. Shortage of time and the frequent unavailability of information are two which are endemic to the job. So, too, are the errors that journalists make when working under pressure. Few newspapers admit to these limitations unless it suits them, such as when they have to grudgingly admit errors to try and avoid a lawsuit. Most prefer to affect a tone of entirely phoney omnipotence – a deceit whose accomplice is the impersonal 'authoritative' voice of a lot of news writing. Add poor attribution and you have something which is trying its damnedest to sound like the voice of God.

There are also limitations on good journalism which are created by journalists themselves, and by those who control or own newspapers. It is one of the great hypocrisies of conventional journalism that newspapers' coverage of events is shaped by the paper's style and something called 'news values' (that is, the yardsticks that journalists conventionally use to judge what is of interest to their readers). Would that it was all as simple as that. Instead, what shapes the quality and nature of a paper's journalism is a whole range of values: the individual journalist's, the paper's owners' or controllers', those of the prevailing journalistic culture, and then those which all of these elements perceive to be the readers' values. And there is a constant conflict between all of these values.

Most individual journalists' values are, at least when they start their careers, pretty much as described in the introduction. But the way they do the job in practice does not always reflect these values.

Other, meaner, values get absorbed from owners and the prevailing culture, and additional pressures are at work: such as the money that can be earned (or the job that can be secured or saved) by compromising those original values, threats to personal safety by the powerful, and the luggage of personal prejudices from which no journalist can entirely be freed. But, if asked to state their values, almost all individual journalists would give the ones they started out with.

Owners' and controllers' values

The values of those who control newspapers are quite another matter. They may pay lip service to concepts of truth, light and the virtuous way, but they are generally in the business to make money or propaganda or both. Whether they are the state, regional government, political party, multinational company, joint venture, solo venture, bank, oil company, wealthy individual, or sponsor, this is what they are about. The way those who control newspapers' purse strings use them for propaganda is so well attested it does not need restating in all its gory details here. Promotion of their own views, exclusion of opposing ones, slanting coverage to fit a point of view or commercial interests and pursuing personal vendettas are major themes of press history.

One example will suffice. It involves William Randolph Hearst, the American newspaper magnate who behaved all his life as if he and honesty had never been properly introduced. He it was who, when a film called 'Citizen Kane' was made patently based on his life, offered money to the studio to have the master and all prints destroyed before distribution. When that failed, he had his gossip columnist, Louella Parsons, ring studio executives and distributors and threaten them with the exposure of personal details. She told them: 'Mr Hearst says that if you boys want private lives, he'll give you private lives.'

Nothing, however, better illustrates Hearst's attitude towards journalism, and that of many other proprietors down the years, than one exchange of cables from 1898. Hearst was very anxious, for personal political reasons and circulation purposes, that there should be a Spanish–American war over Cuba. His main paper, the *New York Journal*, ran slanted, jingoistic stories with lurid, distorted headlines ('Feeding Prisoners To The Sharks', 'War With Spain for Murdering Americans', and 'The Worst Insult to the United States In Its History' to describe a letter from the Spanish Ambassador criticising the US President). He also sent his staff on all kinds of escapades to find evidence of Spanish 'atrocities'. The honest ones filed nothing (and found their careers suffering), others used their imaginations. One of the former was an artist called

Frederic Remington. Finding all quiet, and no bloodshed, he cabled Hearst: 'Everything is quiet. There is no trouble here. There will be no war. I wish to return.' Hearst replied: 'Please remain. You furnish pictures. I will furnish war.'

In so much as any single newspaper ever caused a war, Hearst was as good as his word. When, a few weeks later, the American battleship 'Maine' blew up in Havana harbour with the loss of 260 lives, Hearst ran front-page stories claiming it was Spanish sabotage. While two separate courts of inquiry tried to find the true cause of the explosion, Hearst's paper asserted it was the Spanish without the slightest shred of evidence. These stories, and those urging war, remain a perfect study in press distortion. Here is a summary of the *Journal*'s headlines and coverage for the weeks following the Maine incident:

17 February: 'Destruction Of The Warship Maine Was The Work Of An Enemy'. The cause was unknown but beneath this headline was a seven-column drawing of the ship showing wires leading from mines under it to a Spanish fortress on shore – a complete invention.

18 February: 'The Whole Country Thrills With War Fever'. This on a day when Spanish and Cuban officials were giving the victims a solemn state funeral in Havana and dedicating a cemetery to the United States in perpetuity. This was unreported by the *Journal*, whose circulation passed one million for the first time.

20 February: 'Havana Populace Insults The Memory Of The Maine Victims'. The *Journal* was now devoting an average of eight and a half pages a day to the issue.

23 February: 'The Maine Was Destroyed By Treachery'. More untruths on the sinking, plus the presentation to its readers of a 'Game of War With Spain' to be played by four persons with cards.

26 February: The *Journal* appeals to readers to write to their congressmen demanding war. This, despite the President's statement that the Maine had been wrecked by an accidental explosion of her own magazines. (The official inquiries never identified a precise cause.)

For the next few weeks Hearst concentrated on whipping up war fever and running stories of the destitution that existed in Cuba under Spanish rule. These were not difficult to find, or indeed exaggerate. Meanwhile the *Journal* continued to pour out lies about the Maine. On 11 March it reported: 'the Court of Inquiry finds that Spanish Government officials blew up the Maine'. This was not even remotely true; but it was fuel for the extra editions and banner headlines Hearst was running.

22 March: 'War The Only End To The Crisis!'

28 March: 'War Or Dishonour?' The next day the *Journal* spoke of organising a regiment of American sports champions to be sent to Cuba to defeat the Spanish.

1 April: 'WAR!' It wasn't.

6 April: 'Moving For War!' Reporters from the *Journal* were now scouring America for the families of those killed on the Maine and printing their appeals for vengeance. Such issues of the paper were now routinely covered in depictions of the American flag.

13 April: 'Congress On Verge Of War!'

It must have been almost an anti-climax for Hearst ('I will furnish the war') when Congress finally made its decision on 25 April. Hearst, however, was not finished. On 9 May, besides the paper's title, there appeared in a box the headline 'How Do You Like The Journal's War?'. This tasteless sentiment ran for another day before Hearst was persuaded to remove it. Thereafter he ordered the war reported with uncritical excitement, lent his private yacht to the navy, went himself to Cuba where he filed self-regarding dispatches, and even cabled his reporter in London asking him to purchase a large English boat which could be taken to some part of the Suez Canal and there sunk to obstruct passage of Spanish ships. Luckily the man could not.

By way of an encore, when the short and one-sided conflict was over, he launched a widows' fund, hectored the authorities to grant New Yorkers a public holiday to celebrate the victory (21 August: 'How The Journal Secured The Holiday For The People') and left no aspect of the war or its victims unexploited. He even paid for a fireworks show to tour the country with its depiction in sparks and flames of the battle of Manila. The amount of banners and the show's commentary rather gave the impression that the *Journal* – and not the US Navy – had won the victory. As Hearst said: 'Putting out a newspaper without promotion is like winking at a girl in the dark – well-intentioned but ineffective.' But then Hearst was never one for anything as subtle as a wink – he was always more a heavy breather.[1]

The Hearst episode reveals much about the misuse of journalism for propaganda and profit. Any attempt at accuracy and fairness is deliberately forgotten in the pursuit of stories sufficiently sensational to command huge headlines pandering to a known public prejudice and thus producing circulation. Although Hearst may be one of the more extreme examples, he still perfectly illustrates the imperatives behind the values of owners/controllers and the frequent conflict inside the newspaper between them and the values of good journalism. The latter is often the casualty in this conflict.

The journalistic culture

The controllers' power obviously derives from their economic force, or, in some countries, the authority they have over scarce printing or publishing resources. But they often never need to exert this power on individual journalists in an overt way, so completely have their values been absorbed by the journalistic culture that prevails on a paper or certain types of paper.

This culture is like a trade secret handed down from master to apprentice – a constantly evolving (or degenerating) received professional wisdom. It sets what editors and their executives regard as a good story or dismiss as 'boring', and determines the subjects they think of as 'sexy' and those that are not. It also creates the moral atmosphere of a paper and is thus far more responsible for the ethics that are in daily use on a paper than any theoretical commandments.

This culture determines what is admired in journalists and desired in their work. It has something to do with news value, but is better characterised as 'news instinct'. This can either be a genuine ability to see meaning and interest in what others might overlook, or, in its degenerate form, the artful technique of presenting the mundane as the unusual. This journalistic conjuring trick is normally performed by excluding context, as when, in the early 1980s, the editor of the *New York Daily Post* filled the front page on a slow news day by asking reporters to collect details of every little crime committed in the city, and then wrote them together in one breathless story under the headline 'Mayhem On Our Streets'.

Such dishonest ingenuity can always be recognised by the way a broadly accurate series of parts add up to a totally inaccurate whole. And it is not just admired on the mass-market papers where it originated. It has a wide influence on what is thought to be smart, slick behaviour everywhere. Sleight of hand with the facts, and judiciously selecting information that is then presented out of its true setting is often copied, albeit in a milder form, throughout journalism. Part of this is the unavoidable way in which any reality, which by its very nature is messy and complicated, has to be simplified, or at least have language and coherence imposed upon it, when it is related in words. A lot of journalism, however, wilfully omits context and unduly magnifies this effect for the sake of its own conventions.

The culture of mass-market papers also prizes the writing of 'great intros' and facile narratives. What is involved here is certainly some talent, but also, far more, a stretching of facts and the meaning of words to give an arresting construct. As with the conjuring tricks referred to above, the sneakiness is in the way in which some sort of plausible defence can be mounted of each component. The finished article, however, still amounts to a lie.

Neither is the writing and editing process on more serious, 'quality' papers free of this corruption. There it originates with the desk editors who talk of 'running the story through their type-writers' to 'beef it up'. Often stories do benefit from the attentions of such executives, but frequently this amounts to, and is openly acknowledged as, 'spin': that is, putting a synthetic gloss on a story, stretching the implications of each fact to the utmost and thus producing a misleading overall picture. Indeed, on many papers, the whole writing and editing process, with stories being passed from hand to hand, is like a game of Chinese whispers with the end results bearing less and less resemblance to the truth at every stage.

What is done in the editing process today is liable to be done at the reporting stage tomorrow. Reporters competing to get their stories published anticipate executive values and are prepared (or feel obliged) to adopt practices which are at odds with their private values. This professional schizophrenia is at its most chronic where the prevailing culture is known to favour stories that are comprised of vivid blacks or whites, and not the messy greys and ambiguous mid-tones of reality.

To an extent all journalism favours such stories. A story where A cheats B with provably false documents, and then uses the ill-gotten gains to live it up in the Caribbean is obviously more immediately interesting to all of us than one where A and B are in dispute over a deal, both are claiming to be cheated, and the trip to warmer climes turns out to be a business visit to service off-shore accounts. In any language, for any paper, the first version of that story would be preferred to the second. It is more unusual, it patently has greater news value.

The problem is that such preferences get, understandably, formalised into the journalistic culture. Knowing that simplistic stories of black and white are the most attractive to editors, reporters and executives look for these to the exclusion of more subtle, potentially interesting tales. Worse is the way that this view of what constitutes a 'good, hard story' can affect the research and writing and rob a story of balance. 'Don't check it out too closely' is the cynical, sniggering advice of too many news editors.

The initial versions of many stories that come to reporters are often very black and white, and therefore sound excitingly 'hard'. Further research then often adds qualifying material and context which makes the story softer, 'less sexy' in newsroom parlance. Herein lies the temptation for reporters to consciously or uncon-sciously downgrade the qualifying, contextual material, or, in more extreme cases, exclude it altogether.

It is not a very large step from this to regarding news as something to be packaged to conform to a pre-conceived recipe, or formula. On mass-market papers in particular, editors will be determined to have stories of certain types – light frothy ones or breathless, dramatic ones. Executives will hear of a story in the early stages, decide the kind of headline or treatment they want and then they or the reporter organises the facts or the treatment of them to force the story into the formula. It is journalism by headline. It presents to readers a world where the extraordinary always happens, there are only certainties and simplicities, rights and wrongs, blacks and whites, and only stereotypes exist.

These are the limitations of the journalistic process seen at their most extreme. Many papers do not go this far, but those that do, and those on other papers who have absorbed some of this process, have one standard answer to objections: the readers. No group of people are more often invoked to defend the otherwise indefensible. No group of people have their appetites more regularly or wilfully taken for granted; nor their vocabularies and intelligence more patronisingly underestimated ('Time to go and write my 200 words for people who move their lips when they read', as one British tabloid correspondent always used to say). And, in places where papers are produced for the benefit of sponsors rather than readers, no group of people are more ignored.

Readers' values

In the market-driven press (that is, one that depends for survival on selling papers at a profit) readers are the sought-after, the gods that the paper must appeal to, or wither away through a lack of them. They are the ones in whose name stories and subjects are selected, treatments applied, intros written and re-written, and presentation and design done. Yet, of all the conflicting elements in journalism – those who supply potential information (sources), those who process it (reporters, editors, owners or controllers) and those who consume it (readers) – the latter are the only ones who are not actually present during its creation. Their tastes have to be anticipated.

Newspapers in established, sophisticated markets do this in a variety of ways. They and their journalists build up over the years, through responses they have had to stories, readers' letters, telephone calls, complaints and so forth, an anecdotal 'knowledge' of what their readers want. Or rather what they believe readers want. This internal folklore may or may not produce success and it may or may not be accurate. Unless it is put to the test with some serious research, no one will ever know.

Often it is not. It is instead combined with the prejudices of journalists and executives and owners to produce a highly personalised idea of what readers want, or, what they think they ought to want. Times without number one hears in editorial conferences the phrase, 'What the reader wants is ...'. Too often this is based on the speaker's own preferences and tastes, or those of friends; or, even worse, those he or she wants to impress.

A particular danger here, apart from the general unscientific nature of these assertions, is that very often journalists inhabit circles, and have lifestyles, habits and tastes, that are far removed from their readers. They might, if they are a 'serious' journalist, mix constantly with ·uthority figures and officials and so absorb some of their values. A recent survey in the United States, for instance, found that more than 70 per cent of all news stories in broadsheet daily papers involved the doings or saying of the political elite – bureaucrats and elected representatives.

Another tendency in the United States, parts of Western Europe and elsewhere is that the payment of relatively fancy salaries on many papers has meant journalists breathe a different air, eat different meat and live a life far removed from that experienced by their readers. It takes more imagination than most such journalists have got to appreciate that the restaurants they dine at, the clothes they buy and the vacations they take are not pleasures enjoyed by their readers. And if they do use their imagination, they run the risk of conjuring up a patronising pastiche of their readers' tastes.

Worse still, are the virtual non-attitudes to readers that can be found on papers which are sponsored or have their costs otherwise underwritten. Here the market is not so much readers but more often the sponsor, or potential sponsor. At its basest, it is journalism produced to appeal to or appease the paymaster. The only way out is to produce something that enough people want and so build up a readership that makes the sponsorship redundant.

In all cases – whether it is journalists merely guessing readers' tastes, or simply never having given the matter much thought – the antidote is research. Some papers rightly devote a lot of resources to finding out as much as they can about readers: ages, male/female ratio, incomes, occupations, education, interests, concerns, tastes, how they spend leisure time, spending patterns. They use research companies to find out about these things in great detail and so know, for instance, how many of their readers aged 35–50 take vacations in France, or how many aged 25–35 own a mobile phone. The only problem is that mostly this information is collected for the benefit of the advertising department and is not passed to the journalists.

The research that normally is initiated by the editorial department is into reader attitudes both to the paper and the issues and subjects they might cover. This can either be simple surveys via a form printed in the paper, more scientifically selected 'readers' panels', or by research companies who by structured questioning find out what readers are reading and what they are not (but perhaps claiming to read).

Surveys are, however, strung about with trip-wires for the unwary. They should ask very specific questions on detailed points of the paper's coverage. It is no good asking people if they want more news – of course they will, but what kind? And what would they like less of to make room for it? Then there is the problem of respondents telling surveyors what they think they want to hear, or, even worse, stating preferences that they would like to be thought of as having, rather than their real ones.

Just after 1945, the British *News Of The World* was the largest-selling paper in what was then called the free world. Each Sunday some seven million copies were sold to people who lapped up its diet of murders and sex cases, especially those involving priests and choirboys, teachers and pupils, prostitutes and businessmen. A few 'respectable' features were mixed in. The editor had a hunch that morals and tastes were changing and so commissioned a survey to test readers' tastes. Men were hired to visit readers' homes and quiz them about what they liked, and did not like, in the paper. Since this work was done during the day, it was mainly women who answered the door. None, understandably, were prepared to say to their male inquisitors: 'Yes, I like the rape cases and the indecency, and my husband is very fond of stories about priests and small boys.' Instead, the respondents assured the surveyors that they only took the paper for the respectable features. The editor read the results, and immediately dropped all mention of sex from the paper. After just two weeks, circulation had fallen by 500,000. By the third week, the paper had a new editor, the content returned to its seedy normality and sales eventually reached 8.5 million.

Perhaps that is why some researchers now even use two-way mirrors to observe people reading a paper or uninhibitedly discussing its contents among themselves. There are even visor-like devices which fit on to people's heads, monitor their eye movement and so give a precise record of what they read, merely glance at or ignore.

If the technology or money is not available for those black arts, there are more humdrum alternatives. How many journalists have ever stood and watched people as they select a paper at the newsstands? Or studied them in bars, or on the metro, and observed how they read papers? This is all part of the unquenchable curiosity that journalists should have about readers. It should make them want to talk to them at every opportunity, meet them and get to know as much as they can about them. This is a good deal easier on a provincial paper than a big city or national one.

However, there is always the danger that having found out what readers want, it is not to your liking. Subjects, features, columns and cherished projects that you think important turn out to be unpopular, others which you think uninteresting or trivial or boring prove to be what readers hunger for. This is where journalists either swallow their pride and effect the necessary changes, or shelter behind the traditional response of those feeling threatened by unwelcome research: the methodology was faulty.

This may or may not be right, but readers do have a disorientating tendency to say they like one thing while preferring another, and publicly disdain some forms of journalism while consuming them avidly in private. This is the apparent paradox found the world over: the journalism held most in contempt in any society sells the most. For many journalists it is the truth that dare not speak its name – a realisation that their individual values as journalists and those of some, maybe most, readers are in conflict. Just how much conflict depends on how many copies the paper needs to sell and how much competition it faces.

Advertisers are the other element in the paper's audience, and for smaller circulation papers they are economically more important than readers. This commercial power is what makes many think that they are continuously exercising this muscle to intimidate papers into tailoring their coverage to suit them. The surprise is that the instances of this, and there are many, are not even more frequent. Of course large advertisers have sometimes withdrawn advertising in protest at a paper's coverage (or lack of it), many have threatened to do so and even more have tried a chummy phone call to an editor or publisher to get their way. And some have succeeded.

The dangers of this are greatest when papers, normally provincial ones, are inordinately dependent on one advertiser or group of advertisers. But far more common than this overt pressure is the influence of blocks of advertisers on feature coverage. Editors are often under enormous pressure from the commercial side of the paper to run features on certain subjects because it is known, or anticipated, that this will generate advertising. This can result in some subjects getting more attention than they otherwise would, or, on papers with no ethical restraints, certain companies and their products getting mentioned merely because they are advertisers. A lot of this is relatively harmless enough in itself, but then proves to be the precursor of more demanding attentions.

Universal standards and skills

These limitations on the journalistic process – the ones endemic to information gathering, and those imposed by owners' values, editorial culture and readers' tastes – mean that perhaps the disclaimer suggested for most papers at the opening of this chapter should be a little longer:

> This paper, and the hundreds of thousands of words it contains, has been produced in about 15 hours by a group of fallible human beings, working out of cramped offices while trying to find out about what happened in the world from people who are sometimes reluctant to tell us and, at others, positively obstructive.
>
> Its content has been determined by a series of subjective judgements made by reporters and executives, subject to what they know to be the editor's and owner's prejudices. Some stories appear here without essential context as this would make them less dramatic or coherent and some of the language employed has been deliberately chosen for its emotional impact, rather than accuracy. Some features are printed solely to attract certain advertisers.

These limitations have all the inevitability of recurring bad dreams. In the end, journalists have only one answer to them: to develop universal standards and skills and act upon them. They are our only protection. If journalists do that, they can beat the limitations. It can be done; for every day, somewhere on this planet, it is being done. Reporters are exposing corruption, uncovering negligence, revealing dangers, unmasking criminals, and reporting hard facts that someone wanted kept secret. Papers are publishing information and, to paraphrase the *Times'* editor of a century ago, making it the common property of the people. Even bad newspapers do more good than harm – and you can't say that about governments.

There is, to be sure, a lot of shoddy workmanship and calculated malice in the history of journalism. But there are far more genuine achievements to take pride in: Ilya Ehrenburg's reporting for *Red Star* that first revealed the Nazi extermination camps, John Tyas's exposure for *The Times* of British atrocities against demonstrators in Manchester in 1819, John Hersey and Wilfred Burchett's reporting from Hiroshima that revealed the official lie that there was no such thing as radiation sickness, the *Sunday Times'* campaign for the limbless victims of the drug thalidomide, John Reed's reporting of the Russian Revolution, William Howard Russell's accounts of the bungling of the British army in the Crimea, Carl Bernstein and Robert Woodward's Watergate investigation that proved a US President a corrupt liar, W.T. Stead's exposure of child prostitution, and the unmasking of the violently racist Ku Klux Klan by Roland Thomas of the *New York World*.

All these, and more, were not only legendary pieces of reporting, they were reporting that actually changed the world. But if one was to select one piece of reporting that in its quality and impact represents the best of journalism, one could do a lot worse than go back a century and a quarter to a Central Europe riven by nationalist claims and sickening violence. Any resemblance to contemporary events in that part of the world is, on the part of history, almost certainly not a coincidence.

The story started with allegations of atrocities, the simultaneous lying of several governments, censorship, and a dying empire. It drew in Turkey, Russia, Britain and a nascent Bulgaria, continued with heroism and a war, and concluded with nothing less than the creation of several new nations in the re-drawing of the map of Europe. And what drew all these disparate strands together was a former St Petersburg correspondent, an Irish-American called Januarius Aloysius MacGahan.

Even by the adventurous standards of his day, MacGahan was a thrill-seeker of the first order. In an age when men in an international hurry used the horse and the steamship, MacGahan in five hasty years reported from the Paris Commune (where he was imprisoned), the court of St Petersburg, Central Asia, Cuba, the Arctic, the Caucasus and the Pyrenees. Famously distinguished for his impartiality and sharp eye, MacGahan was also never one to shirk a challenge. In 1875 he sailed through the Arctic's ice-choked waters in a wooden boat, and two years earlier he defied a Russian embargo on reporters to make a remarkable ride over the Central Asian steppes. His goal was to catch up with a Russian military expedition on its way to Turkestan. Cossacks bent on his destruction pursued him for nearly a thousand miles but after 29 days, accompanied by two attendants, sometimes forced to wade knee-deep in sand, and several times lost, he reached the camp. His towering reputation for reliability and bravery reached new peaks.

By the summer of 1876, this 32-year-old reporter was in London with his Russian-born wife, Barbara, and a young son. He was planning a third book and some rest. But his relaxation was short-lived. The *Daily News*, a prominent liberal London paper, contacted him. They had an urgent assignment.

The *News* was in some trouble. A day or so before, on 23 June, they had published a story from their man in Constantinople, Sir Edwin Pears, based on rumours of terrible atrocities in southern Bulgaria against the Christian population by Turkish forces. The British Foreign Office was furious. So, too, was the pro-Turkish Prime Minister, Benjamin Disraeli. Describing the reports as 'coffee-house babble', he flatly denied them, and openly charged the paper with misreporting and, that old standard whine of the politicians, 'irresponsibility'. The Turks, who had imposed a total censorship on events, denied the whole thing.

It was now up to the *News* to prove their charges, or humiliatingly climb down. So they sent for MacGahan and commissioned him to go to Bulgaria and try and discover the truth. By early July, he was on his way; by the middle of the month he was there, investigating and interviewing hundreds of survivors. What he found was beyond even his hardened imaginings: the frenzied and wholesale butchery of some 12,000 Bulgarian men, women and children.

In the first of his dispatches, published by the *News* on 28 July, MacGahan wrote: 'I think I came in a fair and impartial frame of mind ... I fear I am no longer impartial, and I am certainly no longer cool ...'. His most telling account was from the village of Batak. Despite his own remarks about impartiality, it is a model of how the controlled reporting of facts, rather than emotions, is the most effective form of journalism:

> The hillsides were covered with little fields of wheat and rye that were golden with ripeness. But although the harvest was ripe, and over ripe ... there were no sign of reapers trying to save them. The fields were as deserted as the little valley, and the harvest was rotting in the soil.
>
> ... At last we came to a little plateau on the hillside ... We rode toward this, with the intention of crossing it, but all suddenly drew rein with an exclamation of horror, for right before us, almost beneath our horses' feet, was a sight that made us shudder. It was a heap of skulls intermingled with bones from all parts of the human body, skeletons, nearly entire, rotting clothing, human hair, and putrid flesh lying there in one foul heap, around which the grass was growing luxuriantly.
>
> ... In the midst of this heap I could distinguish one slight skeleton form still enclosed in a chemise, the skull wrapped about with a coloured handkerchief, and the bony ankles encased in the embroidered footless stockings worn by the Bulgarian girls.
>
> ... On the other side of the way were the skeletons of two children lying side by side partly covered with stones, and with frightful sabre cuts in their little skulls.
>
> ... As we approached the middle of the town, bones, skeletons, and skulls became more numerous. There was not a house beneath the ruins of which we did not perceive human remains, and the street besides was strewn with them.
>
> ... The church was not a very large one, and it was surrounded by a low stone wall, enclosing a small churchyard about fifty yards wide by seventy-five long. At first we perceive nothing in particular,

... but upon inspection we discover that what appeared to be a mass of stones and rubbish was in reality an immense heap of human bodies covered over with a thin layer of stones.

... We were told there were three thousand people lying here in this little churchyard alone ... There were little curly heads there in that festering mass, crushed down by heavy stones; little feet not as long as your finger on which the flesh was dried hard by the ardent heat before it had time to decompose; little baby hands stretched out as if for help; babes that had died wondering at the bright gleam of sabres and the red hands of the fierce-eyed men who wielded them; children who had died shrinking with fright and terror; young girls who had died weeping and sobbing and begging for mercy; mothers who died trying to shield their little ones with their own weak bodies, all lying there together, festering in one horrid mass.

They were silent enough now. There are no tears nor cries, no weeping, no shrieks of terror, nor prayers for mercy. The harvests are rotting in the fields, and the reapers are rotting here in the churchyard.

MacGahan's reports (which were reprinted across the world and later published as a booklet in many languages) instantly detonated a chain reaction of enormous proportions. Amid the worldwide indignation that followed, the British government was forced to concede their truth, pressure for military intervention built up and, in the spring of 1877, Russia launched a war against Turkey.

Eighty correspondents arrived to cover the Russian side but such were the rigours of the campaign that by its end less than a year later, only four of the original reporters were still in the field. MacGahan, of course, was among them. He had gone off to war with one foot in plaster, after injuring it in a fall. He ignored this, and two further accidents which seriously crippled him, and carried on reporting, watching the fighting from a gun carriage. Six months and two treaties later, the nations of Bulgaria, Serbia, Montenegro and Romania had come into being, Russia was enlarged and the British had Cyprus.

MacGahan, however, was not alive to report it. A few weeks after the end of the war, he went to Constantinople to nurse his friend, Francis Greene, through typhoid fever. Greene survived, but MacGahan caught it himself and on 9 June he died, aged 34. The Bulgarians, who had already christened him 'The Liberator', buried him in Pera, masses were said for his soul in St Petersburg and he was mourned in London, Paris and America. In Sofia a statue was erected to him, and for years afterwards his death was commemorated with an annual Requiem Mass at Tirnova.

Five years later his body was brought by an American warship to New York, where it lay in state in City Hall, and thence was taken to its final resting place in New Lexington, Ohio. That was the year when his wife, who had been the Russian correspondent of the *New York Herald*, crossed the ocean with her husband's body and became the American correspondent for the Moscow paper, *Russkaya Viedmosti*. It was also the year when an official inquiry confirmed, in the cool calm of hindsight, everything that MacGahan had written from the chaotic killing fields of Bulgaria. Universal journalism is nothing new.[2]

> *These Yankees are undoubtedly pushing fellows with a great gift for rooting out facts.*
>
> The Manager of *The Times*
> on J.A. MacGahan

3

News Value

Newspapers are unable, seemingly, to discriminate between a bicycle accident and the collapse of civilisation.

George Bernard Shaw

A newspaper's role is to find out fresh information on matters of public interest and relay it as quickly and accurately as possible to readers in an honest and balanced way. That's it. It may do lots of other things, like telling them what it thinks about the latest movies, how to plant potatoes, what kind of day Taureans might have or why the government should resign. But without fresh information it will be merely a commentary on things already known. Interesting, perhaps, stimulating even; but comment is not news. Information is.

The oft-quoted dictum on this issue was written by C.P. Scott, the editor of the then *Manchester Guardian* in a signed editorial on 5 May 1921. He wrote that the newspaper's 'primary office is the gathering of news. At the peril of its soul it must see that the supply is not tainted. Neither in what it gives, nor in what it does not give, nor in the mode of presentation, must the unclouded face of truth suffer wrong.' This is a tall, if not impossible order. But then he added, and this is the bit that has since been trotted out a million times, 'Comment is free but facts are sacred.'

The real point of this statement is what it says about the comparative values of facts and comment. If, as I have done many times, you take a room full of journalists and ask them who has got an opinion on an important topical news event, every hand will go up. Then, when you ask if anyone has some fresh, unpublished information on this event, almost every hand will go down. The fact is that almost everyone has a comment, be it interesting or not, and very few people have new information. The one is a commonplace, the other is a thing of scarcity and hence value.

So what is news? There are almost as many definitions of news as there are stories. The most common definition of news in Britain is that it is not news if a dog bites a man, but it is if a man bites a dog. This reminds us that news is the unusual or interesting. But there is more to news than that. It is also something fresh, something that people have not heard before. But we can all think of information that would fall into those categories which is not news. For example, I have bought a new car. That is fresh, it is certainly unusual, and I do not want everyone to know (local thieves, the tax authorities etc.). But it is not news because it is only of interest to a very limited circle of people (my friends and family – and possibly thieves and tax men). So news has to be not only something unusual and fresh, it also has to be of general interest.

This last is a better phrase than the one more usually employed – the public interest. This has a particular meaning in political theory of matters which are *in* the public's interest, that is, which affect the public or have an impact and significance for public life. But although that covers a lot of news, it does not cover all of it. There is also what is *of* interest to the public, what it finds interesting, and this is not always the same thing. News of a divorce between two well-known writers is not a matter that is *in* the public's interest, but it is surely *of* interest to the public.

A broad definition of news, then, is: fresh and unusual information on a subject of general interest which has not been heard before. But on the road to a full understanding of news, this definition barely gets us on to the street. That goes the same for any broad definition, which is why the commonly used phrase 'news values' is so unhelpful. It implies that news in general has values which can be applied to it. But news is not an abstract concept, nor a self-sufficient one. It only exists in relation to a number of other factors. These factors relate both to the intended audience and the specific story. They help us decide what we really want to know and – what causes more newsroom argument around the world than anything else – the strength of a story, its news value. And the higher the value, the more likely it is that readers will say 'Wow!' (or words to that effect) when they read it.

Of course, it would be good to think that every story we put in our papers was so interesting and unusual to readers that they were continuously saying 'Wow!', their eyes popping and their mouths opening and closing with excitement. Unfortunately, or perhaps fortunately, life is not like that and a lot of the stories or potential stories we consider are not in the 'Wow!' category. Where they are is somewhere in between the 'story' of my new car and that of 450 people killed when a plane carrying the President crashes on to a city department store. The huge gap in interest in those two happenings is the space in which journalists argue about news. This is where the news value factors come in.

They break down into the specific, which are matters of establishable fact, the significance of which are judged; and the general, which are far more subjective.

Presiding over these factors, and making judgements on them, are reporters and their news editor/editor. They bring their own prejudices to any judgement and, try as they might to professionally isolate these, they will never be able to do so completely. This is most obvious when they judge the basic story subject. I think homelessness is interesting and important, you think it is inevitable and boring. Such subjectivity is natural and fine, so long as journalists are aware of it and do not mistake their opinions for objective truth.

Table 1: News value factors

Specific	General
Story subject	Readers
Story development	Context
(Source)	
(Timing)	
(Knowledge)	

Reporters should also remember that the fact that they have found something out does not make it news. The 'story' they are trying to sell to their editor may have taken days and even weeks to research, they may have had to brave all kinds of difficulties and overcome all kinds of obstacles – but that does not make the story stronger. Only in very exceptional circumstances does the reader care how the reporter came by the story.

Subject

This is the broad category that the story falls under – crime, environment, health, diplomacy, economy, consumer, military, politics and so forth. All subjects are in theory equal, but some are more equal than others. Crime, for instance, has a higher value than fashion because it patently is of broader interest. Each of these first categories then breaks down into sub-divisions, for example crime into murder, fraud, abduction, racketeering, drugs, robbery, blackmail, rape, assault. For the general audience, each of these has its own rough value which is normally based on its rarity in a given society or area. This is where 'context' (see below) comes in. For instance, abductions generally have more news value than assaults because they are rarer.

Development

This is the specific happening or development within the subject and sub-division which is the point of the story. Its rarity is the main part of its value and this exists without any reference to the audience.

It is the straightforward assessment of how uncommon this particular development is. A low rarity value is the chief cause, along with a lack of timeliness, for a story being disregarded or downgraded. The development has three other elements:

Source

The strength or value of the development depends in part on the source from which it was obtained. An opposition politician might tell you that the President is about to resign, but if the President, or one of his close aides, tells you this then it is clearly a firmer story. It will be an even better story if you discover that he is about to resign, but also that he does not want the real reason known – and you know it and pass it on to your readers.

Knowledge

This is a question of how many people know about the development. The highest value attaches to stories which are the first report of a development unknown to all but the source(s), and perhaps their colleagues and private circle. The lowest value attaches to stories which are already in the public arena because they have already been reported by TV or radio or another newspaper.

Timing

News, unlike wine, does not improve with keeping. Timing, however, is not the most important of factors in itself. If you learn of a major development three weeks after it has occurred, the crucial factor is not the time lapse, but how many people have learnt of this development in the meantime. If the story is still not public knowledge, the three-week interval will not significantly reduce the news value. While shortness of time elapsing between the development happening and your report of it can add value, timing is more often a negative factor, subtracting value when there are delays which allow the story to become widely known.

Readers

This is the first of the factors that do not relate directly to the specifics of the story. The audience can be a general or specialised one, but the essential point, echoing part of the last chapter, is to learn as much as you can about them. Unless you do, you cannot possibly judge their interests and tastes and so properly judge the value of the subject and development. It would be like lecturing in a totally dark room to a group of unknown people.

But you should use your knowledge of readers to inform your judgements in general and not influence them incessantly in a detailed way. The day you see news reporting as a commodity to be calculatedly marketed is the day you cease to be a journalist. There is a point where pandering too avidly to what you think are the readers' preferences becomes also filtering to remove stories which do not fit readers' known prejudices or omitting inconvenient parts of them like context, explanations and qualification. This is important. It is part of the journalists' mission to debunk popular myths, and challenge comfortable assumptions. You cannot do that if you are too conscious of readers' reactions, too anxious to placate them. You will end up about as reliable as some eager-to-please lover who speaks only the words he thinks want to be heard.

English satirist Michael Frayn had this in mind when he wrote in *The Tin Men* of a computer being programmed to produce daily newspapers according to the results of mass surveys. People were asked what stories they liked best, how often they wanted them to recur, and which details they enjoyed. Should there be an air-crash story every month or more frequently? Is it preferred, or not, that children's toys should be found among the wreckage? If a murder is reported, should the victim be a small girl, an old lady or an unmarried pregnant woman? And should the corpse be naked, or clad in underclothes?

There are a lot of mass-market papers around the world who, equipped with their own assumptions about readers' appetites rather than any survey results, approach reporting in much the same way as Frayn's imaginary computer.

Context

This is the situation in any given circulation area (society, town, city or region) that relates to the subject and development and helps you judge rarity. This is why the news value of a story will vary depending on where it happens. It explains why a rural Danish weekly will rate the story of a shooting far higher than a New York tabloid would. In one place it is the exception, in another it is an event that happens many times a day.

Sometimes this works in what appears to be the other way, when many instances of a particular development accumulate. For instance, it may not be thought to be news if a dog bites a man. But if a certain breed of dog repeatedly bites people – and badly – then it will become news. Every single event adds to the rarity of the accumulation of cases. This is a reminder of why context should always be reported, and sometimes in substantial detail. Occasionally the context is generally known, but more often it has to be researched and so becomes inseparable from the development in the story. It should always then be reported.

Context is also important for defending journalism against the allegation that it is negative, sensationalist or only interested in bad things. For instance, if you live in a place where people entering hospital are routinely cured and cared for, then it will be news if someone is suddenly neglected and dies. To report that is often condemned as negativist. Apart from the fact that it is not the job of journalists to be either negative or positive, those who make that allegation should ask themselves what atrocious standards of medical care it would take to produce headlines like 'Man Enters Hospital and Lives'.

Once you are aware of these general factors, judging the strength of news values can really only be done on a story-by-story basis. So here are some:

- A new UN peace initiative in Bosnia.
- Government ban on the import of all foreign cars.
- Famous soap opera actress to divorce.
- Opposition politician calls press conference to condemn the president's finance policy.
- Another opposition politician calls press conference to announce he will probably stand for president.
- Four young girls murdered in small area of your city within three days by sex maniac.
- Government announces major new initiative to clean up dirty restaurants.

So what story do you think is the best? What would you put on the top of the front page? Well, of course, it is an impossible exercise unless you know what paper we are talking about and who its readers are. So try it first with your capital city's biggest-selling paper in mind, and then again with the leading paper for the businessman – your equivalent of the *Financial Times* of London, the *Wall Street Journal*, or *Commersant Daily* of Moscow. (For the record my choices would be the murdered girls for the popular and the ban on foreign car imports for the businessman's paper.)

For many years on a national paper in London, I had to make just such a choice of the best stories. I developed a set of guidelines that helped me decide the strength of competing stories. Here they are, although as with any general rules, there will always be exceptions.

At the bottom end of the scale are stories about what people are saying

These are stories about conflicts of ideas or new ideas. These are 'say stories' – nothing has happened, someone has just said something. A classic giveaway of this kind of story is the word 'warns', 'urges', or 'calls' in the headline. A May 1994 issue of the *Moscow Times*, an otherwise excellent English-language paper, once had 9 out of 13 news stories which were say stories. Were they really saying that in one of the biggest countries of the world, and one covering eight time zones, there were only four things that actually happened over a weekend?

There are two common traps for the journalist here. First is the assumption that because a politician says something, we ought to record it. Not true. Every journalist should have the motto on his or her desk, 'They are only politicians'. Just because some middle-aged man in a grey suit has chosen to make a speech or a statement does not make it news. Most speeches and statements are statements of the entirely expected. It is only when they say something we do not expect that it becomes news. A leading reformist, liberal politician condemning the slow pace of change in a society is nothing new. But if he announces his conversion to communism, then it is news.

The second trap is what has been called the pseudo-event: press conferences, interviews and the like. Press conferences are not, as some journalists seem to think, news in themselves. Nothing has actually happened. The world has not been changed one bit. All that has happened is that some politician or celebrity has wanted to make a statement, usually for their own motives, the prime one of which is publicity. The only thing that matters is the content of their message. Treat all such pseudo-events with scepticism.

Next in the scale of news values are stories about what people say will happen

These are stories about threats or demands for action. Such exhortations are over-used by politicians (and in this they are aided and abetted by lazy journalists who find attendance at press conferences so much more congenial than scuffling around looking for genuine stories). But at least they sometimes have the virtue of having good, hard information about a situation imparted along with the hot air and waffle.

Then there are stories about what people say is or was happening

These are stories about research, about people passing on to you what they have found out. Something concrete will have occurred.

At the top end are stories about what has happened

These are about developments, events, accidents, disasters, court hearings and many other hard, real, provable occurrences.

An important concept for judging news value is the number of your readers who will be affected by a story

The more people affected by an event, the stronger the story about it will be. If the readers are affected directly, then so much the better.

The more permanent the effect of what it is that you are reporting, then the better and stronger the story

Something which affects people only for a day or so is clearly weaker than something which affects them permanently.

News v Features

Medieval Christians believed that those condemned to hell had to endure the eternal torture of alternating extremes of intense heat and terrible cold. This bothered theologians greatly. If that was so, they puzzled, would the wicked and the damned have one exquisite moment as cold turned to heat? Would their thawing souls have a fleeting moment of ecstasy? And where, they wanted to know, was the punishment in that?

Similar hair-splitting debates go on between journalists over the divide between news and features. It is worth devoting a handful of paragraphs to this, if only because a lot of journalists think that news reporting is always arid, dry and impersonal, whereas features are rather jolly free-form things. They see the reporter as an earnest collector of 'facts' and the feature *writer* as someone who wanders around thinking of fine phrases which save them the trouble of doing much research.

First, there is no absolute divide between news and features. Of course there are differences – a report of 268 people dying in a fire on one hand and a gardening advice column on the other. One is a news report and the other plainly a feature. But in between these two extremes are the vast majority of stories, and at what point does a news story become a feature? When it reaches a certain length? When it lacks a certain amount of facts? When it deals with certain subjects like lifestyle and relationships that people are really interested in?

For nearly 20 years I have been asking colleagues, editors and students on three continents the apparently half-witted question: what is a feature? I have received plenty of strange looks, but, as yet, no satisfactory definition. Except one: 'a feature is not a hard news story.' True, but hardly a major contribution to journalistic science.

Definitions do not get us very far. Neither does trying to make irrevocable distinctions between news and features. They are phoney and lead to a restriction in the subjects covered and treatments given in news reporting. The false distinction between news and features has, in cahoots with unimaginative, conventional thinking, resulted in the 'news vacuum' phenomena dealt with in Chapter 6. It has also encouraged the idea that features can be a kind of fact-free zone, instantly recognisable from their lack of capital letters.

News stories and features are both reporting and shade gradually from one extreme to another. What is thought of as the conventional hard news approach is but one way of handling fresh information. There are many others, some appropriate to news pages, others less so. They are described in the news editing chapter. There are many ways of writing an article and they are discussed in the relevant chapters without laying down any laws for the treatment stories should receive. Again, the hard news approach is but one way of many.

What are thought of as the traditional approaches to news and features have much to teach each other in subject matter and treatment. Most news pages, especially, could benefit from more adventure and a more flexible approach to stories. How to do this is a recurring theme in this book. Similarly, most 'features sections' would certainly benefit from less of the 'me' columns, less vanity scribbling, and less pieces that are little more than a collection of assertions laid end to end. They need more of the thorough research and sharpness demanded in good news pages. There should be no effective divide between news and features. Best to think of it all as reporting.

> *On this newspaper, the separation of news columns from the editorial and opp-ed pages is solemn and complete. This separation is intended to serve the reader, who is entitled to the facts in the news columns and to opinions on the editorial and opp-ed pages. But nothing in this separation of functions is intended to eliminate from the news columns honest, in-depth reporting or analysis or commentary when plainly labelled.*

> Ben Bradlee, then editor of the *Washington Post*

4

What Makes a Good Reporter

A journalist is a person who works harder than any other lazy person in the world.

Anon

What reporters do is find things out. They go in first, amid the chaos of now, battering at closed doors, often taking risks, to capture the beginnings of the truth. If they do not do that, who will? Editors? Commentators? There is only one alternative to reporters: accepting the authorised version, the one the businesses, bureaucrats and politicians choose to give us.

People outside journalism (and that includes most publishers) think that what a reporter needs more than anything is the ability to write well. In fact, literary ability is only part of the job, and often not the largest part. The essential skills reporters must have are those to root out the best available version of the truth. Without those, they will have nothing worth writing, however smooth their eloquence.

What makes a good reporter, then, is a whole range of skills to find things out and record them in the proper way, some technical equipment, and a lot of mental equipment as well. And then, to make a good one, he or she will also need the right kind of character.

General equipment and skills

Time was when the only supplies a reporter wanted was a notebook and a pen. But to be successful as a reporter now and in the future, you will need a little more in the way of equipment than was good enough for the nineteenth century. You will also need a number of skills, not all of which are taught on conventional journalism courses.

Notebooks

If you need to be reminded that a reporter should always carry a pen, then perhaps newspaper work is not for you. But it is astonishing how many seasoned reporters neglect something as basic to their trade as a notebook. I have seen experienced national newspaper reporters, when asked for their notes, pull out from their pockets a crumpled collection of bus tickets and other scraps of paper covered in hurriedly scribbled notes. That kind of sight rightly worries the hell out of news editors. Neither will it look too impressive if that reporter's story leads to a law case and the bus tickets have to be produced in court.

You need two notebooks: one, as small as will slip discreetly from pocket or handbag when out working face to face with people; the second, as large as possible for working on the telephone from your office. The big size will mean you can take notes a lot better and will not have to keep pausing to turn the page. And speaking of turning pages, get a spiral-bound one, not a stapled or gum-bound one. The pages turn, lie flat and can be torn out without the whole thing falling to pieces. Each notebook should have the date it was first used written on the cover and it should be filed away when full. Then it should be kept for at least as many years as are allowed to elapse in your part of the world between publication of an article and the issuing of a writ for libel.

Shorthand

Unless you are the only human being on the planet who can write as fast as people speak, you will find shorthand invaluable, if not essential. Tape recorders break down, their batteries suddenly fade and there are a lot of circumstances, like press conferences, street interviews etc., where it is simply not possible to use one. There are also an awful lot of people who will say far more to you if they are not being intimidated by a recorder.

An awful lot more will soon tire of the reporter who keeps asking them to repeat things so they can be taken down in laborious longhand. It is like being interviewed in slow motion. Of course, what happens far more often is that you do not keep doing that and your note is incomplete or inaccurate. Shorthand is easy to learn and will be a skill to be used every day for the rest of your life. And for certain kinds of reporting, like court and parliamentary reporting, you will not be able to do without it. If it was good enough for Charles Dickens (who studied it prior to becoming a parliamentary reporter for the London *Morning Chronicle*), it ought to be good enough for you and me.

Tape recorder

Tape recorders are at their best in two situations: for face-to-face interviews and, with the right leads and connections, for recording telephone interviews, the contents of which may be contested later on. As a news editor, when someone claimed to be misquoted by a reporter or when a law suit was threatened, I was always comforted if I knew we could produce a tape recording rather than notes.

But even in interviews with a tape recorder, a notebook should be used as well. Apart from the risk of technical failure, there are two limitations of tape recorders. One is that you cannot do anything other than record voices on them, so you need a notebook to jot down your observations. The other is that listening to the tape afterwards, or transcribing it, is a lot, lot slower than flipping back through a notebook. So use the notebook to record the highlights of what is said and you need only consult the tape for confirmation of detailed facts and precise quotes.

If you are going to use a tape recorder frequently, make sure you follow the procedure you would with a notebook, and date and keep the tapes. And get one that tells you if recording has stopped. Otherwise, there you will be at the office, playing back to your news editor the exciting part of the interview where the government official admits under pressure that your city's water supply is seriously polluted and ... the voice runs out.

Contacts book

Every reporter should maintain a detailed book of contacts, with their addresses, phone and fax numbers. It is tempting to think you will not need that person's number again, but those always turn out to be precisely the ones you need to speak to again months later. When you are the only person in your office, it is 10 p.m. at night and you need some vital information, you will find out how good your contacts book is. It does not have to be a fancy leather-bound organiser (although with those you can helpfully add pages), a simple address book will do. But you should be ruthless at entering every name and number you are given or can get hold of, and use every possible means of getting hold of more. Scrounge them from colleagues and rivals, and when you read papers and magazines note down the names of useful-sounding experts and try to get their numbers. And finally, invest a day one weekend in making a copy of your contacts book for the inevitable time when it is lost.

Camera

A lot of reporters have gone, and will go, through their careers without touching a camera. But on many smaller papers throughout the world, reporters are routinely expected to take pictures. As staff costs increase and specialisation declines, more and more reporters on larger papers will be expected to use a camera. Even if that does not happen to you, the ability to use one will be of direct professional advantage. Every journalist should appreciate what makes a good picture and how it can be taken (even if that appreciation only comes from repeatedly failing to do so), for pictures are the other great component of a newspaper. And the chances are that at some stage in your career, you will be working as an editor of some sorts, handling pictures and making decisions on their use. As a writing journalist you can probably get by without being able to use a camera well, but who wants to just get by?

Computer literacy

You do not have to own one but you should know how to operate one, or rather two: Apple Macs, which are being used throughout the world to produce more and more newspapers, and IBM-compatible personal computers. The great value of computers to reporters is for research. Journalists in many parts of the world now routinely use computer databases which hold huge amounts of information: complete press cuttings services, reference systems and vast statistical records. The equipment needed to access these and other huge computer archives is getting simpler and cheaper all the time. There is more on computer-aided research in Chapter 6. And, of course, the communications work both ways. If you are a freelance, or live in a provincial region, you can use a computer to send articles to national newspapers in the capital of your country, or indeed the capital of any other.

Foreign languages

If you know at least one foreign language well enough to hold intelligent conversations, you will have expanded your journalistic horizons considerably. If you can write in that language, then even better. Speaking a foreign language does not make you a better journalist, but it will mean you are a far more useful one on your paper and it will mean you can do your job in countries other than your own.

Writing to length and deadline

A lot of reporters think it is somehow a mark of a literary talent in full flower to be late and over length. They either imagine that their words are of such extraordinary value that the editor will wait hours over time (or throw out other material to accommodate their verbose story), or they calculate that the editor needs their story, has no substitute and will therefore put up with receiving it at the time and length that the reporter decides. This is unprofessional behaviour and, unless you are God's gift to journalism (and few of us are), it will soon earn you a reputation for unreliability.

Being on time is matter of organising yourself. It is not always easy, but almost every time it is possible.

Being on length (and if there is anything worse than a reporter who overwrites, it is one whose stories are always short) is a question both of organisation and experience. If you are writing on a computer, there is no excuse for being a line over the given length. However, one good tip if you are often writing stories in longhand is to take an exercise book or paper and rule up pages with small boxes into which you write one word. Once you know how many boxes there are to each page, it is a very speedy matter to know how many words (and therefore lines) your story is making.

Attitudes

The most important equipment reporters have is that which is carried around between their ears. Some of these attitudes are instinctive, others have been learnt quickly in a classroom or in an instant in the newsroom, but most of these skills and tools are built up through years of experience; by researching and writing, re-researching and re-writing hundreds and hundreds of stories.

Reporting is one of those trades that you learn by making mistakes. I should know, I've made enough. In my first week in journalism, for instance, I was working on a small weekly paper in southern England and, by a combination of luck and my determination to make an impact, got on to a good story about river pollution. I went off, did the research and then rushed back to the office dreaming of the accolades that would be coming my way when I turned in the story. 'What the hell is this?' shouted the news editor when he read it, 'Where are all the names?' I had been so thrilled with the story that I had forgotten to ask the names of the people I interviewed. There were lots of good quotes but all of them were from 'worried resident', 'water engineer', 'safety inspector' etc. I spent the next 24 hours hardly sleeping, rushing around, getting names, re-interviewing people and repairing most of the damage. And the story lead the paper that week. I have since been so grateful for my stupidity. For I learnt two invaluable lessons in my very first week. One was that quotes are not much good without names attached to them. The other, even more important, was that reporting was a very difficult job. Clearly being enthusiastic and having a good degree was not enough; you also needed the right attitudes. The following are the key ones.

Keen news sense

You need this – and for two reasons. First, in the positive sense of knowing what makes a good story and the ability to find the essential news point in a mass of dross. Second, in the negative sense of not wasting your or your paper's time by pursuing stories that will never amount to much. Often you have to ask yourself: 'What is the best this story can be? What is the strongest news point it will have if I get all the information I need?' And sometimes the answer is that it will not be much of a tale. So drop it.

Passion for precision

As a news editor, this is the one thing I valued more than any other in reporters. Could I rely on their work and trust their accuracy? As a reporter you also speedily appreciate that your reputation for accuracy and not exaggerating, either in print or beforehand, is one valuable commodity. Lose it, and it will be very difficult to regain.

Precision means three things. First, the obvious one of recording and writing accurately what people tell you. Second, it means that you should take care that however accurate each little part of your story, the whole thing is true to the spirit and atmosphere of the situation or events. That means adding background and context. Third, you must not fall into the dangerous and widespread habit of saying, 'Well if that happened and the other happened, then this other thing must be true.' You should not wish but report your stories into print. If there are any gaps in a sequence of events that you are reporting, find out precisely what is missing, don't think that if A happened, then something else and then C, then the missing part must be B. It may not be.

Never make assumptions

This applies to all assumptions – either of logic, identity, fact or motives. Most of the time that you do make assumptions, the chances are you will probably be proved right. That is what makes assumptions so dangerous. They are so tempting to indulge in. But the dangers are obvious. Report only what you know, not what you think you know. That way you will avoid being inaccurate, dishonest and misleading – or sacked.

There was a famous occasion when a British mass-market newspaper was presented by a freelance with a picture of Prince Charles putting his arms around a lady who was not his wife at a time when he was known to be unhappily married. The paper published the picture under a headline that suggested a romantic relationship, because they assumed that was what was taking place. They were horribly wrong. Unknown to them, the picture was taken at the funeral of the woman's child, who had died of leukaemia at the age of four. The Prince was doing what any of us might have done in a similar situation – he was comforting the distressed mother.

Never be afraid to look stupid

However rudimentary your ignorance may be, if you don't know, ask; if you don't understand, request an explanation. Don't worry if anyone laughs at you. The really stupid reporters are the ones who pretend to know, who sit there nodding throughout an interview they only partly understand, and who then try to write the story – and find they can't. The place to show your ignorance is when questioning people, not on paper in your subsequent story.

Be suspicious of all sources

An essential general attitude for reporters, indeed all journalists, is to be suspicious of all sources. Why is this person telling me this? What is their motive? And are they really in a position to know what they claim to know? This complex issue is dealt with in Chapter 6.

Leave your prejudices at home

You cannot be expected to shed all your beliefs and cherished views, but, however much you cannot help them affecting your reactions unconsciously, you should never allow them to consciously affect your work. If you do, you will end up writing biased, dishonest stories. Stories like the one written by the *Washington Post* trainee with decidedly anti-military opinions who was sent off to cover Congressional hearings into the use of defoliants by the United States during the Vietnam War. Scientist after scientist testified that there was no evidence suggesting that one chemical compound, called Agent Orange, seriously affected people's health. Only one witness disagreed, but the reporter devoted his entire story to this person and ignored the testimony of the others. Medical history may in the end prove that one person to be correct, but that is not the point. Reporters are there to accurately relate what happened, not strain everything through the sieve of their own prejudices, cultured and intelligent though these may be.

This invocation applies to newly minted prejudices as well as old ones. Don't let the opinions you form early on in the research prematurely colour your judgement of the story. A great sin of some reporters, particularly those often asked to write colour and atmosphere pieces, is that they will write the intro in their heads on the way to an interview. Their intro may be smart, it may be a beautiful piece of writing, but the chances are that it will say more about them than their subject.

Realise you are part of a process

There are times when it would be good if you could write when you wanted, at the length you wanted and always on the story you

wanted. But you are subject to what editors want. By all means
argue with them, shout at them and try and sweet-talk them, but,
in the end, you have to accept their decision – or go to work
elsewhere. That is professionalism. So, too, is the acceptance of
the discipline of the schedule of your paper. Until your story is on
the page, it is only theoretical raw material. That is why your story
must be to length, on time and, if filed by telephone, you must call
your desk back later to check if they have any questions.

Empathy with readers

Unless people read your story, you might as well be muttering it
to yourself in a darkened room. They will read it if you consider
them – when you write, but especially when you research. What
will readers want to know? What do they need explained? And what
will bring this story home to them? Find anecdotes, show how the
events will impact on readers' lives, or impact on other lives; use
examples that will be relevant to their own experience; above all,
where possible, tell the story in terms of real people. Don't write
stories that are written solely about macro social and economic
concepts and impersonal organisations. Write stories that read as
though they were written by a human being for other human
beings. And finally, if your story has not got people doing things,
or having things done to them, it either needs more work or it is
not a story.

The will to win

Sooner or later the new reporter experiences dawning realisation
that the rest of the world is not run for the convenience of
newspapers. In fact, it often seems to be organised entirely for the
frustration of them. Not only do governments, officials and others
appear to be dedicated to keeping you and reliable information as
far apart as possible; but stories happen at bad times and in awkward
places, telephones are not always available or working; and, if you
are out of the city or country, you can be running out of money,
time, food, drink, and energy. This is where the will to win comes in.
    You need a strong desire to beat whatever circumstances are
strewn in your path, and get to the story and then file as fast as
possible. To be like Ed Cody of the *Washington Post*. Mort
Rosenblum's excellent book, *Who Stole the News?*, tells the story
of how Cody was in Paris one night in December 1988 when word
reached him that a Pan Am jumbo jet had crashed on Lockerbie,
a little town in Scotland. It was 8.20 p.m. and the last flight to Britain
that evening had already left. Cody found a charter operator,
persuaded his foreign editor in the United States to authorise the

cost and, a few hours later, the reporter was in Glasgow. Rosenblum writes:

> Only two cabs were left in the lot, and instinct pointed him to the one on the left. He explained how he had to reach Lockerbie in spite of police roadblocks that had sealed off the area. 'You're in luck,' the cabbie said, 'I'm from Lockerbie.' After a long, fast ride and a few sharp turns in blackness, they were in the middle of town. They split up and met later. The driver had collected as many quotes and telling details as Cody. Then he found a friend who opened his pub so Cody could call Washington. As usual, Cody scooped the pack.[1]

The crash, in which all 259 passengers and 11 people on the ground died, was one of the biggest stories of the 1980s. Cody's excellent job on it (although how did he know the quotes the cabbie gathered were authentic?) was possible because he had the will to win. He may have also had a paper prepared to pay $6,000 for a charter aircraft, but, on most occasions, a reporter's desire to get to the story will not cost as much, and it always brings rewards.

Sense of urgency

Cody, and many others like him before and since, moved fast because he wanted to beat his print and television rivals to the story. There is nothing unworthy about that motive. Readers want the earliest and fullest account they can get. To give them that, reporters have to have a built-in clock set always to their paper's time zone.

Healthy, even a little unhealthy, competition to be first is also part of the fun of the job. And it serves readers well, just so long as too many corners are not cut. Beating the rival agency, for instance, was uppermost in the minds of the Associated Press (AP) and United Press International (UPI) photographers who were assigned to take pictures of the Dalai Lama as he fled Tibet in 1959. Both chartered planes and organised relays of motorcyclists so they could get their pictures from the Chinese borders to the nearest transmitter in India. When the Dalai Lama emerged from his aircraft, the photographers leapt forward, took their pictures and ran to their already-revving planes. After a break-neck race in the air and on the ground, UPI won.

The AP man was devastated. He went back to his hotel room and sat there, full of recrimination about what might have been, and the shame of being beaten. Then he received a cable from his office: 'Opposition's Dalai Lama has long shaggy hair. Yours bald. How please?' The AP guy cabled back: 'Because my Dalai right Dalai.' In his desperation to be first, the UPI man had photographed the interpreter.[2]

Acceptable rivalry has its limits, however, and they were surely reached – and considerably exceeded – by the former *New York Post* reporter Steve Dunleavy when he was a young man on a paper in opposition to his father's one. Both were assigned the same story, and he was so keen to be first to the scene that he immobilised his father's car by slashing its tyres.

Rugged individuality

All but the most cut-throat inter-reporter rivalry is an improvement on the pack mentality which affects journalists in some countries, notably Japan. Here reporters find comfort in numbers. In September 1992, for instance, Japan sent its first troops abroad to be part of a UN peace-keeping mission. The 600 Japanese soldiers were accompanied to Cambodia by no fewer than 300 journalists, all of whom would have to be members of the *kisha-kurabu*, or club for accredited journalists.

In Japan every economic sector, ministry and political party has its own *kisha-kurabu*. Membership is restricted and these clubs control the distribution of news. Foreign journalists cannot become members, but are now allowed to attend club press conferences, so long as they do not ask questions. The clubs provide fully-equipped offices for members, and make life comparatively easy. Herein lies the danger. There are some superb reporters in Japan, but when journalists become spoon-fed, they can lose their appetite for news. Even more dangerous is when information is ladled out via a club, which is always likely to develop its own conventions and rules. Refuse to play by them, rock the boat, and you could find yourself outside the club, and its access to news.

Japan is by no means the only country where this tendency is evident. Authorities like it when journalists behave like a pack. That pack will have its own ways of dealing with its rebels and non-conformists. As governments and others the world over get more sophisticated in their management of news (and more ruthless in their control of what information they distribute and who gets it), there is more and more pressure on reporters to join the well-behaved elite with the privilege of access. At its worst, this is nothing less than a conspiracy of silence.

All around the world, reporters co-operate. They share quotes, pass on phone numbers to help colleagues and rivals. But good reporters should always be prepared to strike out on their own when necessary, to go where no one else is going, and – when it does not work out – take the flak. They are ready to spurn pre-digested meals from the official spoon because they know there is something far tastier to be found if they only go foraging for themselves.

Character

The fact that a man is a newspaper reporter is evidence of some flaw of character.

Lyndon Baines Johnson, US President 1963–1968

Almost any intelligent human being can, if they apply themselves to it, learn how to be a competent reporter. But to rise above that, to be good or great, you must have real talent and flair for either research or writing or both. And you should have, or acquire, the right kind of character. We are not talking psychological reconstruction here. No one needs to rush off and seek corrective therapy or major personality adjustment. They just need to emphasise the right aspect of themselves when doing the job; for if there is one thing that separates outstanding reporters from the ordinary, it is character.

Most of what I know about the personality of a true reporter I owe to one man. He was ten years my junior and I only knew him for a few brief years before he died from leukaemia at the sickeningly early age of 32, but he was as near to perfection as a reporter as I ever expect to meet. He was the chief reporter of the *Observer* of London and his name was John Merritt. This slim, sharp-faced young man had every virtue, and most of the vices, needed in a great reporter.

The first thing that struck me about John, even before I realised what a great reporter he was, was that people liked him. He was open-looking and he could be funny, but the reason people warmed to him was because he was interested in them and showed it with his *outgoing nature*. This did not mean that he toured the world with a fixed grin on his face, oozing phoney friendship, greeting people like a game-show host. But the ability to strike up relationships with perfect strangers was of recurring assistance to him. With rough and ready types (like fellow journalists) he could drink, smoke and swear, and with bishops he could drink tea and talk theology. Whatever he thought of people, he could be easy with them, and make them feel at ease with him.

This pleasantness masked, until he wanted it uncovered, the characteristic which is typical of all classy reporters – *determination*. John had a resolve both to find stories of the right standard and to fight through all the obstacles, delays and evasiveness that he found between him and the finished article. His determination was especially visible when a particular piece of information was proving difficult to find. Then he was prepared to sit at his desk for hours on end, making phone call after phone call, trying all kinds of unlikely places until he had got what he needed.

It helped a great deal that this determination was allied to considerable amounts of that other great reporting quality – *cheek*. He had the audacity to ring that top official at home, ask for a copy of that report or that favour from a perfect stranger. You never heard from him the poor reporter's whine of 'Oh its no good asking for that, they would never speak to me'. He was careful about the timing of his approach, but never shied away from making the call. 'The worst they can say is bugger off', he would say as he picked up the phone to try one last call – and often that call produced the goods. John was never afraid to ask.

Neither was he afraid of much else, least of all threats, hard work, big name officials or governments. This was not due to arrogance (although he had plenty of that at times), but the *passion and sense of injustice* that he brought with him to work. John was not a saint (anybody who disagreed with him in the office was soon aware of his sharp tongue), but he cared deeply about the victims of society and governments. He saw it as a major part of his job to give a voice to those who did not have one.

For him, impartiality did not mean indifference; it did not mean being inoculated against caring about wrongs in society. He believed that anger and a sense of injustice should constantly inspire journalists, informing their judgements about the subjects to be tackled, and powering their enquiries to their end. John could write light stories, but he was distinguished for the stories he wrote about the victims of torture throughout the world, the homeless and their exploitation by greedy landlords, and the appalling conditions in which the mentally handicapped were kept in places like Greece. But he was always professional – he never forgot the difference between a story and a sermon.

He also had, to an extent that was overwhelming at times, *enthusiasm*. It is easy for a reporter to be excited by a big story, but the test of their quality is whether they have the appetite to make the best of the unpromising-looking story. John had this enthusiasm, always prepared to come in early and stay late when necessary. And not just in the office. Reporters who fly at the last minute into meetings or press conferences or any other assignment and then leave at the earliest opportunity may think this is how the grownups behave, but it isn't. Good reporters often get stories by being at meetings early or hanging around late and talking to officials.

Then there was his incessant *curiosity*. He asked questions. Constantly. John Merritt was interested in anything and everything. He wanted to find out why things are like they are, what they are, why they work, or don't work. Wherever he went, he never stopped asking questions. He could probably have found a story in the middle of an empty field.

All reporters are tough, aren't they?

Everyone knows that good reporters are hard; as hard as flint. Cynical, cold, calculating and maybe even a little cruel. The sort of people who can look a corpse in the eye – and smile. A person, in fact, like Ben Hecht, a reporter with the *Chicago Daily News*. In the late 1910s and 1920s he covered every low-life, sordid kind of story that this roaring city of gangsters had to offer. His beat was the mortuary and the police raid, the courtroom and the condemned cell. His daily conversations were with killers and freaks, psychopaths and perverts. He had seen everything Chicago's dregs had to offer and always managed to keep his head and stomach from turning.

Until one day, when he attended the trial of a man who had slaughtered his entire family. It seemed like just another case to Hecht as he sat in the crowded reporters' gallery watching the murderer, a great giant of a man, stand impassive before the judge for sentencing. The judge calmly pronounced death by hanging. But then the giant suddenly came to life. Shouting the words 'Hang me, will you?', he produced from his jacket a long butcher's knife and plunged it into the judge's heart. The judge fell forward gasping out his life.

Stunned silence gripped the court. Everyone, including the hardened Hecht, was frozen. Everyone, that is, except a little reporter from a rival paper called the *Inter-Ocean*. Hecht could see him writing furiously, the only reporter out of 30 who had nerves strong enough to not be diverted from his task. He scribbled on a moment more, filling several small pages, then yelled 'Copyboy!', and a youth sprang forward to take the scoop off to the telephones.

Hecht later recalled: 'None of us in the courtroom had the presence of mind to write a single word, paralysed as we were by the attack. Yet here was this guy from the *Inter-Ocean*, who had nerves of steel, who had never paused in doing his job. I just had to find out what he had written.' Hecht ran after the copyboy, caught him by the arm, and grabbed the pages. On them, written over and over again in a shaky hand, were the words: 'The judge has been stabbed, the judge has been stabbed, the judge has been stabbed ...'.[3]

Whenever you find hundreds and thousands of sane people trying to get out of a place and a little bunch of madmen trying to get in, you know the latter are reporters.

H.R. Knickerbocker

5

Questioning

Newspapermen ask you dumb questions. They look up at the sun and ask you if it is shining.

Sonny Liston

Asking someone questions for a newspaper story is a special skill. It may at times resemble a conversation, but it is not one; it may at times be entertaining to overhear or participate in, but that is not its point. Questioning people for newspapers has one purpose: to collect information.

Interviews, whether in person or over the telephone, are not scripted affairs and you should be prepared for unexpected answers, and to follow their implications and ask follow-up questions. They will often be long, pedantic affairs, with you persisting with a question that you want answered or something that you want to understand fully. And what they are not are opportunities for you to tell that official what you think of him, show off your knowledge or engage your subject in heated debate.

A lot of interviewing is perfectly straightforward. But there are two particular situations that give trouble: questioning those who are uneasy and reluctant to talk, and those who are positively evasive or even hostile. These situations are looked at later, but first, here are some guidelines that apply to asking questions of any source.

General guidelines

Know what you want from an interview before you start

You should always have a good idea of the basic information you want from a source before you question them. Think before you question someone of the final shape that the story might take and therefore the information you will need. During the interview you should continue to think of the shape of your report, and how the new information you are getting is changing that. Above all, be aware of where the information gaps are in your story, and try at all times to fill these holes. This may sound very complicated but in fact becomes second nature after a while. And do not be afraid to write one-word clues or reminders on the flap of your notebook. Apart from making your questions sharper, this will also avoid you having

42

to contact the person again for things you forgot to ask in the interview. And, as we all know, that is sometimes not possible and so you may have to try and write the story without this information.

Do as much research as you can before the interview

You should never be afraid to show ignorance, but that is not the same as being proud of not knowing. Before speaking to someone, find out as much as you can about them, the subject and anything else that may be relevant. Apart from anything else, this will help prevent you being blinded by science or hoodwinked.

The simple questions are the best

There is not a single example in journalism where so-called trick or clever questions produced results. Asking questions like that is normally the sign of someone who is very inexperienced or more concerned with making an impression than getting the best story. Normally the simple questions are: Who? What? Where? When? How? Why? If you have satisfactory answers to those questions you will be well on the way to having your basic research done. In stories which are about events, your main concern should be to build up a chronology of what happened. When dealing with sources who know in detail what has happened, take them back to the beginning of the event(s), or before, and ask them to take you through all the stages step by step. Don't be afraid to keep asking: 'And then what happened?' Get the sequence of events totally clear in your mind. This is vital for incident-type stories, like crashes. At the end of your research, you must be able to run in your head a minute-by-minute video of what happened. If you can't, then your story has holes.

Take them through parts of the story in slow motion

On a lot of incident stories you will be questioning people who have actually been part of the event, or witnessed it. Few of them will be used to giving a coherent account of such things, and they may be excited, shocked, distressed. So when you get to the core action, slow them right down and get every detail that you can. Ask them what happened at every moment, what they saw, the colours, smells, noises. Ask them where they were standing, what people were wearing, what they shouted, what the weather was like.

Check names and positions

Obvious, boring to do, but essential. Ask sources to spell out their names and titles and their ages, addresses if you need them.

Sometimes, if it is a really awkward or foreign name, get them to write it in your notebook. You may think that will make you look silly, but not half as silly as if you get back to your office and find you do not know how to spell their name.

Get as many telephone numbers as you can

This is as basic as getting your subject's name right. Get their office phone number if you do not already know it, their home number if you can and their mobile telephone number if they have one. You may also need their fax number. In some countries, collecting the numbers of someone you are seeing is not difficult because the number is printed on the phone. If it is not, ask.

Get too much information rather than too little

Most times you get only one main chance to interview an important source. Make sure you take full advantage of that by asking all the questions you can. And it is worth bearing in mind that however experienced you are, you never know the final shape of stories until you sit down to write them. It is then that you will be grateful that you asked that extra question.

Do not be afraid to look stupid

We have all been in that situation where someone is talking to us about something and we sit there nodding and agreeing even though we do not have the faintest idea what they are talking about. We are afraid that if we ask them to explain we will look stupid. And then we come to write the story and realise that we really need to understand what it is we have just spent the last few hours pretending we understood.

Never, ever be afraid of looking silly by asking basic questions. First of all, people, even in press conferences, will rarely be so rude as to snigger at your ignorance. And, if they do, so what? Who is the most stupid, someone who pretends to know or the person who does not know and admits it? If you don't know, don't make out you do, ask. Nearly every source is prepared to explain specialist concepts to reporters and most of them will do so happily because someone is interested in their subject.

If in doubt, describe your understanding of a situation

If you do not understand an answer, or if the situation you are reporting on is confusing, then put your understanding to those you question. Never be afraid to say: 'Can I just go over this. It all

began when ...', or 'Can I just see if I understand you correctly
...', or even 'If I wrote that ... would I be right?' This is a standard
technique. It does not imply you are slow-witted. And even if it
did, so what? Better that than an ambiguous, or wrong report.

Ask questions to get information, not opinions or reactions

You are talking to sources to get facts and each question should
be designed to do that. It is very easy to fall into asking questions
about their reactions to something. But reactions are rarely surprising
and so you will not have collected anything that is useful to your
story. The knowledge, for instance, that a right-wing politician dis-
approves of liberal reforms is hardly news. The only exceptions to
this, of course, are when the story is about opinions.

Try to avoid asking cliché questions

To ask someone who has just been involved in a tragedy 'How do
you feel?' is to invite a clichéd answer at best, or a flat refusal to
answer any more questions. If they have just lost their only son in
an air crash how do you expect them to feel? Thrilled? Yet every
day you can see in news stories the most predictable emotions ('I
was excited to win this money', 'We are very upset to be sacked
without compensation') paraded as if they were devastating insights.

Probe for anecdotes

Good anecdotes can add a tremendous amount of life to stories.
Collect them at every opportunity from people you are questioning. But remember that getting people to discharge amusing, ironic,
telling anecdotes is a matter of getting chatting in a relaxed way,
not sitting bolt upright opposite them and saying, 'Now tell me the
funniest thing you ever saw/experienced.' They won't. Their mind
will go a blank. Instead try and get some feel for the areas of their
life/work/activity which are likely to provide humour. For instance,
if you are interviewing airline cabin crew for a story about a new
service and you want a couple of yarns about passengers' crazy
behaviour, then don't say, 'Tell me the silly things travellers do.'
Instead, naturally edge the conversation around to drunkenness,
fear of flying, luggage, complaints about food, kids, strange requests
and so forth.

Don't let them bullshit you

You should obviously ask for all jargon to be explained. But a lot
of phrases that sound like technical talk are, in fact, euphemisms.

Each industry, company or bureaucracy evolves phrases to camouflage reality. An airline will talk about 'passenger underflow', when what it really means is that not many people want to fly with them. An investment fund might issue a statement about a 'net liquidity export situation' when what they mean is that their investors have finally rumbled them and are taking all their money out.

Institutions which deal with dangerous materials, like the military and nuclear industry, are especially adept at evolving this kind of bullshit. Towards the end of the Vietnam War, a US military spokesman, Col David Opfer, told a press conference held after a bombing raid: 'You always write it is bombing. It's not bombing. It's air support.'

In America, following a famous accident at Three Mile Island in 1979, the nuclear power industry came up with a potentially bewildering series of euphemisms to describe bad things. Statements talked of an 'abnormal evolution' at a plant which had led to an 'energetic disassembly' and then a 'rapid oxidation', perhaps followed by 'plutonium taking up residence'. What this meant was that there had been an accident at a plant which led to an explosion and then a fire, followed by plutonium contamination – all of which straightforward words and phrases were banned. Unban them. Ask what they mean.

Listen to the answers

It is easy to be so concerned with rattling off the next question, or taking down the answer, that you fail to really hear the significance of what is being said to you. Ten minutes after questioning someone is often too late to realise the importance – or absurdity – of what they have said. This is especially true when people make extraordinary claims in interviews.

The French novelist George Simenon once told a reporter from the Swiss newspaper *Die Tat* in 1977: 'I have made love to 10,000.' The paper reported the claim with apparent credulity. However, even the least numerate of brains should be able to calculate that, to reach this total, Simenon would have had to make a new conquest every other day for about 65 years – no mean feat for a man of 73 who had also found time to write nearly 100 books. The real total, according to his tolerant wife in an interview some years later, was nearer 1,200.

Review the answers at the end

If at all possible, go back over your notes with people and double-check figures and anything of which you are still unsure. Apart from these overt purposes, this process has two covert ones. First, to see if you can discover any holes or 'information gaps' that have escaped you, and second, to see if you can squeeze a bit more information from the person. Ask them at this time if there is anyone who can support their contentions, or, for that matter, who their critics are.

Never make promises to sources about how stories will be treated

Only the editor is in a position to know how a story will be treated and appear in the paper. A lot of the people that you question will ask this question, but you do not need to answer it. Tell them you are 'just a reporter' and give them your editor's name and number.

Off the record, background and anonymity

This is one of the great daily dilemmas of reporting. People often ask to go off the record, and sometimes you offer it because you fear that otherwise they would not speak to you at all. There are two basic points about this. First, use 'off the record' as sparingly as you can. If you don't, you will end up with all of your sources ones that you cannot name. Second, get it absolutely clear with your source what you have agreed. That way there will be no subsequent argument. Are they giving you material which you will have to confirm and source with another party if you want to use it (background)? Or are they giving it to you on an unattributable basis, in which case you can use it, but not use their name. There are enough journalists who are confused by these terms; make sure that when an interview subject uses a phrase like 'off the record' it means the same to them as it does to you.

The main thing to remember is that you do not accept their reluctance to be quoted without a fight. Keep on at them to go on the record. Argue that the importance of the story depends on verification from named sources. If they persist in wanting to talk 'on background', keep on with the interview and then, at the end, try and find something that they might be happy to be quoted on, and then edge them towards going on the record. Negotiate. And do not let people speak freely to you and then, at the end of the interview, say to you: 'Oh, by the way, that was all off the record.' The rule is: it is only off the record once you have both agreed that. Once you have an agreement, never go back on your word. Do not name them in the story and, if they wish to be on deep background, tell no one except your editor who they are. Especially do not tell your colleagues. There are no bigger gossips in the world than journalists.

One of the main problems with 'off the record' is the way it has been picked up by politicians and their advisers and used for their own sometimes shady purposes. To illustrate this, here is a case that was given at a Harvard University seminar on journalism in Moscow:

> You have been called in for a rare personal interview with a senior presidential adviser. He tells you that everything he will say is off the record. During the interview he tells you about a major change in economic policy. You are excited by the story and rush back to your office and write it, quoting 'well-placed government sources'.

Well, it turns out that the President intends no such change, that the adviser knew that when he spoke to you and was feeding you the story to deal with some other problems that the government had in the Duma. Meanwhile, you look a complete fool.

There are several morals from this story. First, you should have tried to get a second source. Then you should recognise that leaders will often seek to use the press to their political advantage. They will hide behind 'off-the-record' comments in order to pursue their agendas without penalty. Don't let them flatter you into getting away with it. They are only politicians.

A good general rule is that if sources want to make an attack on an individual, organisation or country, they must make it on the record. Otherwise it is too easy for the unscrupulous and cowardly to shelter behind anonymity to make their attacks.

Questioning uneasy sources

A lot of people are rather intimidated by journalists. This is not because they find them frightening as people (although some most definitely are), but because they are not used to dealing with the press. Even if they are, they may be reluctant to talk because they fear losing their jobs or other repercussions. As one who has several times been involved in a news story and therefore a person whom journalists have wanted to interview, I have found it unsettling to be on the receiving end of journalism. You worry about what you might say, or be quoted as saying.

The reporter's first job with people who are uneasy is often to persuade them to talk at all. When doing this, you can be friendly, light-hearted, talk about the public's right to know the information they have; in fact, whatever you may think will work. But do not make promises – about the paper's coverage, for instance – that you are in no position to keep.

Often, however, you do not have the chance to negotiate first. You are 'cold calling', that is, visiting them without any preliminary telephone call to set things up. In these circumstances, just getting past their front door is a problem. The important thing here, as the following quotation illustrates, is to get inside their living room or office. Once you are there, it will be a lot more tricky for the subject to refuse to answer any of your questions. Once inside, the trick is to find ways of staying as long as possible.

This story comes from the book *All The President's Men*, written by Carl Bernstein and Bob Woodward of the *Washington Post* to describe an investigation they mounted which led, eventually, to the resignation of President Richard Nixon. Their reporting, and the story behind it, is looked at more closely in the next chapter. For now, all you need to know is that Carl Bernstein is convinced that the woman who he is trying to interview is a potentially important source about the activities of her employers. This is why he is visiting her in her home and her anticipated reluctance to talk is why he has not telephoned first:

> A woman opened the door and let Bernstein in. 'You don't want me, you want my sister,' she said. Her sister came into the room. He had expected a woman in her fifties, probably grey; it was his image of a Bookkeeper, which is what she was. But she was much younger.
>
> 'Oh, my God,' the Bookkeeper said, 'you're from the *Washington Post*. You'll have to go, I'm sorry.'
>
> Bernstein started figuring ways to hold his ground. The sister was smoking and he noticed a pack of cigarettes on the dinette table; he asked for one. 'I'll get it,' he said as the sister moved to get the pack, 'don't bother.' That got him 10 feet into the house. He bluffed, telling the Bookkeeper that he understood her being afraid; there were a lot of people like her at the committee who wanted to tell the truth, but some people didn't want to listen. He knew that certain people had gone back to the FBI and the prosecutors to give more information ... He hesitated.
>
> 'Where do you reporters get all your information from anyhow?', she asked. 'That's what nobody at the committee can figure out.'
>
> Bernstein asked if he could sit down and finish his cigarette.
>
> 'Yes, but then you'll have to go, I really have nothing to say.' She was drinking coffee, and her sister asked if Bernstein would like some. The Bookkeeper winced, but it was too late. Bernstein started sipping. Slowly.[1]

The woman talked, gave Bernstein some very useful leads and later spoke again to both reporters and proved a valuable contact. This may have had something to do with the fact that Bernstein did not immediately pull out his notebook and begin taking down every word the Bookkeeper said, while pulling faces of delight and amazement. He waited, maybe ten minutes before slipping the notebook out of his pocket and starting to casually make notes.

If, however, people have agreed to talk, the next thing to think about is how to make them feel at ease. This will help you get the most out of them. Here are some tips.

Think carefully about where and how to speak to them

Will it be on the phone or face to face? What will be best for them If it is face to face, where will it be? In a bar? In their office? At your office? Over a meal? In their home? In other words, in which environment are they least likely to feel threatened and, therefore, most co-operative?

Adapt to them

Your aim when interviewing someone is to get them feeling relaxed and helpful. This means not intimidating them or annoying them. This means you may have to adapt your behaviour and appearance a little. You do not have to undergo a personality change for each interview, but you should consider your subject. For example, if you are going to interview homeless people on the streets, you would not wear your best suit or dress. That would make your subjects feel uncomfortable. Similarly, if you were going to interview the Prime Minister, you would not wear jeans and a T-shirt. They would probably be offended at that and think you were more concerned with making a statement about yourself than in getting a good interview – and they would probably be right. With people with whom you would have no natural rapport, you may even have to act a little, and feign interest in them or adapt to them. If they are a formal sort of person, be more formal than your usual self; if they are very easy-going, then you can be too.

Make a judgement about them

What will get them on your side? Flattery? Friendliness? Jokes? Serious talk? Whatever it is, if they are an important source, do it. What interests them? Whatever it is, take an interest in that too. This is always easier if you are meeting them, especially in their home or office. People surround themselves with what is important to them – pictures of their family, paintings of their favourite places, ornaments and mementos. Use these things, ask them about them. Make the person want to help you.

If you have time, try the 'life story' ploy

If your subject is shy, or antagonistic to you, but seems to have time, try asking questions about their life story. These are basic resumé questions – where raised, educated, trained, first worked, success, achievements, overseas experiences etc. It may give you some promising avenues for questioning. If not, it will almost certainly put that person more at ease and more on your side. Almost everyone warms to someone who seems interested in them.

If the interview is in person, don't get out your notebook immediately

There is nothing that will unsettle the uneasy interview subject more than a reporter marching into the room, notebook open, pen poised over it, ready to take down every word they say. Instead, gradually slide it out of your pocket or handbag when they are relaxed and begin writing then. You can even say something like, 'Do you know, I have a terrible memory, do you mind if I make a few notes?' Occasionally your judgement is that any appearance of the notebook will get them to immediately stop talking. In this situation, commit the important things they say to memory and make an excuse to leave the room (such as to go to the toilet or wash your hands). As soon as you are out of their sight, you can then write down the highlights of what they have said.

Be honest about your intentions – but don't tell people everything

You should never fail to declare yourself as a reporter (except in very rare circumstances – see Chapter 7). Neither should you misrepresent your interest in talking to someone. However, you do not always have to explain precisely why you are calling someone. If you have a controversial issue or question in mind, you would often be wise not to spell this out when you start talking to someone. Just say: 'I am just making some general inquiries about this subject.'

Do not come straight out with your main question

Ask some general questions first. These could be questions to which you already know the answer. If nothing else, the subject's answers will tell you what they know and how honest they are. Only when you think they are ready should you ask what you are burning to know. When you do, it may be better to feign indifference to the answer. Dropping your notebook in amazement and exclaiming 'My God! Do you realise what you are saying!' is not the way to react. The thought that they have just given you the story of the decade is liable to produce an almost immediate retraction.

Use the pregnant pause

If the person you are questioning does not fully answer the question, then try a pregnant pause, accompanied by an expectant look. Sometimes they will respond by adding the extra information you need. There is, of course, a limit to the length of time you can try and out-wait them. Delays of more than a few seconds are liable to be construed as idiocy or the onset of some serious disorder of the nervous system.

If all else fails, throw yourself on their mercy

Tell them that you will be in trouble with your editor if you do not get this information. Ask for their help. It often really works.

Keep the conversation rolling

When faced with 'I can't comment', don't attempt to deal head on with their anxieties. In almost every case you will lose that argument because their reasons are to do with their position or organisation and they obviously know more about that than you do. Instead, keep the talk going and try several other tacks. First, reassure them that talking to you is no shocking departure, many other people have spoken to you. Then, without pausing, say, 'What puzzles me is ... Can I ask you if ...'. Try sympathising, but then go straight on with your questions.

Questioning evasive and hostile sources

Some of the ways of dealing with the uneasy subject will also apply to the evasive or hostile subject. Yet, more often, a different approach has to be taken with the potential source who is avoiding you.

Be persistent

Getting hold of such subjects is sometimes extremely difficult. Never give up. Keep calling them, visit their offices. Make them realise that the only way to get you off their backs is to agree to talk.

If telephoning, do not be fobbed off with, 'He will call you back'

Many people have no intention of doing so, despite what they or their secretaries or colleagues say. Do not accept this. Say you will hang on, say you will ring them back or, in a few cases, agree to be rung back – but fix a time for them to ring you back. If they do not do so, ring them back. Better still, ring them back an hour before the set time. Many people will say they will ring you back at 4 p.m. because they know they will be leaving their office at 3.30 p.m.

If someone is stonewalling over a factual answer, put options to them

If, for instance, you need to know how much the government paid for a certain contract and the person who knows is refusing to give you the answer, try putting sums of money to them: 'Is it $6 million?', 'Is it as much as $12 million?' Such questioning often produces results, or good hints. Yet be careful with this technique, make sure people understand what it is they are being asked. It and similar verbal games can lead to confusion.

The most notorious occasion of this was during the *Washington Post*'s Watergate investigation referred to earlier. The reporters had a very good story, but only one source for it. Their editor insisted on two before he would publish. So, late at night, one of the reporters rang the only other person who might be able to support the story. He would not do so directly; so the reporter said:

> I am going to count to ten, if the story is wrong, hang up. If it is correct stay on the line.' He then began counting, 'One, two, three, four, five …' His voice was now getting excited. '… Six, seven, eight, nine … ten.'[2]

He put the phone down and excitedly told his waiting colleague and the editor that they had confirmation and the story ran. The only problem was, it was not true. The late-night contact had misunderstood the instructions from the reporter and thought if he stayed on the line, he was letting him know the story was not right.

Occasionally, try pretending that you know more than you do

If you strongly believe something to be true, but cannot get confirmation of it, ring a source and say you are just calling for confirmation of the facts, or comment on them. For instance, try asking the official *why* something happened, rather than *whether* it happened. They often then start explaining rather than denying. This, however, is something only experienced reporters should do.

Watch out for non-denial denials

A non-denial denial occurs when an accusation is put to someone and, instead of denying it, they make a statement which insults the person who is making it, or the reporter, or both. Asked, for instance, if the government contract has been neglected and millions of dollars over-spent, the subject would reply: 'Your sources do not know what they are talking about.' That is not a denial of the claim. It is often the classic ploy of the person with something to hide – but don't rely on that.

Watch out for uninvited denials

Unlike the situation described above, people with something to hide can sometimes go further than your question requires them to go. When asked for a comment, for instance, they deny things you never put to them. Be alert to this, it sometimes comes out of the blue and is the first indication you have that they have something to hide.

Do not use 'set-up' questions

These are the questions that try to trap someone, not with information, with a verbal trick. The fact that the trick is not very original does not stop it being used. It is a variant on the old 'have you stopped beating your wife?' question, to which the unwary might answer 'yes', implying they used to beat their wife but have now seen the light and stopped, or 'no', meaning they never started but instead conveying that they still beat her.

One of the occasions when this was used most flagrantly was when rumours were flying around Britain's national papers that Prince Edward, the Queen's fourth child, was gay. The *Daily Mirror* pursued him to New York and, at a public event, shouted out the question: 'Are you gay.' The Prince was naive enough to say 'No', and the next day's *Mirror* appeared with the huge front-page headline: 'I'm Not Gay Says Edward'. The impression readers were left with was that Edward was indeed gay, but was now strenuously denying it.[3] Nasty reporting.

Ask them to imagine how 'no comment' will look in the paper

If an official is refusing to comment or answer questions, ask them to visualise how this will look in the paper. But don't make it sound like a threat. Make it sound like you are trying to save them from a public relations disaster: 'You know the readers will see "X declined to comment" and they will think you have something to hide. Now I know that isn't the case, so can I just get your answer to …'.

Only be aggressive as a last resort

Sometimes, however hard you try, people will persist in refusing to speak to you or comment. Only when you are convinced that nothing else will work should you ask them if they really want to be quoted in the paper as having declined to comment. Very rarely this produces a sudden and full answer to your questions. But more often it is your admission of defeat, and their way out.

Finally, remember that a person may refuse to talk to you one day, and be more amenable a few days later. If they are an important source, try again.

Press conferences

Press conferences are obviously a special case when it comes to questioning. You are not alone, you are not face to face and you often have little time. If that is the case, and you have to file a story immediately after the conference ends, then make sure you or other people ask the questions you need answered. That can sometimes mean being aggressive, shouting your question so that you are sure it is heard, or standing up to ask it.

A lot of people who call press conferences seem to imagine that the event is one where they can hold court before a group of docile note-takers. No reporter should ever let that idea take root. These events may be organised solely for the purpose of generating publicity, but that does not mean you have to play their game. You decide what the story is, not them. Never mind what they think is the message of significance, is there another, better story?

Similarly, some press spokespersons show an extraordinary reluctance to give a clear answer to even the simplest questions. Consider this, from a White House press conference given by American President Richard Nixon's press secretary Ron Ziegler in 1974. He was asked if certain tapes which may have recorded the President discussing illegal actions were still intact. (The courts had ordered the White House to hand over these tapes for use as evidence.) The question seemed to demand a straight 'yes' or 'no'. Instead, Ziegler gave the following 99-word reply:

> I would feel that most of the conversations that took place in those areas of the White House that did have the recording system would in almost their entirety be in existence, but the special prosecutor, the court, and, I think, the American people are sufficiently familiar with the recording system to know where the recording devices existed and to know the situation in terms of the recording process, but I feel, although the process has not been undertaken yet in preparation of the material to abide by the court decision, really, what the answer to that question is.

This statement is, of course, unintelligible nonsense, and no reporter, either in the press conference or writing the subsequent story, should let spokespersons get away with that kind of non-answer.

Life is going to be a lot easier if you have some time and can save your own questions for after the press conference. In that case, do not let the person who can answer them leave the room until you have asked and been answered. That can sometimes mean standing between them and the door. Don't be shy of doing that. Any person who regularly gives press conferences will be used to this. You are not there to make friends but get a story.

Another tip is to watch and try to note if there is another reporter there who seems to know a lot about the subject. After the conference, engage them in conversation. Most reporters cannot resist showing off what they know, who they know and thereby passing on some valuable leads. Don't take other people's reporting on trust. But you will often pick up some good ideas to follow up from such conversations. This is a reminder that often the real benefit you derive from press conferences is meeting people and making contacts rather than the ostensible story.

Personality interviews

The bigger the personality, the less time you will often have. And very big ones could well have press agents in attendance, who try to set limits to the subjects you can ask about. It is your job to evade such controls where possible. You are a reporter, not a courtier. If time is very short, don't waste it by asking questions that can easily be verified by a little pre- or post-interview research. Instead, especially if you are writing a profile, it is often a good idea to ask questions that will enable you to compare the personality with their public image.

If you are new to such interviews, here are some general questions which are often useful probes for unexpected answers, or areas of life that the subject is willing to open up about. Some of these questions are useful ice-breakers for any kind of face-to-face interview. They are based on a list filed by Jeremy Martin to the CompuServe Journalism Forum, an excellent source of professional debate and tips.

- When did you get your first kiss?
- Who was it and how did it happen?
- What is your first memory?
- What was the first thing you learned?
- Who taught it to you?
- Who was the biggest influence on your mind, when you were a child?
- What was your mother's/father's best advice?
- Who has had the most impact on your life?
- What didn't you learn in school?

- What have you had to teach yourself?
- What was your first job?
- What was your worst job?
- When did you decide on your career?
- What would you have done if not that?
- Who was the first person you cared for?
- What was the first thing that you bought?
- What was your first car?
- Did you buy it yourself?
- Who was your first love?
- How long did it last?
- What do you do when you are nervous?
- What are you compulsive about?
- Have you got a bad temper?
- What do you cook?
- What do you eat/not eat?
- Who is your best friend?
- What is your worst habit?
- What are your good/bad habits?
- What makes you cry?
- What makes you angry?
- What makes you smile?
- Would you prefer another name?
- What do you study?
- How often do you read?
- How does driving make you feel?
- How many hours a night do you sleep?
- What do you do if you wake in the night and can't get back to sleep?
- What do you have dreams about?
- How do you answer the telephone?
- What does your answerphone message say?
- What do you do every day?
- What is your ideal day off?
- Have you ever felt cheated?
- Do you handle your money in detail?
- Do you love your work?
- What gifts do you think you have?
- How do you challenge yourself?
- Are you challenged now?
- If you have a setback, how do you react?
- Where will you be in one year?
- When do you plan to quit?
- Who have you hurt along the way?
- Who would be your favourite party guests?
- Do you like Christmas?

- What is your favourite cliché?
- What is your favourite song/book/film/singer/artist?
- Who do you admire most?
- What is your favourite drink?
- What will you not eat?
- What could you never do?
- Where is your favourite vacation place?
- Where would you live if you had total freedom of choice?
- What is your favourite cartoon character?

The most guileful among the reporters are those who appear friendly and smile and seem to be supportive. They are the ones who will seek to gut you on every occasion.

Ed Koch, Mayor of New York

6

Sources

When the call comes in the middle of the night, a fireman only has to put on his pants and extinguish the flames. A correspondent must tell a million people who struck the match and why.

Mort Rosenblum of Associated Press

The best stories come from nowhere. They come out of the blue when you are least expecting them, and are so extraordinary that no one would dare make them up. Who, after all, a few years ago, would have thought that they would be writing a story about a Russian passenger plane that crashed because the pilot let his teenage children take the controls?

But stories like this are in a different class from most of what fills our newspapers. They are events, accidents, incidents and catastrophes of national or international importance. In most cases they happen and are very quickly known about by all media. At the opposite end of the spectrum are those many stories which can be anticipated in advance, such as press conferences, formal announcements, elections, the release of reports, openings, closings and court hearings. These are diary stories, recorded in a news desk diary and coverage of them planned in advance.

Journalists cannot do much about influencing whether there are disasters or court cases to cover. But off-diary stories are different. Most of them do not have any kind of public existence until a reporter recognises the potential of a few disparate facts and begins sniffing around. So where do good, off-diary stories come from?

Well, they don't, unless in exceptional circumstances, come from commercial press releases, press conferences (because they are diary events for all media with nothing more dramatic happening than a speech), most of the mail that arrives at your news desk or from people who call you up and say 'Have I got a story for you!' Neither do they ever come from that regular supply of lunatics, paranoids and obsessives who seem to be attracted to newspaper offices the world over with their tales of being followed, transported to outer space or persecuted by the government.

Good, exclusive, off-diary stories come from opening up your mind to unconventional sources and subjects and thinking beyond the narrow confines of what most journalists regard as a news story. They come from realising that every area of life is full of potential stories. They come from a determination to fill the 'news vacuum' – that great cavity which exists when journalists think too rigidly of news as something official, and regard the really interesting aspects of life (relationships, families, working etc.) as belonging in the features sections. They are wrong. If it is new, unusual and interesting to your readers, then it is a story, or at least potentially one. Such stories come from something you hear in a bar, see on the street, discover in a long, otherwise boring official report, or unearth in a million and one other places. They can be found, in short, anywhere. Since that statement is only a limited amount of help, let me try and give some concrete suggestions.

Potential sources

Contacts

It helps if you keep up a regular relationship with your contacts and do not just ring them when you need them. You may also need to cultivate them socially, or occasionally pass information to them. Do this well, and in a friendly spirit, and your contacts will remember you when they have a good story and will call you with it. Less regular contacts will also remember you if your reporting was good and accurate when last you dealt with them.

Politicians

These should be among the prime contacts of reporters. They are a lot closer to what is happening inside the local or national administrations than you are and, if you develop a relationship with them, will give you stories. Generally these will only be those which help their own causes(s), but, providing you recognise that, many of these stories will be no less genuine. Build a really good relationship with them and they may start to assist you in all kinds of ways. A governing party politician whom I knew was instrumental in smuggling into Iraq one of the *Observer*'s top foreign news experts so he could investigate reports we were receiving about atrocities committed against the Marsh Arabs by Saddam Hussein. Without my relationship with that politician, her contacts with rebel groups in Iraq and their bravery, we would not have been able to get inside southern Iraq and the world would not have heard about these atrocities.

Official reports

It is difficult to stifle a yawn when you see the cover of most official reports. But in many of them, perhaps buried away on page 94, is a real piece of dynamite. In fact it will probably be deliberately buried away on page 94 in the confident expectation that most journalists will not be bothered to read that far or that closely. Be the exception. You will be rewarded.

Pressure groups

These are the organisations, like Greenpeace, that are privately funded or charities, that exist to promote a particular good cause. They may operate in the field of the environment, civil liberties, wildlife conservation, transport, women's rights, health, children's welfare etc. In every country in Western Europe there are thousands of such groups, all of them researching, producing reports and willing to help any journalist who is interested in their subject. For many European reporters, especially those who operate in a special area, these pressure groups are one of the chief sources of good, off-diary stories.

International organisations

There are thousands and thousands of international organisations pumping out reports, statistics and data, holding conferences and seminars and staffed by experts who never hear from a general newspaper reporter from one year to the next. This is a great shame. Organisations like these are one of the great untapped sources of stories. And by no means just stories about global problems. Much of their work is studying or working on specific problems in particular countries. Go to a library, look up the organisations covering your area of interest and make contact. The United Nations, for example, has bodies dealing with women, disasters, children's welfare, health, disarmament, training, economic development, human settlement, the environment, oceans, trade, refugees, peace-keeping forces, population, food aid, food growing, atomic energy, civil aviation, labour, shipping, telecommunications, industry, copyright, meteorology, indeed almost every subject under the sun.

Universities and research institutes

Whether it is pioneering medical research, a study of your region's wildlife or an investigation into why men wear certain colour ties, there will be stories here that no reporter would dare make up. And many of them will be totally unexpected. For example, one space research institute outside Moscow has been for years studying what personality types are truly compatible so that they do not put people together in the Mir Space Station who will begin fighting as soon as they leave Earth. Written for the general reader and applied to how people get on inside an apartment, rather than a space ship, you would have a story that should interest anyone.

Specialist and academic journals

Providing you have the expertise to read them, all the above remarks apply to these. Your country's underground press is also worth reading regularly. Such publications' reporting is often unbalanced, but one thing is certain – they have access to unconventional sources. Some of the best stories surface first in such papers.

Esoteric magazines

These are not ones written for an academic audience, but for ordinary people with special interests. Many of them deal with worlds (like that of the treasure hunter or vegetable grower) which most us would never normally enter. But buying a copy of these magazines or papers lets you enter that world. I rarely buy one without seeing some story in the editorial or advertising they carry that would be of interest to the general newspaper reader. A computer magazine might have a story about a new computer virus that is threatening commercial data systems the world over; a car magazine one about a new auto-theft racket; a sex newspaper might have an advertisement that leads you to investigate child pornography.

Classified advertisements

Any journalist who does not read the classified advertisements in any paper they can get their hands on is missing one of the best sources of human interest stories there is. After all, this is where the parts of the human race that are not journalists often communicate with each other. For instance, on 2 May 1962, the following ad was placed in the *San Francisco Examiner*'s classified columns by a Mrs Gladys Kidd:

> I don't want my husband to die in the gas chamber for a crime he did not commit. I will therefore offer my services for 10 years as a cook, maid or housekeeper to any leading attorney who will defend him and bring about his vindication.

One of the city's most famous lawyers, Vincent Hallinan, saw the ad and contacted Mrs Kidd. Her husband was about to be tried for the murder of an old antique dealer after his fingerprints had been found on a bloodstained ornate sword in the victim's shop. During the trial, Hallinan proved that the dealer had not been killed by the sword. He also established that the prints and blood of Kidd's found on the sword got there because he once fooled with the sword while out shopping with a friend. The jury found Kidd not guilty and Hallinan refused Mrs Kidd's offer of servitude. There are countless lesser examples of stories found in the classified: from the woman in Russia so poor that she was trying to sell her son, the exotic animal smuggling ring that was advertising rare pets and so on.

Police and other emergency services

An obvious source, but, for the provincial paper especially, a really productive one. National papers, which are less interested in crime stories unless they are of a great magnitude, may well find it better to develop contacts with specialist branches of the police, like those who deal with fraud or organised crime.

Follow-ups

These are a staggeringly neglected source of stories. There are basically three types of follow-ups: following up small news stories which look as if they may develop into something a lot larger, immediate follow-ups just after something has happened, or delayed ones when some good length of time has elapsed. A lot of reporters think follow-ups are likely to be unproductive, but this is not the case.

Observation

Keeping your eyes and ears open as you walk along the street, or just go about your normal business, and being ever alert to a story, will produce plenty of results. My first major story was about homeless people on the streets of the city in Britain where I lived. It was the result of noticing them late at night in doorways and parks, and asking the basic reporter's questions: who? why? etc.

Anniversaries

With the aid of a good reference book, or a record of interesting anniversaries you have compiled yourself, you will have an endless supply of light stories. The anniversaries can be simple births and deaths, major historic events or more unusual, social anniversaries like inventions of household objects, first appearance of well-known brands of goods or other landmarks of everyday life. Nor do anniversary stories have to be light. Researching the five-year anniversary of a major news story for a background piece can often turn up some buried report, neglected group or something else that makes a good hard story.

Meeting people

Useful as the telephone is, you will pick up far more stories if you go out of the office and meet people face to face. They will trust you quicker, tell you more and also chat casually with you. This is important. Most non-journalists (and a few practising ones) have no idea what makes a good news story. It is only when they are talking to you informally before or after a meeting, interview or whatever, that they may mention something which is a far better story than the one you originally came for.

Being known as open-minded

If you have a reputation for fair and balanced reporting and for being a journalist who is willing to take risks to do your job honestly, you will find people coming to you with good stories. In 1968 after Soviet dissident Aleksandr Ginsberg was jailed after a closed trial, his wife Ludmilla called a press conference. The night before it was due to be held, all the nearly 100 Western correspondents in Moscow were contacted by the government Press Department and warned that 'severe measures' would be taken against those who attended. The following day only four had the courage to go to the Ginsberg apartment, among them Raymond Anderson of the *New York Times*. A few months later, in July 1968, Anderson was given a document by a friend, who had received it from Andrei Amelrik, a dissident historian. Inside the package was the now-famous essay challenging the Soviet system written by Dr Andrei Sakharov. After a few more adventures and inquiries, Anderson established that the document was genuine and he sent it out secretly for it to make headlines around the world. A scoop – and all because he was known to be both brave and fair.

Other newspapers

There is an enormous amount of nonsense written by academics about newspapers and other media feeding off each other, or, as they call it, 'inter-media cognizance' or some such pseudo-scientific phrase. However, a great many good stories come from a journalist spotting a small item in another newspaper, investigating and finding there is a lot more to the subject or issue than the first paper thought. And many important stories have only been fully revealed because individual papers working on them independently each found different pieces of the jigsaw which *collectively* completed the picture.

This, however, is not the same as using other newspapers' stories as reliable sources that need no further corroboration. This is plainly dangerous in any circumstances. It is, for instance, common to be given a story from another paper and asked to stand it up. You should try and match it, and not merely regurgitate it. Don't just lift it as if it is a standard truth. If you are unable to get any new source of your own to substantiate it and your editor is insisting on a story, then quote it with attribution and tell readers of your attempts to verify it. Better still, get an acceptable source to comment on the report. Don't ever use unconfirmed reports as the basis for a story.

The only other justification for using other journalists' work as a source is where you are writing about the atmosphere surrounding a story and wish to quote their articles. In these situations, do not use 'press reports' but specify the paper or, if there are lot of them, write 'several dailies, including (name papers) reported that ...'.

The most feeble source of all (unless they are the only eye-witnesses to some drama) is the word of other journalists, rather than their articles. It suggests that you never left the bar. If you have good reasons to quote other reporters do not use vague phrases like 'informed sources', which try and conceal who they are, but write 'journalists (with names) covering (specify story) for (name papers) say that ...'. If that is not possible, apply the same wariness you would to using any other anonymous source.

Basic research

The most dispiriting words you can hear a reporter say are, 'I can't find out.' This may be true, he or she cannot find out. But what is rarely true is the phrase they invariably add, 'I've tried everywhere.' In 99 cases out of 100 you can be absolutely certain that they have not, and you will be able to suggest at least two more places to try. There will nearly always be somewhere where you can get the information you want. The golden rule is: never give up and never be afraid to ask. You will often be amazed at the help you can get.

Basic research is uncontentious factual information, given willingly by someone authorised to give it. Often the most obvious source will be the best one – government or regional departments, official organisations and international bodies. The degree of helpfulness you will find at national organisations obviously varies from country to country. The political system and culture has a huge impact on this. People in fully democratic societies have widespread opportunities to vote on everything from national, regional and local governments to sometimes even the person running the local fire service. This and the stake they feel it gives them in their society makes them demand information on how it is running and how they are being served. And they want it told them in a direct way.

This demand for information has forced governments in these countries to impart far more than they would otherwise choose to give (although by no means enough). National and local governments have created an entire branch of the public relations industry devoted to pumping out information, some of it suitably doctored for public consumption. In such information-rich societies, readers demand summaries, highlights and precision, not vagueness. And the journalist has so much readily available material for the general run of non-controversial stories that there is no excuse for not supplying it. Indeed, it is easier to supply it than not.

But unless you work in a totally controlled system, staff in official and semi-official organisations can be surprisingly helpful if they think there is someone interested in their subject or work. This also applies to some of the less obvious sources of basic research. These include embassies, commercial companies, experts at universities and institutes, pressure groups, the police and other newspapers and international news agencies.

Such organisations are often a fund of assistance and, the thing you most often need, telephone numbers. For instance, two of us were once trying to trace a museum of Russian culture in Romania. Our first source knew the region where it was, but had no name or telephone number for it. We tried all the obvious places to no avail, and then one of us tried the local police and the other the regional newspaper. In minutes we had both collected the relevant name and number.

On another occasion we heard of a Russian professor who was being held by the immigration authorities in San Francisco in the United States, pending deportation in unusual circumstances. It looked like a good story. The problem was that we had no telephone numbers for her representatives or the American authorities; the US embassy in Moscow was closed and we had to produce a story within the hour. After a couple of false starts we called the Associated Press office in Moscow, got a number for their office in San Francisco, telephoned them and immediately got numbers for everyone we wanted, plus the professor's American husband and those organising a campaign on her behalf.

Commercial companies, especially but not exclusively those in the West, can also be helpful. Imagine this situation: you are in your office at 10 p.m. at night and hear that one of your nationals has been arrested for armed robbery or gun-running in Florida. What do you do? The US embassy in your city is closed, your consulate in Miami is not answering the phone and the FBI office in New York knows nothing about the case, and neither does the Associated Press office in the city. When that happened to me, I called the American Express office in Miami, claimed to be a card holder (which was true, but need not have been – they would never have checked) and asked if they could give me numbers for the local police, district attorney's office and prison. Again we soon had our story. These are obviously not common problems, but they do illustrate what you can do before whining to your news desk that you cannot find out and have tried everywhere.

Books and directories are another source of information, but they need to be treated with care. Make sure you are consulting an up-to-date edition and that it is produced by someone who is in a position to know. You have to evaluate written sources as you would any other. The written source that should be treated with the most care is newspaper cuttings. If they are from your own paper you will at least know if that article was subsequently corrected or the subject of legal action. Extreme care should be taken when using all other cuttings. Just because it has appeared in print does not mean it is correct. That obviously applies just as well to computerised press cuttings and other databases.

Then there is the Internet – 70,000 computer networks all around the world, including libraries, databases, commercial companies, NGOs, universities etc. It is an extraordinary research facility, providing you know where to look, or start looking. This knowledge takes a lot of time to acquire, but for the freelance who has no ready access to a large paper's library, it is well worth acquiring. No journalist living within easy reach of a service provider should hesitate to get hooked up. Do so, and ask one of the many Internet search tools to find references to the subject you are working on and you will be amazed how much free information is there. You can now, armed only with a modem, computer and the right software, sit in the middle of Russia and write a thoroughly up-to-date piece on Brazilian soccer. I have done so. What you cannot find on the Internet, you can e-mail people for.

Contentious sources

There are two types of sources of which reporters should be immediately suspicious: those who pass on hearsay or rumour and those who approach you or your paper unprompted. No one in their right mind would be anything other than very wary of such sources. But they are only the most extreme form of contentious sources, a phrase which covers anyone who is telling you something other than the most straightforward, checkable, factual things. Contentious sources

are those giving you information that will or could be challenged,
or which is not given by an authorised person, or which has been
leaked – or which is being given by an authorised person. Contrary
to what they would have you believe, officials have not been injected
with truth serum before speaking to you – in fact, rather the reverse.
In dealing with these sources, you should bear the following
guidelines in mind.

Ask yourself what their motives are

Although it sometimes happens, people are rarely helpful to
newspapers because they are saintly. They want to damage their
political or commercial or personal opponents, they want to advance
some cause (or harm a rival one), they want revenge or to cause
trouble. These, and many other murky motives, are likely to be what
made them help you. Ask yourself (and occasionally them) what
those motives might be. Most people will have some reason to see
a particular story in print. That does not mean the story should
not appear, but it should warn you to take care.

Ask yourself, and them, what the other side to the story might be

The story as initially presented to you is rarely as black and white
(and, I am afraid, as strong) in reality. Ask sources if there is
another side to the story, or if they are forgetting to tell you any
qualifying information. And never stop asking yourself that question.
Crazy, horrendous, absurd things do happen; but experience
teaches that most stories are not as neat as most sources would have
us believe.

Are they in a position to know what they claim to know?

Sometimes the answer will be no. This is far more likely to be the
case if they are speaking to you 'off the record'. People granted this
facility often take advantage, exaggerate and make out they know
more than they ever could. Yet a lot of named sources frequently
claim to be 'in the know' when they are in fact only marginally so.
You are particularly vulnerable to these when you are reporting a
situation or subject about which you are almost totally ignorant.
The classic case of this is the coverage by the Western press of the
Soviet Union in the two years following the 1917 revolution.
Western correspondents were barred from Russian soil and so
papers sent them to Riga where, 300 miles from Petrograd, they
attempted to cover the events happening there and in Moscow. The
reporting was confused, hostile to the Bolsheviks and almost totally
inaccurate. This was not surprising for most of it was based on what

the correspondents were being fed by former Tsarist generals and officials, deposed politicians and tipsters who could produce 'news' for cash. All claimed to be 'in the know'. Virtually none of them were.

The sensational and distorted stories coming out of Riga prompted Walter Lippmann and Charles Merz to make their famous study of the surrealistic *New York Times* coverage of Russia between 1917 and 1919. They found that in these two years, the paper reported: the Bolshevik government had fallen or was about to fall (91 times); Lenin and Trotsky were preparing to flee (four times); Lenin and Trotsky had fled Russia (three times); Lenin had been imprisoned (three times); Lenin had been killed (once).

The paper's coverage reached new comic heights in October 1919 when an anti-Bolshevik force involving the Finns, White Russians and others, attempted to capture Petrograd. On 18 October, the paper headlined its report: 'Anti-Red Forces Now In Petrograd', then four days later: 'Anti-Red Forces Near Petrograd' – an invasion which was apparently working in reverse. Accuracy only reared its head on 24 October when the *Times* reported that the 'Anti-Red' forces had almost ceased to exist.

Insist on documents where possible

You know yourself how difficult it is as a reporter to accurately convey the essence of complicated issues and information on paper, never mind in conversation. This ought to make you constantly wary of what people tell you. Ask if there is any documentation to support what your source is telling you. If they will not let you have their copy, ask if you or they can photocopy it; if they will not let you do that then at least ask if you can read it in their presence. Be extra suspicious of sources who refuse. And then still be suspicious of the documents until you are satisfied they are genuine. Ed Behr tells a cautionary tale in his book *Anyone Been Raped Here and Speak English?* of the agency given photographic evidence of atrocities by one side in an African civil war. The pictures are of a woman being raped by soldiers. All very convincing until the local bureau chief had the sense to ask for the contact strip. They showed the harrowing rape scenes and then, in the final frame, the 'victim' with her arms round her 'attackers', smiling and posing for a group photograph.[1]

If you have any doubts, seek a second source

You should use and trust your instincts at all times, especially if you have any doubts about a source or about the information they are giving you. Almost every story I have published as a news editor and then regretted, I had worries about before publication.

I ignored these concerns. Don't. Follow your instincts. Ask sources if there is anyone who can confirm what they are telling you. If you do it pleasantly, and they are honest, they will not object. In certain circumstances, where the story is of such importance or so contentious or involves very high-level people, you should invariably seek a second source.

Don't fall into the trap of believing the story just because it would be a good story if true

The courts, and some ruined careers, bear testimony to stories that were wished, rather than reported into the paper. Be precise, be meticulous and establish that each part of the story's jigsaw happened – and happened in the way you are being told it did. Don't catch yourself saying, 'Well, it must have happened like that.' Or, even worse, 'Everyone else is reporting that, it must be true.'

In the autumn of 1989, when then-Czechoslovakia was on the brink of what was to become the 'velvet revolution', a young woman told reporters that state police officers had beaten to death a student called Martin Smid. The story was reported locally, and people began to visit the spot where Smid died, which soon began to acquire the aura and status of hallowed ground. Reuters wrote the story, and Agence France Press said that three young men had been killed.

The Associated Press failed to have the story. Its desk chiefs were not happy with their Prague bureau and demanded they catch up fast. Their local man was Ondrej Hejma, a guitarist who combined journalism with rock music at the expense of neither. Taking none of the earlier Smid reports at face value, he began digging. He and his wife, a doctor, toured local hospitals and mortuaries trying to find someone who had treated Smid, dealt with his body – anything. He found not the slightest shred of evidence for the Smid story and several days later the rival agencies were forced to report that Smid, whoever and wherever he was, had not died on that Prague sidewalk.[2]

The more passionate the source, the less they should be trusted

This does not mean they are lying or exaggerating, although it is distinctly possible. What it means is that people are generally less reliable for precise facts on the issues and causes about which they feel most strongly. Question such sources very carefully. They often fit facts to their theories and are blinded by these attitudes into ignoring vital facts that may put another construction on the story. But the vehemence of sources can be useful to you. On contentious stories, being verbally attacked by both or all sides is one good indicator that you are getting the story about right. As Daniel Marcellin of Radio Metropole in Haiti once said: 'We know when we are getting close to the truth. It's when the number of death threats from both sides is more or less the same.'[3]

Do not accept anonymous sources

This does not mean you should refuse to talk to them. But an anonymous source is, for the purposes of actually writing a story, not a source at all. It is merely a tip, a lead to tell you where to research. Even in these cases, you should insist on knowing their identity. Otherwise if you print the story and it is challenged or proved to be wrong, you have no means of producing your source – in court or anywhere else.

National newspapers often have anonymous sources come to them and offer stories about the private lives of politicians and celebrities. Prostitutes, ex-lovers, gay or straight, are the most common of these types of sources. They often do not want to give their names and, even more often, ask for payment (see below). They even sometimes claim to have pictures or tapes of the encounter(s) in question. However convincing their account, however plausible they seem, never accept such stories without confirming extra sources. The chances are high that you are being set up to play an unwitting part in a revenge ploy or dirty tricks operation.

Never pay money for stories

This is easier said than done in some places where officials routinely expect payment for co-operating with the press. But if it is at all possible to do your job without making such payments, then do so. The trouble is that paying people money for information does two undesirable things. First, it creates an information market which will spread to all kinds of unexpected areas quicker than you could ever imagine. Just a few years ago it was rare for people to ask newspapers for money in any circumstances. Now, following some well-publicised cases, many people demand cash, especially ordinary people who have suddenly been swept into the news.

In some countries, like Britain and Japan, this practice is becoming a disease – and one which is primarily spread by newspapers' willingness to pay. What happens then is that these people will sign exclusive deals with one newspaper and no other journalist can then get to them. This restricts the free flow of information and it prevents these people from being questioned properly. It means that the only version that sees the light of day is their 'authorised' one. Truth is therefore materially damaged by the creation of such information markets. This is not a question of ethics; it is a practical matter. You buy up one person on one story one day and you can hardly complain when other people on other stories refuse to speak to you because they have been bought up by other papers on other days.

Second, payments offer a source a direct inducement to exaggerate or improve the facts. They know that the stronger the story, the more you will pay; so they elaborate, embroider and flesh out a few facts with their fertile imaginations. This is especially the danger with stories about politicians and celebrities. A few years ago Britain's most popular newspaper, called the *Sun*, paid money to a gay male prostitute for a story about Elton John. They published it on 25 February 1987, but there was no truth in it and they later had to pay £1 million libel damages to the rock star and print a front page apology.

Beware also of sources trying to sell you tape recordings or videos

There now follows a warning from Britain. The money paid there for stories by some popular papers is so high (the *Sun* spends millions of pounds a year on payments to sources and freelances) that there are even one or two people who earn a living as professional newspaper hoaxers. The best of them is probably a film stuntman called Rocky Ryan, alias Major Travis, Peter Bernstein, David Oppenheimer, Rocco Salvatore or one of the other false names he regularly uses. He sold the *People* (a mass-market Sunday newspaper) a story about sex and drugs orgies among a Himalayan expedition, and to other media a tale that Gorbachev had resigned two years before he actually did (with the result that millions of dollars were lost on the foreign exchange markets) and a story that top Nazi Martin Bormann was alive and well and living on a kibbutz in Israel.

He also made $18,000 by concocting transcripts of a phone conversation between Prince Charles and Princess Diana and then stung papers into paying for this. He got an actress friend to phone the *People* to say a friend in the security services wanted to talk about the royals. She gave a number in a smart part of London, and when the paper rang the telephone was answered by another friend who said he worked for British intelligence. He explained that they had been bugging Prince Charles's phone. He said he was prepared to sell the transcript of the phone conversation for $7,500. The *People* bought it, as did other papers. The reason they fell for it was that the hoaxers were giving them a story they wanted to believe was true – the art of the confidence trickster down the ages.

Be scrupulous about getting the other side

This means not only keeping balance in your story and research at all times, it also means playing fair with people. If they are being criticised or accused of doing something, you should not only put these claims to them, but also give them time to reply. Ten minutes before deadline is not good enough. Quite often they will only have a 'no comment' for you however much time you give them. But there will also be occasions when what they say will give you new information that changes the story or at least puts an entirely different construction on it. This is not just a question of being fair and balanced; it is also a question of being safe.

Finally, don't be in a rush to get into print with difficult stories. In Britain the atmosphere is so competitive that there is continuous temptation to publish a story before it is all checked and ready. We have all fallen prey to that. If I have learned one useful thing from working from Americans, it is to only publish a story when you are totally happy with it. Anything else is not worth the risk.

Beware appeals to your 'responsibility'

Short of formal censorship, appeals to reporters to 'think of the consequences of this being published', to 'show responsibility', are the oldest trick in the would-be suppressor's book. Such pleas are normally a good indicator that the story is true and that the person making it does not want you to publish. You should always resist. You are a journalist, not a civic propagandist. Outside of wartime, where advanced publication of troop movements may be of use to an enemy, it is difficult to think of any story that should be deliberately suppressed – ever. In wartime, governments will appeal to journalists' patriotism and use the excuse of national security to deny reporters access to information, the story and the truth. What they do tell is always liable to be disinformation.

Specialist reporting

National and large regional papers have a certain amount of specialist reporters. These are the people who only ever write on one subject, such as education correspondents or crime correspondents etc. Subjects covered in this way include defence, foreign affairs, diplomacy, home affairs, health, environment, arts, education, science, religious affairs, heritage, politics, media, transport, fashion, industry, economics. And these are just the ones who work for the general news department; other departments, like business and sport, will obviously have others.

There are many advantages for a paper in having a good team of specialists. But both they and the paper should be aware of some of the problems that can arise when a reporter spends a lot of time with the same subject and group of contacts. Specialists must avoid becoming insiders in the business or area they report on. If that happens there will be a considerable risk that they will start seeing stories from the point of view not of the reader, but of the people about whom they are supposed to be reporting. Specialists must retain proper, reader-orientated news instincts and not allow stories to be for the benefit of the bureaucracy they are supposed to be covering.

Specialists must also guard against using the jargon of the area they cover. This is one of the most common failings in specialists' stories and is an early sign that they may be turning into 'insiders'. There is an additional danger here, and that is that specialists must not write stories that only the insiders in their area would be interested in. If a specialist tells a news editor that their story is 'for the benefit of a few hundred people', then that is the time to switch them to another specialty, back to general news or out of the paper altogether. Neither should specialists get so close to their contacts that stories are suppressed. While outright suppression for sinister motives is very rare, more common is the situation where a specialist keeps a story to him or herself in return for the promise of a bigger story later on. Be wary of being asked to do this, and if you are an editor, be even more wary of any reporter you catch doing this.

Finally, here is a story that illustrates as clearly as any could the dangers – to reporter and paper – of a specialist getting too closely involved with contacts. It concerns one Alfred 'Jake' Lingle, who was a police reporter for the *Chicago Tribune* in the 1920s. Lingle was highly thought of at his paper. A lot of well-informed stories about organised crime in that city came from him and his contacts, and he built a legendary reputation with readers and colleagues. Lingle prospered and, thanks to what he said was a bequest of $50,000 from his father, the $65-a-week reporter dressed well and maintained several homes. His fertile supply of crime stories, however, was suddenly stopped on 9 June 1930. As he entered a train station on Randolph Avenue, Lingle was gunned down in the street in broad daylight by a man dressed as a priest.

The killing had all the marks of a gangland professional hit. Lingle's paper was outraged.

> The meaning of the murder is plain. It was committed in reprisal and in an attempt at intimidation. Mr Lingle was a police reporter and an exceptionally well-informed one. His personal friendships included the highest police officials ... What made him valuable to his newspaper marked him as dangerous to the killers ... To the list of those who were killed in the St Valentine's Day Massacre [when seven died in a gangland feud], the name is added of a man whose business was to expose the work of the killers. *The Tribune* accepts this challenge. It is war. There will be casualties ... Justice will make a fight of it or will abdicate.

The *Tribune* backed these fine words with a $25,000 reward for information about the killers, other papers followed suit, and Lingle was then accorded the accolade of a civic funeral, complete with military bands and guards of honour. Tens of thousands of Chicago citizens lined the streets and bowed their heads in respect as the cortege passed.

But not long afterwards, some hitherto unknown details of Lingle the 'innocent hero' began to emerge. It turned out his father only left him a few hundred dollars, not $50,000. When Lingle was shot he had over $1,000 in cash in his wallet and was wearing a belt-buckle encrusted with diamonds. It was, apparently, a gift from Al Capone, the most notorious of the city's organised crime bosses. Moreover, his bank account showed deposits of more than $60,000 in the previous 18 months.

One of his joint accounts was with City Police Commissioner, William F. Russell, who resigned in disgrace immediately. He and Lingle had been friends since their youth and the crime reporter had been selling his influence over Russell to other police wanting transfers and promotion, to politicians, hoodlums and major gangsters like Capone. He was a frequent guest at Capone's retreat on Palm Island, Florida, and had day and night access to this, perhaps then the most feared man in the United States.

But Lingle liked to gamble, and gamble big. Despite several successful attempts to fix dog races, he was soon losing $1,000 a week at the tracks and at Capone's illicit casinos. By the summer of 1930, his gambling debts with the organised crime boss totalled more than $100,000 – worth $1 million plus at 1995 values. His attempt to extort money from members of Capone's own gang was, for the crime boss, the final liberty that Jake Lingle was ever going to take. The killer in priest's clothing was hired.[4]

Three weeks to the day after Lingle was shot, his paper was forced to admit:

> Alfred Lingle now takes on a different character, one in which he was unknown to the management of the *Tribune* when he was alive … He was not and could not have been a great reporter … He was accepted in the world of politics and crime for something undreamed of in his office and he used this in undertakings which made him money and brought him to his death.

> *All day long, Hollywood reporters lie in the sun, and when the sun goes down, they lie some more.*
>
> Frank Sinatra

7

Investigative Reporting

> *The image of the reporter as a nicotine-stained Quixote, slugging back Scotch while skewering City Hall with an exposé ripped out of the typewriter on the crack of deadline persists despite munificent evidence to the contrary.*
>
> Paul Grey

There is a school of journalistic thought that curls its lip and sneers at the very mention of the words 'investigative reporting'. It argues that since all reporting is investigative, the phrase is meaningless.

If only that were true; but some reporting is investigative only in the most basic sense. It is the journalistic equivalent of the single-cell creature and bears about as much resemblance to the subject of this chapter as amoeba do to humans. Anyone who doubts that is referred immediately to the final section of this chapter which deals with the work of the remarkable German Gunter Wallraff. Investigative reporting is substantially different from other kinds and there are three features that distinguish it.

Distinguishing features

Original research

It is not a summary or piecing together of others' findings and data, but original research carried out by reporters using often the rawest of material. It can be extensive interviewing, or matching and comparing facts and figures. In many cases the fruits, and originality, come in discovering patterns and connections in the information that no one has observed before.

The subject involves potential wrong-doing or negligence for which there is no available evidence

Often you have suspicions of wrongdoing or negligence but have no proof and neither does anyone else. You need to accumulate evidence, and this will require far more time and prolonged effort than ordinary work. It may also involve more than one reporter. Clearly you will not spend this time unless the subject is a matter of importance to readers.

Someone is trying to keep the information secret

This is a feature of a lot of reporting. One definition of news, after all, is 'something that someone does not want you to print'. In day-to-day reporting, however, there is, for all kinds of practical reasons, a point at which you stop and report what you have found or not found. Investigative reporting starts at the point where the day-to-day work stops. It does not accept the secrecy and the refusal of officials to give the information. It finds out for itself.

Investigative reporting can be done in almost any subject or area of public life. Two broad categories, however, are particularly fruitful: activities and organisations that do their work in remote places or otherwise away from the public gaze; and people and institutions that suddenly get thrust into the spotlight, appear to have 'come from nowhere' and around which speedily grows a mythology. They are people and institutions which seem to have no background. But they will have, and in that background is almost sure to be a good story.

Companies and financial institutions, especially of the 'get rich quick' variety, are a highly fertile ground for some journalistic digging. Sink your spade into a newfangled and highly publicised investment scheme and you can bet your salary that there will be dirt there. The Romanian pyramid funds of the early 1990s are a prime case of a missed opportunity. One that was not missed, and a classic example of this type of reporting, was the story of Charles Ponzi, or, as he liked to call himself, The Great Ponzi.

A lot of people believed him. More than 40,000 Americans plunged their savings into his scheme, lured in by his pledge to pay them, within 90 days, $2.50 for every $1 invested. Despite warnings from financial experts that his sums just did not add up, Ponzi was, at one point in 1920, raking in $200,000 a day. In just 18 months, he had collected more than $15 million.

It was all based on currency exchange rates. His company would take your investment, and send it overseas where his agents would buy International Postal Union reply coupons at depressed rates and then sell them in other foreign outposts at a higher rate. That was Ponzi's story, and thousands joined the rush to have their money earn money faster than they could. The reality, of course, was that he was paying new customers with the money from old ones. In the whole life of his company it traded in foreign currency with only $30 of the original $15 million.

But the flood tide of people who crowded the sidewalks outside his offices, queuing for the chance to invest everything they had, did not know that. It seemed, in the words of one of these hopefuls, that he 'had discovered money itself'. He hadn't, of course. He had merely found that if you offer people a big enough return on their money, and wave a few libel writs around, you can postpone the day of reckoning for a long time.

But not indefinitely; for other things were being discovered. Reporters from the *Boston Post* newspaper were discovering his past. 'The Great Ponzi', it turned out, was better known to the authorities in Canada as prisoner no. 5247, the number he bore while jailed for forgery. He had also done time in Atlanta for smuggling aliens. His company duly collapsed, and Ponzi went to jail for four years.[1]

Investigative reporting skills

Investigative reporting can be undertaken by anyone with the determination to see the job through and handle all the inevitable frustrations. It requires no special skills. But there are a few things that make the job easier and you more efficient at it.

Knowledge of law on public access to information

What is the law on this in your country? Do you know what public records and documents you are entitled to see? This is vital. Some investigations have turned on secret documents being passed to journalists. But many more have resulted from reporters discovering that certain records or registers are kept and that they have a right to consult them. Most bureaucracies will not exactly advertise the existence of such information, and then they will erect all kinds of barriers to prevent people bothering to consult them – by making them only available at certain times, or storing them in out of the way places.

A reporter who once worked with me in London discovered in the small print of a government report the existence of a certain register. It listed all the rights of access to private estates that had been granted in return for the wealthy owners of the estates receiving tax concessions. Neither the officials (because they had given tax concessions) nor the owners (because they did not want members of the public tramping all over their estates) were keen to have this register publicised.

Once the reporter learnt of its existence and established that we had the right to examine it, she went through the lengthy process involved and consulted it. She was then able not only to report the details of the access to these estates, but also to investigate the deals done between the owners and the government. None of which would have been possible were it not for her finding about about the register in the first place and securing the rights to see it.

This was in Britain, which has a tradition of secrecy about official documents. It is not exactly alone in this, but there are other countries that now have freedom of information laws which have opened up a vast amount of records to citizens. Very few ordinary people will know of these records and even fewer will consult them. All the more reason for journalists to make it their business to know what is kept and what can can be seen.

In the United States, the 1966 Freedom of Information Act, strengthened in 1971, has opened up all kinds of documents – some very obscure – to journalists. As a result of their use in investigations, all manner of scandals have been uncovered by the press:

- Unreported accidents at nuclear sites.
- X-ray machines at cancer-detection centres which were emitting 25–30 times the correct level of radiation (within months of disclosure, all such centres in the United States had reduced amounts of radiation).
- Security guards at sensitive weapons plants who had records of instability or had committed criminal offences.
- Anaesthetic drugs routinely given during childbirth even though they could – and did – cause brain-damage to babies.

There was also the paper in Louisville, Kentucky which obtained federal inspection reports on nursing homes showing the abuse of residents. As a result, new state legislation was introduced, many homes closed and owners of several charged with fraud.

There are many, many other cases that could be cited. They all show the value of journalists discovering what records are kept, examining them and using them in their investigations.

Knowledge of standard reference sources

In all but the most furtive of societies there is much more information available than the average journalist realises. A lot of this can be be traced through standard, if not commonly available, reference sources: such as lists of official publications, reports from legislatures, lists of public bodies, company ownership reference books, or registers of bodies receiving government funding. Any reporter, especially those intending investigative work, should make it their business to know what information such reference sources hold.

Contacts

All reporters obviously need contacts, but investigative reporters more so. And they need a particular type of contact – not just those who can give them information or point them in the right direction for it on a specific story, but those who can be useful on a range of stories. People like lawyers, officials in telephone services, car registration centres; those who can give advice and access to official records.

Computer literacy

Increasingly all such records and registers referred to above are held on computers. This, in places like Europe and the United States, has led to the rise of computer-assisted investigative journalism. For example, the *Providence Journal* in Rhode Island, America matched a computerised list of all those registered to drive school buses with those convicted of traffic offences and drug-dealing, and the *Atlanta Journal-Constitution* in Georgia won a Pulitzer Prize in 1989 for a series analysing racial discrimination in bank lending.

This investigation, by Bill Dedman, repays study; not because its subject has any great global significance, but precisely because it hasn't. It is a piece of local city reporting, although a particularly fine one. It did not bring any governments down, reveal any criminal corruption or save any lives. To someone who is white and living a long way away from the United States, it might appear to be small beer compared to the problems that affect their country. But the *Journal-Constitution* series is worth looking at for its methods, organisation and attitudes. It is the story of a journalist determined to report a situation into print, rather than wish it there or just repeat the hearsay that was coming his way.

The investigation started with an off-hand remark by a white housing developer. He said he was having trouble building houses in the black areas of South Atlanta because banks would not lend money there (something that would be illegal, if done for discriminatory reasons). He added that he had been told that loans were even hard to come by in affluent black areas. It is the kind of remark that reporters hear every day – general, unsubstantiated and seemingly impossible to prove. But Dedman had his curiosity aroused. He wanted to see if there was a way the charge could be stood up.

First he talked to some academics who worked in this field, and they told him that banks and savings and loan companies must file to the government the location of every home loan, by amount and census tract. As Dedman later wrote: 'All we at the paper did, to put it simply, was to cross-index the federal computer tapes with a federal census tape, looking especially at comparable black and white neighbourhoods.' This was easier said than done. The first three days were devoted entirely to putting spaces between the numbers on the computer so they could be read properly.

For the next five months, Dedman checked loans made by every bank and savings association in Atlanta over a five-year period – a total of 109,000 loans. There was also another study looking at real estate records. Yet the effort was worth it. Dedman discovered that banks and other institutions were making five times as many loans in white areas as in black areas. By examining bank policies and practices, he also found that they were not looking for business in black areas and were otherwise discouraging black borrowers. Blacks, in turn, could only resort to unregulated mortgage companies and loan sharks. As he says, 'Only then did I turn to anecdote.' He talked to blacks and whites to get personal experiences and give his series real lives, and to show how the policies of banks affected people.

When he went to the banks, they were predictably reluctant to talk. One replied to Dedman's request for information thus: 'Some of the material you have asked for does not exist. Other parts of the material exist but are confidential. The rest of the material exists and is not confidential but is irrelevant to your subject matter.' It is the unmistakable voice of someone with something to hide. Another bank tried to sneakily combine an appeal to local patriotism with a thinly-disguised plea to the paper's publisher, Jay Smith, to kill the story. He wrote: 'I'm sure that Jay Smith would recognise any article alleging racial discrimination by Atlanta financial institutions as another unmerited potshot at our great city ...'. And he sent a copy of the letter to Smith.

Finally, when Dedman had enough material for a series (which he would call 'The Color of Money' after the Hollywood film), his editors came into the picture. As Dedman wrote later: 'I think I know the key to the effectiveness of "The Color of Money". The editors took out what I thought were the good parts. When I wrote that Atlanta's banks were red-lining [a pejorative word for marking-off areas to be discriminated against], editor Bill Kovach marked through it. "Just use the numbers," he said, "Let the facts speak for themselves."'

On Sunday 1 May, the series began with a story of several thousand words headlined 'Atlanta Blacks Losing In Home Loans Scramble':

> Whites receive five times as many home loans from Atlanta's banks and savings and loans as blacks of the same income – and that gap has been widening each year, an *Atlanta Journal-Constitution* study of $6.2 billion in lending shows. Race – not home value or household income - consistently determines the lending patterns of metro Atlanta's largest financial institutions, according to the study, which examined six years of lender reports to the federal government.

Among stable neighbourhoods of the same income, white neighbourhoods always received the most bank loans per 1,000 single-family
homes. Integrated neighbourhoods always received fewer. Black
neighbourhoods - including the mayor's – always received fewest.
The study was controlled so any statistical bias would under-estimate
the differences between lending in black and white areas.

The story went on to contain the following: explanation and denial
from bankers, details of the survey with further news points
(including the fact that the only bank which specialised in lending
to blacks had the lowest default rate in the whole country), explanation of the law relating to bank loans etc. Elsewhere in that
day's paper was a story about individual blacks who were well-
qualified for a loan but had had found trouble getting one. The
rest of the series was as follows:

Monday 2 May: Detailed story on bank policies, the history of discrimination by them, plus more case histories including the black
Vietnam veteran who was refused a loan which would have cost him
$100 a month less than his rent. The article also detailed the process
of home purchase and how it related to blacks.
Tuesday 3 May: Detailed explanation of the law on banking and its
regulation and practice over the whole country, plus history of
efforts by black groups to change Atlanta banks' policies. There were
also follow-up stories which established that discrimination was
being practised nationally.

The results of Dedman's series were immediate. Nine days after
it ended, Atlanta's nine largest banks began pouring $77 million
in low-interest loans into black areas. Some institutions also went
positively into black areas looking for business, hiring black staff,
advertising in black media and even taking their executives on a
bus tour of the areas. And eleven months after the series was
printed, the US Justice Department began investigating 64 Atlanta
banks and financial institutions for possible breaches of the discrimination laws.[2]

Dangers of investigative reporting

Except for a very small number of isolated examples, investigative
reporting in Western Europe and the United States carries no
greater personal danger than boredom. Endless hours of wading
through documents and records, whole days eaten up by sources
who prove fruitless – most of the job involves drudgery rather than
glamour. In a lot of other countries, however, the risks are a little
more serious.

- In Russia, *Moskovski Komsolets* reporter Dmitri Kholodov was investigating army corruption. An anonymous source rang him one day in the autumn of 1994 and said that a bag of documents had been left for him at Kazan Station. Kholodov collected them and took the bag back to his office. When he opened it, the bag exploded, killing him.
- Investigative journalist Julia Plotnekova, who worked for the newspaper *Kvek*, went missing in Moscow on 24 April 1992. Her body was found in a forest two days later. Money and jewellery had not been stolen. Some saw the murder as a warning to other journalists investigating organised crime.
- In the summer of 1992, Peruvian reporter Adolfo Isuiza Urquia investigated drug dealing for the daily *La Republica*. In August he named a major drug trafficker who was being protected by ·the armed forces. 'The army does not want to fight terrorism because it lives off drug trafficking', he wrote. A few days later, on 27 August, his body was found in the River Huallaga. He had been tortured and stabbed.[3]

The list of journalists killed in the course of their investigations, even if confined to just the last few years, could fill many pages. There is no doubt that in countries where organised crime is widespread, investigative reporting is a potentially lethal profession. Anyone considering digging around in these areas should carefully weigh any risk involved. Dead reporters can't report.

How to run investigative operations

The subjects for investigations come to papers in all kinds of ways: as tips from contacts, by accident, a seemingly routine story that subsequent information indicates is far bigger, a reporter's own observations, a run-of-the-mill story which escalates bit by bit, or one where every question you ask throws up other, increasingly important, questions.

The case with perhaps the most famous journalistic investigation of all was Watergate. It began in June 1972 with a break-in at the Democratic Party's headquarters in the Watergate Building in Washington. It ended just over two years later with the resignation of the most powerful man on earth, President Richard Nixon. The role of the President and his staff in the original burglary and much else besides (phone-taps, slush-funds and, most important of all, the cover-up of these illegal activities) would never been known had it not been for investigative reporters. The two who did most were Carl Bernstein and Bob Woodward of the *Washington Post*.

When they started working on the story, in a mood of mutual distrust, it was a routine crime story. Five men had been caught breaking into the Democrat HQ to plant a listening device. Woodward went to the courtroom the following day and noticed a prominent lawyer taking a great interest in the case. What was he doing there? Woodward also learnt at the court that several of the men had worked for the Central Intelligence Agency. They were also carrying large amounts of cash on them when arrested, and two of them had notebooks, inside which was a telephone number for a man who worked at the White House.

From these slender – but promising – beginnings was launched a series of stories that were finally to prove the Nixon administration's complicity in a whole raft of illegal activities. Bernstein and Woodward were feted, wrote a best-selling book, and a Hollywood film was made of their investigation. But that was the final outcome. Before that were a thousand frustrations, the abuse from Nixon supporters and officials who feared and suspected their reporting, the wasted days, weeks and months pursuing false leads, the mistakes (some of which got into print), the countless hours searching records for that one vital piece of information, the self-doubts, the criticism and envy of colleagues, and the late nights, all nights and weekends of their own time spent on the case.

There are valuable lessons to be learnt from their experiences. Indeed, their book, *All The President's Men*, is probably the best detailed description of reporting in the English language. It tells the story of two reporters edging slowly, and not always in a straight line, towards the truth by painstaking research and a healthy obsession with accuracy. The following guidelines on investigative reporting are based on their work, the study of other cases and my own limited experiences.

Find and file every document

The moral of every investigation ever mounted is to lay your hands on every document that you can and throw nothing away. You just never know when documents, notes, reports – indeed anything you accumulate – will be useful. Months after you acquire that apparently innocuous report, something might give it sudden significance. Bernstein and Woodward, the Watergate reporters, filled four filing cabinets after just a few months.

Write up every interview and file the notes

This is especially important if there is more than one of you working on an investigation or it is a lengthy one. It pays to swap notes of interviews to see if you have missed something of significance. Typed (and filed) notes are also a lot easier and quicker to consult. This practice also allows executives to participate better in the discussions of the story (see below).

Be persistent

Read the story of any investigation and the persistence of the reporters is the thing that strikes you. During the Watergate investigation Woodward and Bernstein often spent days going through records, sat at their desks making phone calls all weekend, or waited outside lawyers' offices all day for the chance to see a perhaps vital source. On one occasion they obtained a list of the hundred-or-so people who worked at the Committee to Re-elect the President, the seat of much of the wrong-doing. Since they obviously could not visit these people at their offices, they spent many weeks calling on them at their homes after their normal day's work at the paper.

Re-interview 'old sources'

As long as an investigation is in progress, there is no such thing as an 'old source'. People who are working in the area you are investigating will often remember things they should have told you, receive new information, or be able to make sense of new information you are getting. Each one of these is reason enough to call them regularly. Woodward and Bernstein each kept a separate master list of phone numbers of contacts. This eventually amounted to several hundred names. They were each called at least twice a week, every week, for well over a year. As they wrote in their subsequent book: 'Just the fact that a certain source would not come to the phone or return calls often signalled something significant.'

Cultivate sources who really are in the know

During the Watergate investigation, Woodward contacted a man who worked at a senior level in the government to ask him if any word of the wrong-doing had reached him. It had. He knew an enormous amount, and clearly regarded it as his duty to assist the exposure of the conspiracy. However, he had the bureaucrat's natural suspicion of the press and was also concerned lest stories based on knowledge only he and few others had was used without other sources.

He therefore agreed to help Woodward, but only on certain conditions: he would only guide the reporter in the right direction, anything he told them would have to be corroborated by another source. Meetings between him and Woodward took place in underground car parks, late at night and were only arranged at his behest. Such was the eventual quality of the help that he gave that Woodward agreed to these conditions.

The source revealed his identity to no one and an executive at the *Washington Post* christened him 'Deep Throat' after the title of a fashionable pornographic movie which featured a woman whose speciality was oral sex. Deep Throat's identity remains a mystery to all but Woodward still.

It is, of course, given to few reporters to know and have the co-operation of such a well-placed source as Deep Throat. But the moral of Woodward's dealings with him is that if such a source sets certain rules, you should stick by them. That does not mean you should accept everything they say; Woodward argued with his contact frequently. But whatever is finally agreed should be adhered to.

Executive support

The news editor/editor must commit staff and other resources to the project. The editor should be prepared for the project to take a long time and possibly result in no story. Publishing something just because a lot of time has been spent on it is a sure way to have a disaster on your hands. When it is finally printed, the story should be watertight.

The executives and reporters will also have to make a basic decision early on about whether the investigation will be a series of stories published as they are written, or a 'big hit' operation printed only when all the research is complete. If the latter, a deadline should be set. It is easy for investigations to simply drag on for months, with the reporters always claiming that they need 'just one more week' to finish their research. You should also remember that interim stories can sometimes produce people to come forward with more – or even the vital information.

Yet whichever way it is being published, the investigative operation should be closely monitored by an executive. A key part of this role is to ask questions continuously of the reporters about the story. Such executives should act as devil's advocates and also keep going over evidence with reporters. They should be the fresh mind on the case.

Going undercover

This should never even be considered unless you are very experienced, and have discussed your plans fully with an executive on your paper. It is very time-consuming (the story had better be worth it), and might be highly embarrassing and a waste of the story if you are discovered. Sometimes it is physically dangerous. Going undercover is like going behind enemy lines without identity papers; it carries the same perils, not the least of which is that you may be publicly disowned by your paper if discovered. And it is a very rare form of reporting. Most times there is a better way of collecting information.

However, there are a few occasions when it is the only way to write a story. Your investigation may depend on finding out about the treatment of a certain group of people and access to that knowledge is denied to everyone but those people. It may be that you believe the situation inside an organisation or institution or company is being falsely portrayed and always will be to any reporter.

There are many risks to going undercover – both to your reporting and to you personally. First, it always involves some deception, so the wrong-doing you are reporting had better be serious enough to justify that dishonesty. Second, if you are investigating criminal activities undercover you may well be drawn into participating in these, which makes your actions even harder, if not impossible, to defend. Third, the physical dangers in such a situation can be immense and last long after you have surfaced to write your story. If you are undercover with people who might harm you, it is essential that you keep your editor informed about your movements and who you are dealing with.

There is an additional risk when you are investigating an illegal trade and posing as a buyer or seller, in other words as an *agent provocateur*. Apart from the dubious morality of that, you also become part of the story and so change it. If you were posing as a wealthy buyer, for instance, you would be distorting the market. The most flagrant case of this was in 1994 when stories began to emerge of weapons-grade plutonium being offered for sale on the German black market. A lot of this material was alleged to have come from Russia, but this has never been established. What then happened was that a number of reporters thought they would make a name for themselves by probing this trade. Some posed as sellers, others as buyers with unlimited money. As if this was not bad enough, some journalists working undercover as 'buyers' then ran into others impersonating sellers. None discovered the true identity of the other and so their published stories were not of the the 'trade in death' as they claimed, but of two over-enthusiastic journalists fooling each other – and themselves.[4]

Yet there are some instances of undercover investigations producing memorably good stories. At the end of the nineteenth century, *New York World* reporter Nellie Bly (real name Elizabeth Cochran) feigned insanity to get inside the asylum at Blackwell's Island and wrote a shocking exposé. Her findings were later published in her book *Ten days in a Madhouse*. Her reward from her publisher, Joseph Pulitzer, was an assignment to beat the round-the-world journey time of 80 days set by the fictitious Phineas Fogg in Jules Verne's novel *Around The World In Eighty Days*. She did it in 72 days 6 hours 11 minutes and 14 seconds.

Less well-rewarded was the editor of the *Pall Mall Gazette*, W.T. Stead. He exposed child prostitution in Victorian London by 'buying' a 13-year-old girl from her mother and, under the strictest of supervision, spending enough time alone with her to prove that she could have been put to almost any immoral purpose. The point of his famous series on child prostitution was to reveal its extent and campaign for a change in the law. This campaign had the support of many leading figures, including bishops. They, however, could not prevent Stead subsequently being one of the first people prosecuted under the law. The authorities jailed him for three months on a technicality for buying the girl at the centre of his story. He later visited Russia and founded the Peace Crusade. This strange, red-bearded and eccentric man (he sometimes caught mice, fried them and ate them on toast) was drowned when the *Titanic* sank in 1912.

Since then, journalists have gone undercover mainly to expose the treatment – or maltreatment – of various 'victims' of society like the homeless, mentally ill or drug addicts. This involves a degree of acting and perhaps the adoption of disguise. The master of this genre is a German called Gunter Wallraff. His aim is to enter worlds forbidden to a writer. He uses false papers, an invented life-story, new clothes, new spectacles or contact lenses, ways of disguising his hair and teeth. For, as he says, his task is 'to deceive in order not to be deceived'.

He styles himself 'the undesirable journalist' and, as far as his targets are concerned, not without good reason. He worked for two years in five factories, volunteered for civil defence exercises, played the part of an informer for the security services and the political police, tested Catholic theology and morality by posing as a man who had been making napalm bombs, led the life of a homeless man in a hostel or an alcoholic in a mental hospital, and imper-sonated a ministry adviser to find out how many armed units are available to German industry for factory protection. As a 'German financier of the extreme Right' he discovered plans for a coup in Portugal, and, as a 'tabloid reporter', worked on and exposed the methods of the mass-market *Bild*.

Scrupulous about notes and records, he tapes everything and photocopies all documents that he wishes to quote. As he says: 'I decided to conspire in order to take a look over the wall of camouflage, denials and lies. The method I adopted was only slightly illegal by comparison with the illegal deceptions and manoeuvres which I unmasked.'

One of his more striking – and simple – investigations was into the training by large companies of paramilitary forces for factory protection, a phrase which could cover anything from deterring thieves to the use of violence and intimidation to defeat industrial action. Having received some further evidence that this was being done with the connivance of the Federal Association of German Industry (BDI), and receiving a tip-off that these corps were receiving weapons, and the training to use them, Wallraff decided to make inquiries.

He telephoned the Continental rubber works in Hanover, introduced himself as a journalist and asked to speak to someone about 'civil defence preparations and shooting practice' at the factory. He was put through to a Herr Bockenkamp who was emphatic: 'Sheer nonsense. We don't even have a works security force as such. All we have is a works fire brigade.' Wallraff asked about the civil defence courses recommended in the official, but secret, BDI documents. Again Bockenkamp was adamant: 'It's nothing. Nothing behind it at all ... It's a good job you checked.' Some time later, disguising his voice slightly, Wallraff phoned as 'Herr Krover', an official of the non-existent but plausible-sounding Civil Defence Board of the Federal Ministry of the Interior. The conversation went like this:

Bockenkamp: Bockenkamp here. A very good morning to you, Minister.
Wallraff: Are you specially charged with preparations for the Corps?
Bockenkamp: Yes.
Wallraff: Are you in a position to intervene in the event of wildcat strikes or other disturbances which might, for example, arise over wage policy matters?
Bockencamp: Yes, we've made all the necessary preparations. I have complete plans worked out for every plant, and also the personnel ...
Wallraff: ... What's the position on weapons?
Bockenkamp: I've got seventy men here licensed for firearms, and the corresponding weapons ...
Wallraff: ... Have you detected any underground activity?
Bockenkamp: Yes. At least as far as the Greek workers go. But I have them under continuous surveillance. I find out everything through my interpreters who are partly German, partly Greek, and are able to attend their meetings ...
Wallraff: ... That's very good to hear. Perhaps you'd like to give a talk sometime at one of our conferences. Report on how it works in practice?

Eventually Wallraff uncovered an extensive network of paramilitary training groups being prepared by some German companies. Much of the activity was aimed at immigrant workers, and conferences had been held on the subject with police forces. All of this, plus the weapons training, was routinely denied when Wallraff called people later as a journalist. Following publication, he was prosecuted for 'false impersonation and unauthorised use of title' at Frankfurt Magistrates Court in December 1969, but was acquitted.

To those outside Germany, perhaps his most devastating story was one that required no disguise at all. He investigated the sentences that certain Nazi war criminals actually served and discovered the following:

> Case 2: Doctor Walter Sch. was sentenced to death in 1947 for killing mental patients at the Eichberg sanatorium in Frankfurt. The sentence was commuted to life imprisonment. Six years later, in 1953, Dr Sch.'s life imprisonment was over.
> Case 5: Adolf W. poisoned at least 900 inmates of the hospital and nursing home at Hadamar. He was sentenced to death in Frankfurt. The sentence was never carried out. Six years later he was free again.
> Case 9: Adolf R. was found guilty in Karlsruhe of the mass extermination of Jews in the Minsk region. He was sentenced to life, plus 15 years, in 1949. He was released in 1962.
> Case 12: Paul H. ordered the shooting, hanging and gassing of concentration camp prisoners. He was sentenced to nine years imprisonment in Bochum. After three years he was free again.
> Case 19: Wilhelm G. had Jews and communists shot near the Lithuanian border at the outbreak of the war. In Dortmund he was sentenced to five years' imprisonment. Three months later he was set free.

And so it goes on, for case after case. Like virtually all of his work, it was published in magazines, booklets or books. Not newspapers. Wallraff's investigations consume a great deal of time, more time, perhaps, than many newspapers would grant a staff reporter. But his results are impressive and his methods worthy of more attention than they get in the world of conventional journalism.[5]

As Professor Dr Eugen Kogon wrote in his Afterword to the original published report of the factory defence corps story:

> First a word about the journalistic method used in this case to ascertain the truth. Since it concerned illegal measures of a reactionary kind, which had to be tracked down, no straightforward request for clarification would have penetrated through the smokescreen of lies. Only the appearance of conspiring, of belonging to

the body of accomplices, made an insight – the first step – possible. As with dictatorships: the uniform alone allows access.

Our conception of realism must be broad, political and rising above conventions. A realist means someone who unmasks the complex causality of social relations ... who stresses the moment of evolution in every subject; who makes everything concrete while he facilitates the work of abstraction.

Bertolt Brecht

8

New Ethics

A gifted man who isn't interested in money is very hard to tame.

Alistair Cooke of the BBC

There is more nonsense written and spoken about ethics than any other issue in journalism. It is every non-practiser's favourite subject, mainly because it provides such a neat opportunity to take a swipe at those who do practise journalism. There is also the perpetual spectacle of the high-minded in the business attempting to teach their morals to the fast and loose at the popular end. They stand as much chance of having an impact as someone trying to advocate celibacy to a group of sailors arriving in port after six months at sea.

And then there are those organisations who decide that what the journalists in any emerging democracy need first, before they get typewriters, cheap printing, computers or light bulbs, is lectures on ethics. Teach primitive democrats this, goes the argument, and very soon they will be transformed into clones of *Washington Post* reporters. All of this, and similar, tripe is due to an almost universal misunderstanding. What ethics conventionally are and what they should be are two very different things.

What is normally meant by ethics? Well, to some journalists they are a code of principles to which all in the press should adhere, or at least feel guilty about if they do not. To others, normally those who do their job in more rough and ready circumstances, they are an irrelevance; something for journalism professors to argue about. This divide is something found universally. You find it in Africa, Russia, Australia, the United States and Europe. These kinds of ethics, then, and attitudes to them, vary more according to the kind of paper you work on and the market it operates in than the country you live in.

The vital factors in determining these ethics and whether you follow them are pay, and competition and the culture on your paper. The first is obvious. Pay a staff journalist $3,000 a year and he or she may have to accept all kinds of dubious freelance assignments and bribes to write puffs to earn a proper living; pay them $100,000 a year and they can afford to take a moral stand on almost anything. There are, of course, exceptions, like the highly paid reporter who is thus so afraid of losing the lucrative staff job that he or she will be prepared to do all kinds of things to keep it. Generally, however, the higher the pay, the more a journalist can afford principles.

Competition is important, too. Intense competition between newspapers for readers can tempt editors to put pressure on staff to cut ethical corners. And competition between journalists for work obviously encourages some to do things they would otherwise not do. When it comes down to it, if you think of ethics as a question of morals, you will only be as moral a journalist as your paper and its culture lets you.

So these journalistic ethics are either the codification of prevailing behaviour and culture, or an irrelevant exhortation to standards of behaviour that are doomed to be unmet. Either way, there is not a great deal of point in them.

Better then not to think in these terms, but another. We should forget arguments about who is more virtuous. Nor should we be preoccupied with matters of taste and fashion as they are in the United States, with their multi-pointed, sub-sectioned ethics codes about sexism and racism (for these are ever-changing; as then, of course, are the codes). Instead we should think of ethics as defining not just principles, but what are safe practices for journalists. We should seek guidelines that help us decide how to make our work as reliable as it can be and least open to challenge.

Our aim is to devise a way of working which enables us to justify our actions with a clear conscience. That way we will keep our reputations intact; for, in the end, the only thing that determines our worth as journalists is our reputations. You can let an editor take away your social life or your proper allocation of sleep, but never your reputation.

So these new ethics are not exhortations to the journalistic equivalent of celibacy; the advocacy of virtue for its own sake. They are specific pieces of advice founded on the argument that honesty, plain dealing and the removal of conflicts of interest are the best ways to do this job because they are the safest ways to do it. In that way they can be applied to all journalists, regardless of their personal morality or that of their papers. They are universal.

These new ethics flow from an unwritten contract that should always exist between newspapers and their readers in a free society: every story and feature in the paper is there as a result of decisions made free of any political, commercial or non-commercial pressure. They are not there due to any exchange of favours or money, but written and edited in a spirit of free enquiry, and chosen for publication entirely on their own merits, be they real or imagined. In other words, they are honest.

General guidelines

Journalists should serve only their papers and their readers

If you want to be a propagandist, go and work in public relations, the government or politics. The journalist should owe no loyalty to anyone or anything else; not a political party, a source, a commercial interest, a non-commercial interest or a particular cause, however worthy. Balanced journalism is difficult enough to do without such conflicts of interest. The *Washington Post* newspaper has a rule that its journalists cannot take part in any political activity. That includes marching on demonstrations. So when several *Post* reporters were spotted on an abortion rights demonstration, they were told they would not be allowed to cover anything touching on the abortion issue.

Every story should be an honest search for the truth

It is a non-negotiable fundamental of reporting that each story should be an open-minded attempt to find out what really happened, and be accompanied by a willingness to print that truth, however uncomfortable it may be to our own cherished beliefs. Thus, journalists should not accept work which seeks to bolster a point of view in the face of evidence or undertake reporting which aims to support a preconceived theory.

You would think this so self-evident that it would not need stating. But every day you can read reporting which stretches and strains the facts to fit a particular thesis. One of the worst examples in recent memory was committed by the *Sun*, Britain's biggest-selling daily. For reasons best known to himself, the then editor became convinced that Aids was a disease limited to drug addicts and homosexuals. On several occasions government statistics were wilfully manhandled to support this view. The most flagrant occasion was the publishing of a story whose headline was 'Straight Sex Cannot Give You Aids – Official'. The report said, among other absurdities, that the chances of getting Aids from heterosexual sex were 'statistically invisible. Anything else is homosexual propaganda.' Promised for the following day's paper was 'Aids – The Hoax of The Century'. Eventually, the volume of protests at this coverage produced an apology – which the paper ran at the bottom of page 28.

Here, and this is no isolated case, was reporting that deceived readers and possibly even endangered them. Preconceived theories have no place in journalism. Newspapers should be at war with closed minds, not employing them.

No inducements to publish should be accepted

This means not only money and free gifts, but also the promise of advantage or preferment. It specifically means two things. The first is hidden advertising, where journalists or their papers take money for writing public relations pieces about firms or people which then appear in the editorial columns parading as normal stories. This has in recent years become a widespread practice in some countries like Russia and the temptation to write hidden advertising in places where pay is very poor is understandable. But that does not make it journalism, and that is what is wrong with it. It is advertising, PR, puffs, whatever you call it, dressed up to look like journalism. It is a deception, and a corrupt one.

It is damaging and dangerous on several other grounds. First, it breaks the basic contract with readers. Such stories are purporting to be normal editorial but are in print only because money has changed hands. Second, such deceptions will eventually break the trust in the paper's honest pursuit of truth that should exist between readers and papers. Third, hidden advertising deprives papers of much-needed legitimate advertising. Fourth, the widespread nature of the practice makes many editors suspect that their staff have taken bribes to write about a company when their story may be a perfectly honest and legitimate one. Fifth, editors and publishers will, like hotel owners paying waiters low salaries because of tips, use hidden advertising as an excuse not to pay journalists properly. Sixth, if hidden advertising is acceptable, then why are such stories not labelled 'advertising' or some line carried at the end to make it plain that the company mentioned has paid for this story? The reason, of course, is that if this was done, firms would soon stop paying for hidden advertising and have to buy open advertising. And, seventh, it establishes that the journalists who do it have their pens and minds available for hire. What will they accept money for next? Writing favourable stories about criminal groups? Keeping stories about wrong-doing by firms and others out of the paper? That is but a short step or two away from the collection of information with the deliberate view to selling its destruction or non-appearance in print. In other words, blackmail.

(Lest anyone think this a good original money-making scheme, an American publisher called Robert Harrison got there first in the 1950s with a magazine called *Confidential*. It specialised in Hollywood scandal and, by paying large sums for tips and information, he and his investigators obtained decidedly intimate details of the stars' private lives. Each story was well-researched and Harrison's staff were not fussy about their methods, hiring prostitutes to trap victims, secretly taping and filming encounters and confessions. Sales of *Confidential* soared, and eventually hit four million – an American record. But soon the temptation to sell the negatives, tapes and other evidence to wealthy stars proved too strong. The inevitable court case happened, a staff member killed herself, the editor shot his wife and himself in a New York taxicab, Harrison sold the magazine and both he and it went into a richly-deserved oblivion.)

Hidden advertising is very rare in Western Europe. What is common there is the acceptance by journalists of what they call 'freebies', that is, free trips with vacation companies, free meals from restaurants or free tickets from theatres, all given so that journalists can review them. The danger of this is that the writer will feel obliged to write a favourable piece. This need not be so, and the dangers can be minimised and faith kept with the reader if it is made plain somewhere in the piece or in a footnote that the ticket/trip/meal or whatever was given free to the newspaper.

Journalists should not allow advertisers to influence, directly or indirectly, the paper's editorial content

It is not uncommon, especially on smaller, less profitable or provincial papers, for advertisers to try and use their commercial weight to bully the paper. This pressure should be resisted at all times. It normally comes from the paper's advertising department who will say to the editor that they have this important client who is or has spent a lot of money on ads and it would be helpful if some 'good coverage' can appear. For instance, a few years ago the *Riverside Press-Enterprize*, a paper in California, published a total of 11 news pieces and 22 photographs of a new department store called Nordstrom's in six days before, during and immediately after its opening in the town. These 400 column inches appeared in the same week as 20 full pages of ads for the store. A coincidence? Unlikely.

More rarely, groups of advertisers can act in concert to try and force the paper to change its coverage. When I took over as editor of a provincial paper in Britain, one of the things I did was to stop the *automatic* reporting of all court cases involving shop-lifting because they were so common as to be boring. Within a week, all the department stores in the city approached the publisher and told him that unless reporting of all shop-lifting cases was restored they would withdraw their advertising, which was considerable. They wanted the coverage to resume, they said, because it acted as such an effective deterrent to would-be thieves. Luckily the publisher supported me. The advertisers' threat was not carried out.

The danger of giving in to advertisers' pressure, whether individual or collective, is that your content ceases to be freely decided on. You would also find that what is granted to one advertiser would soon be demanded by many. Give in once, and you would never be free of the pressure.

Stories should not be submitted for approval or vetting to anyone outside the newspaper

Showing the subject of a story the finished article before publication is a common practice on many papers. The excuse made is that this gives a chance for any errors of fact to be corrected and so save the journalist from error. But surely it is not up to the subjects of stories to save journalists from mistakes; that is for journalists to do themselves. Showing someone what will inevitably be described as 'the draft' of a story gives them the idea that they are being given it for their approval, and hence, possible alteration. It is the journalists' job to produce accurate copy, not something that is the basis for negotiations with the subject.

Many times a source or subject will say something to a reporter that they subsequently regret. There is not a lot of point in journalists training themselves to question good information out of people if they then offer them an subsequent opportunity to withdraw it. And does any journalist seriously think that when a source or interview subject requests sight of the story before publication that their motive is to help the journalist? Of course not. Giving someone outside the paper a look at a story before publication is not only an invitation to censor or pressure the journalist to change an honest account, it leads to the expectation that this practice is routine and a right. Once word goes round that people can request sight of a story, they will all want to do it.

Always quote accurately

This is vital, as even the smallest liberty can change emphasis and meaning. The excuse given is, 'It's what they meant to say.' Well, how do you know? If your source has spoken in a clumsy way, put what they said in reported speech. Many journalists working in the political field regularly tidy up the language of politicians. They think it is part of their job to take the inarticulate ramblings, the incoherent, ungrammatical sentences of politicians and turn them into neat, rounded sentences. It is not. First you would be quoting inaccurately: what you said they said is not what they said, and that is dishonest. Second, if the politician in question is an ignorant oaf who cannot speak his own language properly, let the readers know. Otherwise they might vote for him.

There is one other unsafe practice with quotes and that is the habit some reporters have of putting statements to people, getting a 'yes' answer or a nod and then putting that statement in direct quotes as if it was said by them. For instance, 'Do you agree that the government has mishandled this situation and is now trying to cover that up?' And when the subject nods, the reporter writes in his story, 'He then said, "The government has totally mishandled the situation and is now in the middle of a cover-up."' Any such exchanges should be in reported speech, making clear what the question was and the extent of the reply.

Making up quotes ought to be as patently ill-advised as sticking a wet hand in a light socket. But some reporters seem to feel that the obvious wrongs of this are somehow suspended when they are doing a story which involves, or would enlivened by, a few words from the man or woman in the street. Dishonesty is almost the least of reasons for not doing this. First, no reporters' imagination will be the equal of the bizarre and often naturally comic voice of the public. Second, the kind of reporters who go in for this, and specialise in filling their pieces with such details as 'overheard on the metro', invariably have no more idea of how people actually speak than someone who has been deaf from birth. The normal retort to such 'inventive' reporters is that they should be writing fiction. But, actually, they shouldn't. Ideally they should not be writing anything.

Do not use your position to threaten or gain advantage

A journalist has power. It should never be abused, either in the course of a story, or in one's daily life. Prosecuting personal disputes by implying exposure or reference to high-placed connections is bullying, and unsafe bullying at that. How could you ever come to write a future story about any person or organisation you have threatened in this way? How also could you write about the connections you have used in your threat? You will be in their pocket for the favour you owe them. Neither should you use your newspaper's headed notepaper to write a letter demanding preferential treatment, compensation for some alleged negligence or faulty service. It implies to the recipient, apart from anything else, that your paper exists as a sort of private protection racket for its staff.

Do not promise to suppress stories for friendship or favours

It sometimes happens that you are asked by someone to 'forget' a story, or part of it, in return for some favour, or, in some countries, money. It is clearly wrong to accept such an offer, for the same reasons as it is wrong to put in a story for favours. When friends are involved, refusal might be more delicately phrased, but just as swift and sure. So should it be with colleagues, as the following two stories illustrate.

The first case comes from Oregon in the United States where a few years ago a local television station reported that the long-time chief of staff of the state's Republican senator, had served for 25 years as director of a bank that collapsed and was bailed out at a cost to taxpayers of $100 million. It was suggested that the man's involvement with the bank may have influenced the senator's position on bank deregulation and the subsequent bailout. The story was picked up by the Associated Press and was the talk of the state, but the main newspaper in the state, the *Oregonian*, chose to ignore it. It also ignored allegations a week later that the chief of staff's official travel, at taxpayer's expense, had included 52 trips to New York, where he published an annual guidebook to the city that had earned him more than $1 million.

The paper's reluctance to write this story may have had something to do with the fact that the chief of staff wrote a weekly column for the paper. It eventually published parts of the story only after the *Washington Post* gave the revelations national exposure.

Contrast this with a paper called the *Daily Item* in Sudbury, Pennsylvania. Among the daily stories from the police in one issue was an uncensored account of charges filed against a town resident for driving under the influence of alcohol and driving at an unsafe speed. The item included the man's name, age, address and occupation – editor of the *Daily Item*. Which paper would you trust most, the *Item* or the *Oregonian*?

Do not trick people into giving information

Reporters should always make plain their identity as a reporter. Otherwise you will be tricking people into giving information under false pretences. That is not only dishonest, it is also unsafe. As you will know yourself, people are often very free with talk until they realise you are a journalist or that you are taking an interest in what they say. Then they become a lot more guarded and start to qualify their information. This is because they are now having to take some responsibility for the quality and veracity of these facts. So if you do not tell them you are a reporter, they are liable to exaggerate in a way that people often do in informal conversation. Only in very special circumstances should you hide or change your identity, as discussed in the chapter on investigative journalism.

Do not invent or improve information

Inventing information is obviously wrong and dangerous. So, too, is even a little light doctoring of the facts, embellishment of the truth or temporary amnesia about certain details that inconvenience the main thrust of the story. Your report will be a cheat. This applies with equal force to photographers and the dishonest 'set-up' picture, where an event or situation is staged to imitate some alleged reality.

Some news photographers in Western Europe also have been known to carry around in their cars certain 'props' to insert into pictures. A well-known ploy, for instance, used to be to always have a child's shoe, or teddy bear available, so that if the photographer was covering a disaster like a train or air crash, they could set this prop among the wreckage for the 'poignant' picture. Such pictures have now become a cliché. Besides, there was always the danger that the passenger list, when finally issued, would reveal that there were no children aboard.

Never reveal sources

Much information is given to journalists on the understanding that the identity of the supplier will never be revealed. It is vital, especially when dealing with authorities which are angered that such information has been revealed, that you keep secret the identity of your sources. To reveal them is a betrayal of a promise made and will mean that fewer people will take risks to supply journalists with information. In some circumstances it might also get your source the sack, a spell in jail, or worse.

Always correct your mistakes

Journalism is the first draft of history, and is often written under great pressure, without access to all the sources and in a very short time indeed. So it is not surprising that mistakes are frequently made. Newspapers should always correct these as soon and as fully as they can. It is honest to do so, your readers will be better informed and they will be grateful for that and admire your candour. The sneaky pretence that you do not make mistakes is patently absurd and fools no one.

You should not benefit personally from the articles you write

You are compromised if you accept favours from the people you cover, or if you benefit personally from the articles you write. Let me illustrate this with a case given at the Harvard Ethics workshop previously mentioned:

> You have become personal friends with a city official, who is a neighbour. He invites you to join in purchasing a washing machine that your two families can share. He can obtain this machine, which would ordinarily be beyond your financial reach, because of a good relationship he has with a local factory

director. He says that, in return, the director would like a positive story about his enterprise.

The workshop notes then ask the question, 'What do you do?' A rhetorical question if there ever was one, perhaps better phrased: 'Would you trade your reputation, honesty, integrity and ability to cover freely this factory for a half share in a washing machine?'

The other highly dangerous practice is to use the information you have acquired in order to make a commercial gain before the story is published – a temptation more likely to be faced by business reporters. A few years ago, for instance, a reporter for the *Wall Street Journal* called R. Foster Whinans co-wrote a column based on information from sources that traded stocks. He decided to sell information to his friend who was a stockbroker.

He was paid $31,000 to leak the contents of the column to several stockbrokers, enabling them to buy and sell shares in companies before this information became public and thus would affect the price of the stock. The brokers made about $690,000 from the leaked information. Whinans and the brokers were eventually caught and found guilty in court of violations of the Securities Exchange Act by misappropriating confidential information. Whinans was sentenced to 18 months in prison, five years' probation, 400 hours of community service and a $500 fine. It is to prevent abuses like this that many Western papers make their financial staff declare their investments and financial dealings.

Grey areas

The above issues are clear-cut ones. But there are a lot of issues in reporting that are more complicated. Hard and fast rules are difficult to design and apply. Take phoney by-lines, for example, a practice that is widespread but thought by many to be unethical. Since the story purports to be written by someone who does not in fact exist, it is plainly a deceit. It is also unsafe where the story may be challenged, or even end in a law suit. Who do you produce in court? An actor taking the name of the fictitious reporter?

Another issue about which you cannot be dogmatic is privacy. There is a great deal of difference between the public interest and what the public may find interesting if presented in a sensational enough way. Journalists must have very good reasons for invading someone's privacy and also be aware of the consequences of such reporting. Public figures, when they become such, can be regarded to have sacrificed most of their right to privacy. If they are asking for our votes and our taxes to pay their wages, we do have a right to know about them and their lives. This justification is, however, normally applied in a partisan way: a general rule of journalism seems to be that papers defend the privacy of those they admire and invade the privacy of those they seek to destroy.

A sensible, safe and correct guideline is that the person should be a public figure and that the invasion of their privacy must have a legitimate justification of the public interest, and not merely the interest (that is, curiosity) of the public. If a man standing for public office makes a great deal of public fuss about morality and the virtues of family life, but you can prove that he has a string of mistresses, then I think it is right for you to publish a story. His double standards are clearly relevant to public life. If, however, you learn about the sex life of a private citizen, then however fascinating it is, I do not think that is a legitimate target for a story.

A few years ago in Britain a policeman began an affair. His wife learnt about it and persuaded him to give up his mistress. The jealous lover then told a national paper and her account was printed under the headline, 'The Love Life of a Detective'. As a result, the couple's child was teased at school, the husband had to give up his job and the family had to move. Some may think that a fitting punishment for his original sin. I do not think so, and neither would I like to have to justify that reporting.

An issue which comes up less frequently is where journalists get involved in wrong-doing in order to investigate it. This is not a good idea. Breaking the law in pursuit of a story is both wrong and unsafe. It removes whatever moral legitimacy their reporting may have otherwise had. But sometimes reporters investigating drug-dealing, crime or prostitution learn information that they should ordinarily pass straight to the police.

You need a lot of experience to judge this, but I think you can justify pressing on with your inquiries and not telling the author-ities, on two conditions. First, that the safety of no innocent citizen is threatened by your silence, and second, that you pass on to the police your information as soon as you can. (This condition about the safety of citizens also applies to the situation where journalists are accused of merely spectating in disaster or war situations and not doing anything to help those who are in danger. My rule would be that if you can have any influence on the outcome of a situation you should follow your normal instincts and act to help.)

Never accept a free ticket from a theatre manager, a free ride from the chamber of commerce, or a favour from a politician.

H.L. Menken

9

Writing for Newspapers

The most essential gift for a writer is a built-in, shock-proof shit-detector.
Ernest Hemingway

Newspapers are not literature. But then neither is most literature. Writing for papers is different from writing a novel or short story, but not as different as some would like to think. All good writing has some things in common. It is clear, easy to read, uses fresh language, stimulates and entertains. Those things are as true of the well-written newspaper story as they are of the well-written novel. And they are true whatever language you are writing in.

Now for the bad news. Learning how to write is hard, lonely work. We all know people who say they want to write. What they often want is to merely walk around saying they are writers. What they do not want to do is to put their butts on a chair and not get up until they have covered some paper or a computer screen in words. That is what you have got to do. Many, many times. And the way you progress and develop whatever talent you have is to write hundreds and hundreds of stories and make mistakes. You leave vital things out and put irrelevancies in, write half the piece, then realise it is going wrong and have to start again, write clumsily, pompously or stiffly, turn in work that is confusing or trite, and commit to paper or screen whole paragraphs so silly that if you had to speak them, your voice would trail off in embarrassment mid-sentence.

Now for the good news. After a while, by hanging around a good newspaper and listening; by reading, studying the good and the bad and being your own sharpest critic, you begin to see a way. There will still be times when you take a long time to get a story to work, but by and large, the more you write, the more fluently you write. Writing is like a muscle, it will be a lot stronger if you exercise it every day; you will waste less time in false starts and chasing down the wrong route, less time in writing stories at the wrong pace for the length they should be and less energy trying to think of a fancy phrase when a simple one will be better.

And you find that essential thing without which no one can call themselves a writer – your voice. No more will you be experi-

103

menting with a style that is over-elaborate, too formal or too colloquial. Instead, you will have found a natural style that suits you, is consistent, has rhythms and expressions recognisably yours and – the crucial test – if read aloud would sound like an only slightly tidied up version of your speech. It will be your own. Not put on, not affected and not borrowed. Of course it will owe something to the writers you admire, your background, education, reading and so forth. But it will be your individual use of words and idioms, and your own particular pattern of sentence lengths. This, and the rhythm within sentences and over several of them, will be like a signature. Only more readable.

Planning

The most important part of writing is what happens inside your head between finishing your research and putting the first word down. You have got to think about your material and decide what it is about and what you want to do with it. Composition is not merely the business of arranging words, it is the business of organising thought. It does not matter how wonderful you are at conjuring up colourful phrases or witty remarks, if you have not got a clear idea of what you want to say it will show.

This is easy enough on some cataclysmic event or short, straightforward news stories, but most journalism is not like that. Stories are complex, not as strong as you would like, or they are long features covering many different aspects, or commissioned pieces where you are not very sure that the subject is all that interesting to the reader. Then you have to think hard about what the story is actually about. And it is sometimes not immediately obvious. A feature, for example, about a man collecting and keeping exotic frogs in his apartment is superficially about amphibians, a subject in which not a lot of people are automatically interested. But it is also a story about eccentricity and obsession, about how a hobby has taken over his life (and his home). That is a far more promising topic than frogs.

The other thing you have to work out is the treatment for the story. Is it hard news? A soft news story or light human interest? Told chronologically or by covering each aspect in turn? All these different ways of handling the story (and there are many more) affect the construction, the main framework of which you need to know before you start. In the case of simple news stories, planning what you want to say and the order you want to say it in can be done quickly in your head. But with longer, or more complex, articles you need a written plan. Never be afraid to make a plan on paper. It is not the sign of an untutored novice, but someone who wants to get it right. It does not have to be very detailed –

just the main building blocks of the story in order, with maybe a few notes of how to link them.

Construction is dealt with later in its own chapter, as is the intro, that all-important first paragraph. Those sections discuss how you can grab the reader's attention immediately and sustain it through the piece – both obviously essential features of good writing. There are, I think, six others: clarity, fresh language, honesty, precision, suitability and efficiency.

Clarity

Each story must be clear in thought, organisation and language. If it isn't, then it needs re-thinking or re-writing. You don't just have to take my word for that. French novelist Stendhal wrote, 'I see only one rule: to be clear. If I am not clear then my entire world crumbles into nothing.' British writer H.G. Wells put it less dramatically, 'I write as straight as I can, just as I walk as straight as I can, because that is the best way to get there.' Of no writing is this more true than that for newspapers. They are often read in distracting, noisy surroundings by people with other demands on their time and easier, albeit inferior, ways of getting news. Specific points to watch for are detailed below.

Achieve clarity before you have even put a single word down

To explain something to others, you must first fully understand it yourself. Until you do, don't write it down.

Be careful to include each stage in a narrative, each event in a sequence and each step in an argument

Jumping from A to C leaves the reader having to work out that B happened in between. That's annoying, confusing and sometimes misleading, especially in the cases when B actually happened out of place. And don't make leaps of logic. You may understand your thought processes but the reader will not unless you explain them.

Don't assume readers have special or prior knowledge

When you as a reporter have spent a lot of time delving into a specialist or technical area, it is easy to forget that the reader knows only as much about it as you did before you began your research. Don't. And on stories that run for many days, weeks or months, don't assume that the reader has a photographic memory of what has gone before or has sat dutifully making notes while they read your previous stories. They haven't. Instead, work on the assumption that until something has passed firmly into general knowledge, readers will need reminders and recaps.

Explain all jargon

The normal instruction on this subject is to avoid using all jargon, whether it is scientific, technical, bureaucratic or whatever. I think this is a mistake. Some jargon is useful. It takes readers inside a formerly closed world, adds to their knowledge of the language specialists use and, especially with bureaucratic jargon, shows the often-ludicrous phrases that officials dream up and thus their mentality. For these reasons, and for lovers of irony, it should never be banned from stories. What, however, should be is the failure to explain in everyday language what the jargon means.

This is not to say that jargon should often be used, even if it is explained. Journalists, especially specialist reporters, can easily slip into using jargon because they want to display their knowledge and sound like an insider. Well, by all means do so at a dinner-party if you think it will impress people, but not in your paper. Trying to come across as an insider or writing for insiders is elitist and obscurantist, neither of which characteristics are wanted on newspapers. A number of journalists are prone to trotting out computer jargon. For them writing is 'randomly-accessed user-friendly input', and the trouble with that, as you can see, is that if you use the language of computers, you end up writing like one.

Then there is commercial and political jargon, which these days is perhaps the most damaging kind of all. It is widespread, sometimes difficult to detect, and journalists are especially prone to repeat it unthinkingly. Spokesmen for large companies say that their 'operation' (firm) is 'undergoing temporary cash-flow difficulties' (running out of money) due to 'market positioning problems' (people are not buying what they make) and so there will be a 'rationalisation of the work force' (people will be sacked). Government officials talk of 'correctional facilities' when they mean prisons and 'an in-balance between the supply and demand for domestic units' when they mean that there is a housing shortage.

These are euphemisms, a form of linguistic dishonesty which is particularly common where public relations people proliferate. They play on the natural tendency of politicians and business leaders to, if not lie, at least try and hide the truth when under pressure. The result is the contemporary obsession by those in authority with 'presentation'. If this has not yet happened in your country, then wait a while. It will soon come.

Ensure your sentences are totally clear

Beware especially of writing sentences that oblige readers to revise their opinion of what you are saying. This means they have to go back and read it again. Don't make them do this; instead, go back and re-write it. Of course, it is a frequent device in writing to lead the reader to expect one thing and then deliver another. Surprise is important to keep the writing lively. But that is done deliberately and it is not the same as inadvertently taking yourself by surprise.

Avoid tricky writing and tricky language

Any writing that is self-consciously clever is almost certainly self-evidently bad. The idea is to communicate your meaning to others, not to keep it to yourself. So if you find yourself writing a showy phrase that you are particularly proud of, strike it out; if you have to verbally explain a passage to someone, change it; and if you feel tempted to use words to display your erudition, resist.

One final word on clarity – simplicity

This virtue is normally urged on journalists when they are writing, especially for mass-market newspapers. It is good advice, up to a point; and that point is where simplicity becomes simple-mindedness. Some papers, particularly in Britain and Australia, severely under-estimate the literacy of their readers, with the result that they use a vocabulary and language which is restricted and stylised.

They defend this on the grounds that they know their readers – a questionable assertion. If they actually knew them, they would know that in speech and thought their customers' minds operate several levels above that of the paper. If anyone doubts that, they have only to compare the vastly more complicated language and vocabulary of television that their readers cope with every day. When simplicity means linguistic in-breeding, it is time to let in a little new blood.

Fresh language

The whole point of articles in newspapers is to give readers something they have not had before – information, insights, observations, thoughts. It is therefore a terrible waste to give them something new, but write it in language that is tired and worn-out through over-use. Do that and you will not have the impact you expect and readers will feel even the newest material has an old, familiar ring to it. Points to watch out for are the following.

Regard each story as an individual, new thing

Don't fall into the trap of formula writing, where you say to yourself, 'Ah, here's a he said – she said argument story' and then trot it out to a well-worn pattern. Of course there is a limit to the types of stories around, but that does not mean you must make all which bear a similarity to each other conform to a set formula. Professor John Carey, in his introduction to *The Faber Book of Reportage* writes: 'Massive accumulations of standardised language and hackneyed story-lines lie in wait, ready to leap from the fingers to the typing page.' As he says, reporters have to see their story and tell it, as if for the first time. In this sense, beware especially a story which appears to write itself. If that starts to happen, stop, think and you write it instead.

Avoid all clichés

And, for once, here is something that is as easy to do as it is to say. Clichés are words and phrases that are familiar, too familiar, so recognising them should not pose any problems. A good rule is that anything you suspect of being a cliché undoubtedly is one and should be removed. Some are in general use, others seem to be purely confined to newspapers and are dealt with later in this chapter. But whatever they are, they are expressions so old and worn-out that they have ceased to have any impact.

Those that are similes pose an especial danger because their automatic use means they are often applied in the wrong place. For instance, describing a crash scene as 'like a battlefield' is both unoriginal and wrong, as those who have seen both accident scenes and battlefields will know. But whether they are similes, metaphors, catch phrases or single words, the cliché (a feature of which is that it is out of your head and on to the page or screen almost before you have realised it) should be deleted and something fresher put in its place.

Avoid all automatic words

These are normally adjectives which some reporters instinctively link with certain nouns. All deals have to be 'huge', all reports 'shock', all murders 'brutal', all concern 'widespread' and all wants 'long-felt'. The adjective has become like a parasite living on its host and over-use has meant that such descriptions have long since ceased to have any effect. There are also phrases which seem to be used automatically in certain circumstances. Each country's newspapers have them. In English-language papers, for instance, disasters always have investigators 'sifting through the wreckage' and civil disturbances overseas have 'baton-wielding police' and 'stone-throwing demonstrators'. These are not just automatic, but clichés and used so frequently that they cannot possibly be accurate in all cases.

Be very careful with puns

An outright ban would be a bit severe, because once in a while (say every three years) somewhere in the world a journalist comes up with a good fresh one. But meanwhile, many millions more that are anything but fresh get published. They normally take two forms, either where the writer on a certain subject thinks of every possible word associated with that subject and loses no opportunity to fill the story with them (as in 'Tennis Player Nets Fortune') or where the story, normally a light one in a mass-market paper, seems to consist of nothing but word play. To those in the know, such puns are an infallible giveaway: in the first instance that the story is being written by someone with no imagination or judgement; in the second that the story is not worth the space it has been given.

There are no absolute rules in writing, but one that comes pretty close is: never write the obvious. If you go to Las Vegas, don't write about the slot machines; if London, try to get to the end of the piece without reference to rain or Big Ben; if Paris, leave observations on the way women dress to someone else. So, too, with language. They cannot put you in prison for writing a light story about cats which avoids all play on words like paws, nine lives or tail.

And contrary to the myth peddled by newspaper journalists whose stock in trade are puns, they are not at all difficult to write. If they were, there would be very few of them in newspapers. A good general rule would be to allow someone else the glory of being the once-every-three-years hero who comes up with a pun worth repeating, and remove yourself from that competition by never writing with them.

Work hard at creating new similes, metaphors and phrases

Whenever you find yourself reaching in a semi-automatic fashion for a phrase, simile or metaphor, stop and think. Think hard about the real nature of what it is that you are trying to convey and try and find a phrase that fits the bill perfectly, not just the nearest off-the-shelf option. Experienced writers have all kinds of devices where they deliberately and cleverly invert or fool around with familiar phrases to give them new life. But they also put a lot of brain power into trying to describe something or communicate its nature exactly, and that means the hard work of inventing a phrase especially for it.

They also fight and argue with editors for the right to use colourful language. Sometimes this is necessary when you work on a paper which seeks to force a literary straitjacket on its staff. The editing staff at the *New York Times*, for instance, used to be notorious for the dead hand they would lay on the prose of its writers.

Consider the experiences of Molly Ivens in the late 1970s. She once wrote that a man had 'a beer gut that belonged in the Smithsonian'. The copy-editor changed it to, 'a man with a protuberant stomach' – accurate, but dull. Then, another time, she wrote that a guy 'squawked like a two-dollar fiddle', and it appeared in the paper as 'an inexpensive musical instrument'. Editors who do things like that to fresh language should be working in a museum.[1]

Beware the fashionable word or phrase

Language has its vogues, just like hem-lines and hair-styles. Each new fashionable word or phrase, however, rapidly becomes irritating to read. So do your writing a favour – be a trend-setter rather than a trend-follower. Use your own words, phrases and voice and let others mimic the passing fancy. As the style book of the London *Daily Telegraph* says: 'If you are tempted to use a word because all the smart writers are using it, change the word, your reading matter or your job.'

Honesty

There is something about the process of journalism which often mitigates against truth. The lack of time to collate a totally comprehensive account, the difficult or impossible access to all the sources and information, and the need to write the story to a finite, often quite short length – all these factors prevent us sometimes presenting an account that is as complete (or accurate) as we would like. That is fine as long as we are aware of these limitations and don't claim that we are presenting the definitive account in each story. And it is fine if we are doing all we can to overcome these limitations and difficulties.

But often when writing and editing news stories, journalists do things which actually put even more distance between their story and the truth. Writers know what editors prize as a strong news story and in writing the story as strong as they dare, they often make omissions and use language which exaggerates or 'hypes' the story beyond its true value. And, on popular papers especially, if they do not do that, the chances are that an editor will. Avoiding this sometimes inadvertent, sometimes deliberate process is not easy, but here are a few points.

Write only what you know to be true

This is obvious and should not really need saying, but it does. Quite a lot of reporters when challenged on a part of a story will say, 'Well, it must be true.' Suppositions like this might be good enough for a chat in the kitchen with a friend, but not for newspapers.

All stories should be a conscious effort to be balanced and true to both the detail and spirit of the material

This is a tall order. It is not just a question of making sure you have included both sides (normally there are more than two) to the story, and quoted accurately. It is a question of making sure what you have put in the story accurately reflects what you know to be the whole picture. You may, for example, spend a great deal of time interviewing someone who is perfectly even tempered, except for their response to one question. Of course you are entitled to report that touchiness, but even if you quote it with total accuracy, the whole piece would be dishonest unless you indicated that their general mood was benign. Anything else is slanted selection with a dishonest purpose.

Do not hype

This is the process whereby journalists use words that convey a stronger meaning than the material justifies. A lot of it is done automatically to conform to what the writer thinks are the required journalistic conventions, and thus is also a cliché. But whether his intention is conscious or not, the effect is to over-cook the story. Words like 'sensational', 'shock', 'dramatic', and 'disturbing' are used to describe things which are normally a good deal less than sensational, shocking, dramatic and disturbing. As one commentator once said: 'When you hear something described by a journalist as disturbing, you know you cannot take it seriously.'

There are two other bad aspects of this habit. First, all these words involve a value judgement, which has no place in a straight news story. And it is the worst kind of comment – a sneaky comment posing as an legitimate description. It does not declare itself, but goes under an assumed identity. Second, let the facts speak for themselves. If the story is sensational, shocking, disturbing or whatever, tell the readers all about it and let them judge for themselves. Good journalism involves not only the readers trusting the paper, but the paper trusting the readers.

The final trouble with this sort of breathless, exaggerated language is that it bears no relation to the language real people use. And in almost every country, many newspapers have evolved this 'journalese'. In Britain, for example, it is a world where two people disputing a point are 'confronting' each other, and where 'amid extraordinary scenes' (anything remotely out of the ordinary) 'soap-stars' (any actress who has has a walk-on part) have 'miracle' babies (used to describe infants born in anything but the most routine circumstances) which are 'dashed' or 'mercy dashed' to hospital to be operated on by 'hero' doctors. Reporting in journalese is dishonest, at least several steps removed from reality and, because it is so over-used, ultimately has no impact on readers. It is a fossilised art form, performed to a set of rituals. It has stopped evolving; stopped being relevant. It has no life. Replace it with fresh, honest language.

Beware of using simplistic, black and white headline language in stories

There is a great deal of difference between writing that brings an issue or subject to life, and writing that gives the material a phoney life. A prime example of this is using words that have no shades of meaning, but are either very black or very white. This is best explained by relating briefly the roots of this in European mass-market newspapers. Over the last 50 or so years on such papers, headlines have become progressively larger in size. The unavoidable result of this is that the words used in headlines have got much shorter. And there is one great trouble with short words: in almost every case they are far less good at conveying shades of meaning than longer words. They tend to deal in extremes of meaning, black and white and not grades of grey.

Thus if you and I hold different opinions on a subject and discuss it, we could be said to have a disagreement. If we are sufficiently interesting for a popular paper to want to report our debate, how will they describe it in their headline? Well 'disagreement' cannot fit, neither can debate, because all they have room for in type 4.5 cm high is a word of four letters. So our disagreement becomes a 'row' or a 'feud', something very different. Or we have a 'bust up', or I 'lash' you, or 'rap' you or 'blast' you, none of which happened. Typography and design has made a dishonest account of our meeting.

In British tabloid papers, regional papers and some quality ones, annoyance (meaning you are not pleased) is invariably now 'fury' (suggesting anger beyond control), an arrangement (meaning an informal agreement) is a 'deal' (meaning a far more formal agreement, with definite overtones of a financial, possibly even shady, side), bad luck is a 'curse', criticise is 'slam', failure to attend is 'snub', internal dispute is 'civil war', possibility is 'threat', proposal is 'plan', replace is 'oust', traffic jam is 'road chaos' etc. All of these samples (and there are many more to choose from) are shorter, more extreme and more brutal. And in most circumstances where they are used, they are downright misleading. It is as if the story is being translated into another language by an angry man with a limited vocabulary.

This inaccuracy might be confined to the headline were it not for one thing: the language of today's headlines is the language of tomorrow's news stories. Editors and their senior executives control the culture of a paper partly through the language of headlines, which they approve. Reporters read the words used for headlines on their stories and, wanting to be thought in tune with the culture of the paper (and their editor) or a 'bright, lively' writer, they adopt it. And provincial reporters see such language in popular capital city or national papers and they imitate it, often badly. And then even some flagging quality paper, wanting to make its image more youthful, or its appearance more lively, will adopt larger headlines and thus imbibe some, if not the worst, of these excesses. Thus, in varying degrees, does the whole journalistic stream become polluted. If the language of your papers has not yet been invaded by the little black and white words, keep a wary eye out for them.

Do not assume motives

As a reporter, as opposed to a commentator, your job is to find things out and report them, not deduce them. If someone does something and their motive is relevant, ask them, don't assume it. Reporting is not a parlour game.

Precision

Journalism should be the enemy of imprecision. Stories should be written to answer questions in the readers' minds, not raise them. And the questions a reporter should be trying to answer, and answer precisely, are:

What? – What has happened?
Who? – Who has it happened to? Who has done it? Age, appearance, position, credentials and any relevant background.
Where? – Where did it happen?
When? – When did it happen? What time, day, month?
How? – How did it happen? Explanations.
Why? – Why did it happen?

Other points to watch for are:

In all cases, abolish the abstract and use the particular

We as reporters are the ones who should be taking the sweeping generalisations that people make, investigating them and relating our detailed findings. So writing which is not specific is not wanted. Reporting that talks of 'criminal structures' and 'official organisations' without naming them is no good. As a news editor you get to know such stories instantly – by running your eye down them and looking for capital letters. If they have few, you just know that this is a piece about generalisations. So use specific words, concrete ones, name names, make lists and pin things down. You have to be careful where in the story you itemise these details, but they should be there. And don't just call a building 'tall'. How tall is it? In metres, please, plus some graphic idea of what that means.

Use known quantities rather than unknown ones

Writers often use words like 'really', 'considerably' and 'very' to express values or scale. But how much is 'very'? Be precise, use known values.

Don't use vague adjectives

There are some phrases in common use (so common that they border on the cliché) which communicate only vague ideas. 'Expensive tastes', for example, tells you that these tastes are not cheap, but that is all. What does expensive mean here? What the reader wants to know are some concrete examples of what the money is being spent on, preferably with brand names and prices. Similarly 'fast cars' – is it a Porsche, a second-hand police car or a Ferrari? And luxury – what is that? The answer is it is different things to different people. Tell the readers something that will mean the same to all of them. This applies also to descriptions of people. 'She is tall and attractive.' Oh yeah? What does that mean? But if I write that she is blonde and stands 6 feet, then we both know what we mean. 'She is intelligent' is meaningless, except as a general indicator that she is not actually mentally handicapped. But if I write that she has a degree in politics, we begin to learn something concrete.

Avoid euphemisms

This is the language people use to hide from reality. They speak, for instance, of someone 'passing on' when they mean dying, they refer to sex as 'being intimate with'. Victorian England was a rich source for the more absurd euphemisms: 'nether garments' for underwear, 'maleness' for penis, 'in a state of nature' for naked, 'smallest room in the house' for toilet, 'in an interesting condition' for pregnant. Even now, people invent words or phrases to describe the things they feel uncomfortable with, whether it is death, sex or their own emotions.

Journalists should not use euphemisms, unless with irony. But that does not mean that every last detail of sex cases, or killings has to spelt out. Most newspapers are produced for a general readership which embraces an enormous range of people and different sensitivities. You should neither write for the most shockable, prim and proper, nor for the most bloodthirsty.

When writing about violent deaths, be they the results of crime, war or accidents, use your judgement about how graphic you can be without making your readers feel sick. Precision does not have to mean gloating. It means being accurate, and describing things in sufficient *relevant* detail, without becoming insensitive. You should have a reason for giving the detail that you have. In some situations, like plane crashes, readers will not be surprised to learn that the force of the crash or explosion has dismembered and mutilated the corpses. You need only spell out what is necessary.

In other situations, like war or terrorism, people need the horrors of what has been done brought home to them. You will do this all the more effectively if you use measured, cool language. Here is Robert Fisk, then of *The Times* of London, describing the scenes he found when he went to investigate reports of a massacre of Palestinians at a refugee camp at Chatila in September 1982:

> They were everywhere, in the road, in laneways, in backyards and broken rooms, beneath crumpled masonry, and across the top of garbage tips. The murderers – the Christian militiamen whom Israel had let into the camp to 'flush out terrorists' fourteen hours before – had only just left. In some cases the blood was still wet on the ground. When we had seen a hundred bodies, we stopped counting.

Eight paragraphs into his report, Fisk then openly addresses the question of describing the horrors he found:

> What we found inside the camps at ten o'clock next morning did not quite beggar description, although it would perhaps be easier to retell in a work of fiction or in the cold prose of a medical report.
>
> But the details should be told for – this being Lebanon – the facts will change over the coming weeks as militias and armies and governments blame each other for the horrors committed upon the Palestinian civilians.
>
> ... Down a laneway to our right, not more than fifty yards from the entrance, there lay a pile of corpses.
>
> There were more than a dozen of them, young men whose arms and legs had become entangled with each other in the agony of death. All had been shot at point-blank range through the right or left cheek, the bullet tearing away a line of flesh up to the ear and entering the brain. Some had vivid crimson scars down the left side of their throats. One had been castrated. Their eyes were open and the flies had

only begun to gather. The youngest was perhaps only twelve or thirteen years old.

On the other side of the main road, up a track through the rubble, we found the bodies of five women and several children. The women were middle-aged, and their corpses lay draped over a pile of rubble. One lay on her back, her dress torn open, and the head of a little girl emerging from behind her. The girl had short, dark curly hair and her eyes were staring at us and there was a frown on her face. She was dead.

Fisk's report continues for another eleven paragraphs. Neither in these or the preceding thirteen is there is single word of comment, or emotionalism. You can be sure that is not because he feels no emotion, but knows that as soon as the reporter lets that infect the writing, then the impact – and veracity – of the story begins to diminish.

Sex

For many years newspapers all round the world used the language of the nunnery to describe anything remotely sexual. Readers had to guess, rather than know, what was being described. Phrases like 'intimacy took place' and 'improper suggestion' were not only imprecise but also often left the reader with the implication that far worse had happened than actually did. One of the most abused terms was 'interfered with', which once led to the headline in a British paper: 'Girl Stabbed 65 Times But Not Interfered With'.

Yet the replacement of such bashful language with a clearer one is not a licence to write soft pornography. Detail should be given to explain and not to arouse. You will also find that being forced to describe events in a way that is acceptable to the broad band of your readers will frequently produce original and evocative writing. Here is Ben Hecht, an American reporter from the 1920s, writing the final line of a story for Chicago's *Daily News* about a priest who regularly made love to a girl in the basement of his church – until, one day, he accidentally kicked the gas jet open and died while having sex: 'Preoccupied by love, he had smelled no fumes than those of Paradise and given up the ghost while still glued to his parishioner.'

Suitability

Suitability is matching the style, tone and pace of the story to the subject. By no means all subjects require special handling, but others need treatment that is sensitive. Most are obvious. Matters of life and death, for example, should always get serious treatment (unless you are writing a column and specialise in bad taste). Here are a few guidelines for the more straightforward situations.

Stories of action and movement should be written with real pace

The language and construction should be taut, the verbs active and direct, sentences economical and there should be few adjectives. There are few better illustrations of this than Sergei Kurnakov's description of the frenzy in St Petersburg, August 1914 in the hours after Germany declared war on Russia. It is a model of how to write something that reads at the same fast pace as the events it reports:

> When I got to the St Isaac Square it was swarming with people. It must have been about nine o'clock, for it was pretty light yet – the enervating, exciting twilight of the northern nights.
>
> The great greystone monstrosity of the German Embassy was facing the red granite of St Isaac's Cathedral. The crowds were pressing around waiting for something to happen. I was watching a young naval officer being pawed by an over-patriotic group when the steady hammering of axes on metal made me look up at the Embassy roof, which was decorated with colossal figures of overfed German warriors holding bloated cart horses. A flagstaff supported a bronze eagle with spread wings.
>
> Several men were busily hammering at the feet of the Teutons. The very first strokes pitched the mob to a frenzy; the heroic figures were hollow!
>
> 'They are empty! A good omen! Another German bluff! Hack them all down! No, leave the horses standing!'
>
> The axes were hammering faster and faster. At last one warrior swayed, pitched forward, and crashed onto the pavement one hundred feet below. A tremendous howl went up, scaring a flock of crows off the gilded dome of St Isaac's. The turn of the eagle came; the bird came hurtling down, and the battered remains were immediately drowned in the nearby Moika river. But obviously the destruction of the symbols was not enough. A quickly organised gang smashed a side door of the Embassy.
>
> I could see flashlights and torches moving inside, flitting to the upper storeys. A big window opened and spat a great portrait of the Kaiser at the crowd below. When it reached the cobblestones, there was just about enough left to start a good bonfire. A rosewood grand piano followed, exploded like a bomb; the moan of the broken strings vibrated in the air for a second and was drowned; too many people were trying to out shout their own terror of the future.

There is not a spare word in this description. Each detail is fixed precisely with the minimum of adjectives. Like all the best writing, it defies editing.

If the events in the story are stark and horrific, resist the temptation to over-write

Not that you should over-write in any situation, but the lure to do so is always greater when your material is extraordinary. Let the events themselves make the impact. And do not try and add drama by characterising the events in any way. Do not, for example, write that the story is 'sensational', 'disturbing', 'extraordinary'. Present the story without such comment and let the reader judge.

Here is a good example, part of an account by Henry Wales of the International News Service, of the execution of Mata Hari, the famously erotic dancer, who inflamed all of Paris, and, if the more lurid stories are to be believed, slept with many of its male population. She was shot as a German agent by the French in October 1917.

Wales, an eye-witness, describes how she was woken; requested, and was granted, permission to write two letters; dressed herself in a silk kimono, stockings, black velvet cloak, floppy hat and black kid gloves, and then declared: 'I am ready.' She was then driven to the grounds of the fort and stood in front of a mound of earth, piled about 8 feet high to catch any stray bullets. Wales then wrote:

Mata Hari was not bound and she was not blindfolded. [She refused to wear one.] She stood gazing steadfastly at her executioners when the priest, the nuns and her lawyer stepped away from her.

The officer in command of the firing squad, who had been watching his men like a hawk that none might examine his rifle and try to find out whether he was destined to fire the blank cartridge which was in the breech of one rifle, seemed relieved that the business would soon be over.

A sharp, crackling command, and the file of twelve men assumed rigid positions at attention. Another command, and their rifles were at their shoulders; each man gazed down his barrel at the breast of the woman which was the target. She did not move a muscle.

The under officer in charge had moved to a position where from the corners of their eyes they could see him. His sword was extended in the air.

It dropped. The sun – by this time up - flashed on the burnished blade as it described an arc in falling. Simultaneously the sound of the volley rang out. Flame and a tiny puff of greyish smoke issued from the muzzle of each rifle. Automatically the men dropped their arms.

At the report Mata Hari fell. She did not die as actors and moving-picture stars would have us believe that people die when they are shot. She did not throw up her hands nor did she plunge straight forward or straight back.

Instead she seemed to collapse. Slowly, inertly, she settled to her knees, her head always up, and without the slightest change of expression on her face. For the fraction of a second it seemed she tottered there, on her knees, gazing directly at those who had taken her life. Then she fell backward, bending at the waist, with her legs doubled up beneath her. She lay prone, motionless, with her face turned towards the sky.

A non-commissioned officer, who accompanied a lieutenant, drew his revolver from the big black holster strapped about his waist. Bending over, he placed the muzzle of the revolver almost – but not quite – against the left temple of the spy. He pulled the trigger, and the bullet tore into the brain of the woman.

Mata Hari was surely dead.

If the story deals with strong emotions, understate rather than overstate

This does not mean you should leave anything out, but that you should avoid language that strains for effect. A heart-rending story, for example, always works best low-keyed.

Beware of humour

In all these instances above it is usually fairly easy to avoid the pitfalls. But there is one area where journalists get into all kinds of suitability problems: comedy, or attempts at it. If it is on the stage or in a book, humour should have no taboos. Death, cancer, sex, hunger – none of these should be fenced off in some propriety zone. Those, however, are the subjects in general. They are a very different matter from having a laugh at some specific person's misfortune in a news story for the following day's paper. Giving a light-hearted treatment to a story which involves injury, distress, or upset is never a good idea. It is insensitive, and actually pointless. If there is a genuinely comic element to the story (of however questionable taste), people will find it and laugh anyway, especially if the tale is told straight.

Most journalists would agree that humour is very difficult to write. The trouble is, it does not stop them attempting it. Indeed so much writing in newspapers is humorous in intent, if not effect, that the failure of journalism textbooks to address this issue borders on the criminally negligent. Just the two words: 'think twice' would be valuable. Of even greater worth would be for them to point out one of the basic truths of humour, because that at least might stop at the drafting stage a lot of the laborious, creaking efforts that get into print. And this truth is: being funny on paper is a God-given talent, and he did not give to it to many of us.

Writing humour is like singing in tune. If you can do it, you don't need to be taught; if you can't do it, no amount of teaching will help you do it. And comedy out of tune, like singing, is excruciating to experience and embarrassing to do. Or should be. However, if you have got the talent, it comes relatively easily. Your ear will recognise instinctively the rhythm that humour writing must have above all things, and the words that are almost funny in themselves. Your instinct tells that jokes are funnier when delivered with a straight face rather than the literary equivalent of a red nose, whirring bow-tie and a grin that splits your head in half. Your eye will see comic possibilities where everyone else sees what is merely on the surface. Your inspiration will be able to call upon all the little cultural, social and historical references that make a joke.

If you have got a good comic idea for a piece that is suitable, then work on it. It has to be tightly written, so tightly that no one word is spare. It has to surprise the reader, which is why anything remotely predictable (like puns) or anything that is telegraphed ahead is no good. And it has to have the punch line at the end of the sentence. Right at the end. Not in the penultimate phrase. Finally, if you are giving an article a particular humorous treatment or framework, that has to be strong enough to carry the whole piece right to the end. The soundest policy always is to let the humour flow naturally from the events and innate absurdities of your subject, rather than being a 'joke' that you impose on it from outside. Here, for example, is an intro written by *Wall Street Journal* reporter Tony Horwitz. Just after the end of the Gulf War, he filed a piece about Kuwait, the invasion of which by Iraq had started the conflict. Kuwait is an oil-rich, semi-feudal state presided over by a fabulously wealthy royal family. This is what Horwitz wrote: 'The emir of Kuwait, Jaber al Sabah, returned home yesterday, 15 days after the liberation of his land, and 10 days after his furniture.'

The moral of this section is that if you have any doubts about a joke or allegedly funny line, leave it out. If you have no doubts, then imagine standing on a stage delivering it to an audience of 500 readers. Only if you still think it will get a laugh should you go ahead with it.

Efficiency

In the last century and quite a way into this one, journalists in Britain and the United States were paid by the line. This system of payment gave birth to a generation of journalists who could write impressive amounts about nothing and almost endlessly about very little. And this in turn produced a bloated style of writing whose chief characteristic was its exponents' ability to never knowingly write one word where four or five could be deployed. As a result, their pompous and excessive language (goalkeepers, for instance were known as 'custodians of the sacred turf' and the ball was 'the elusive leathern spheroid') made a lasting if inadvertent contribution to British humour. It was writing so spectacularly inefficient that, in its way, it was almost admirable.

Thankfully, journalistic style (and, in most cases, systems of payment) have moved on a little. These days, payments to freelances in Western Europe obviously reflect length, but no one gets paid by such a rigid formula. Payment by the word has long since been recognised as a way of bribing people to write badly. But enough of the lineage men's spiritual descendants live on to make a few notes about writing efficiency worthwhile.

Make every phrase and sentence do a job of work

They must either convey fresh information or otherwise help move the piece forward. If any part of the story does not do this, cut it.

Avoid wasteful constructions

Every language has phrases that are used in speech to give the speaker time to form fully the thought that is coming. In English, examples would be: 'It is a well-known fact that ...'; 'Indeed, there is no doubting the fact that ...'; 'We can also observe that ...'. Avoid these and avoid also the leisurely constructions that slow a piece down. Journalism, especially news reporting, has to have pace. It can't if sentences like the previous one are constructed thus: 'It is an essential requirement of most journalism – features, sport, profiles and features, but particularly news reporting – that they should move forwards with that quality known as pace.'

Write without looking at your notes

You will write more quickly and more efficiently if you do so without looking at your notebook every five seconds. You should not even start to write unless the story is clear in your mind, and if you write without notes only the essential material will go in. The details, spellings and figures you can check with your notebook afterwards. There will almost certainly be one or two points you will add as a result, but the main draft will be written far more efficiently from your head than by copying out large chunks of notes.

Ruthlessly hunt down all obvious and silly remarks and remove them

Even the most experienced writers find themselves writing the most pitifully obvious things sometimes. These are often links between paragraphs that you have struggled over, and, in your desperation to try and weld one part of the story to another, you find yourself writing the purest nonsense. Only the other week I cut from a story the phrase, 'Of course, a ballet dancer's life is not all applause ...'. Well whoever thought it was? You often find that you do not need these links at all. Most readers can handle a small change of direction if it is accompanied with a change of paragraph.

Use the active, not passive voice

People and things do and say things, so it is always best to write this directly. Thus: 'Moscow International Airport will open another runway in 1998' and not 'It has been established that another runway will open at Moscow International Airport in 1998.' Certain verbs, like come, leave and give, are frequently used for the passive voice as in: 'The demand came when Yeltsin asked ...' (better to say 'Yeltsin demands ...'), 'The earthquake left 3,000 people dead ...'. ('The earthquake killed ...') and 'The move gave a boost to ...' (better is 'The move boosted ...'). The active voice is not just more efficient, it is also, as the name suggests, more active.

Use quotes sparingly

You can write a lot more efficiently than most people can speak. For example, instead of 'A United Nations spokesman said, "We utterly deny this claim is or ever was true"', just write, 'A United Nations spokesman denied the claim.' Generally you should always use reported speech to convey information. Quotes personalise and give immediacy to a story but they should normally be reserved for reporting lively exchanges, allowing people to comment, or to give an impression of them, their opinions or feelings. They are not to be used as mere padding. There is more on the handling of quotes in the chapter on construction.

Shorten quotes only by visible deletion

There is only one honest, safe way to shorten quotes and that is by omitting phrases and sentences, but making plain by dots that you have done so. For instance, 'I think it is outrageous that we should be asked to do this ... We have no intention of giving in. We are going to fight this all the way.' Never just remove the surplus words and join the parts together as if they were said in continuous speech. If you still cannot achieve the brevity you require, use reported speech.

Use bullets and lists to itemise points in a story

This can be overdone in a paper, but is very useful when you have a long catalogue of points to make. For example, instead of taking several long paragraphs to describe the effects of, say, government spending cuts on transport, itemise them like you would on a shopping list. But beware of doing this and then finding that you have to mention most of the points again in order to add detail to them. Put the detail with the list.

Avoid meaningless modifiers

Phrases like 'serious danger', 'unconfirmed rumours' and 'unduly alarmed' are, if you think for a second, complete nonsense. What, after all, is unserious danger? And if a rumour was confirmed it would no longer be a rumour, it would be a fact and an attributable one. Such automatic phrases can be cut down to the second word, along with other meaningless modifiers like 'rather unique'. It either is, or is not, the only one of its kind, and if it is not, then it is not unique, rather, slightly or otherwise.

Avoid tautology

This is the use of words that say the same thing twice. For instance, '*Some* of the remarks *included* ...' and 'it is an *essential condition*'. In both cases (and many others that could be given) only one of the italicised words is needed.

Do not use quotes to restate points already made in reported speech

This is a common and wasteful habit, as in: 'The ministry denied this. A spokesman said, "We do not accept this allegation."' Write one or the other, preferably the first.

Get to know the words that can be used instead of long phrases

'The subject to which I refer', for instance, amounts to the one little word: 'this'.

Finally, a useful exercise is to take a few of your recent published stories and, with a red pen, reduce the number of words used, without eliminating any essential fact. You will be surprised how wasteful you have been. That is why it is a very good experience for a writer to work a period as a sub. There is nothing like the discipline of telling complex stories in 250 words to teach you efficient writing.

Revision

Writers have to be their own fiercest critics. It is essential that you read back what you have written, looking for any flaws, and revise it if you are not happy. Normally, by the time the story reaches another pair of eyes it will be too late – either for improvement or your reputation. Some writers prefer to get some sort of version of the whole story done before subjecting it to perhaps heavy revision. Others, perhaps those who know more clearly what they want, revise as they go. The timing does not matter, what is important is that the revision is comprehensive, and not just a superficial search for spelling mistakes.

George Orwell, the author of *Animal Farm* and *1984* whose writing was noted for its clarity, thought there were four questions that any writer should ask of each sentence. This sounds laborious, and would be if this questioning did not become automatic and almost subconscious after a while. His questions were:

What am I trying to say?
What words express it?
What image or idiom will make it clearer?
Is the image fresh enough to have an effect?

Then, by way of important afterthoughts, he added two more:

Could I put it more simply?
Have I written anything avoidably ugly?

Those writing regularly will soon learn to ask those questions of their writing with no more conscious effort than they use to move their eyes from left to right as they read. I would, however, suggest that a couple of questions are knowingly asked of the drafted piece:

Are there any loose ends, is everything explained properly?
Does it read flowingly?

If it does, then leave it alone, resist the temptation to throw in a few more colourful phrases, as if you were a cook tossing a few more currants into a cake. And if it does read awkwardly, it may need more than a bit of light tinkering to put right. Punctuation, for instance, is not a quick way to give the kiss of life to dying sentences. Re-write and re-structure until you are happy.

And then cut it. Are there any words, phrases or sentences that slow the piece down? Beware especially of anything that sounded good when you wrote it. As Samuel Johnson once said, 'Read over your compositions and, when you meet a passage which you think is particularly fine, strike it out.' Such parts often don't work as well as you think, or are just unnecessary padding.

This is what you should be hunting for when revising. I rarely come across an article (especially one of my own before submission) that could not be improved by cutting. It is like tightening the nuts and bolts on a piece of furniture. If left undone, the thing would be loose and unstable. (You may be grateful to know that this chapter was originally twelve paragraphs longer than it is.)

The joys of writing

Inexperienced journalists can be almost overwhelmed at times by the problems of writing something clear and interesting that people will want to read. Older writers are not exactly immune from this sinking feeling, too, and to hear them speak of the pains of composition you would think that no sane person would write, unless at the point of a gun. The great American sports journalist, Red Smith, for instance, once said, 'There's nothing to writing. All you do is sit down at a typewriter and open a vein.' To which another American, Gore Vidal, probably gave the definitive reply when he wrote, 'When I hear about writer's block, this one and that one! Fuck off! Stop writing, for Christ's sake. Plenty more where you came from.'

Sure it is sometimes a real sweat. Of course, there are stories which seem a confusing and worthless jumble until you have spent many hours wrestling them into shape, and there are times of sheer panic as the deadline approaches with the thing only half done and ill thought. But the pleasures of capturing something and pinning it down in words, your words, are immense. So too is the thrill of starting a piece with an assortment of disparate information and finding a pattern to it and new ideas about it as you write. It also beats working for a living.

You will have to write and put away or burn a lot of material before you are comfortable in this medium. You might as well start now and get the necessary work done. For I believe that eventually quantity will make for quality.

Ray Bradbury

10

Intros

Always grab the reader by the throat in the first paragraph, sink your thumbs into his windpipe in the second, and hold him against the wall until the tag line.

Paul O'Neil, American writer

The intro is the most important paragraph in the story. It can make people want to read to the end, or turn them off and send them hurrying to another article. And they will not be slow to do this. Newspapers are often consumed fast, by people with little time to read them, in places and conditions not designed for relaxation and contemplation – trains, metros, cars at traffic lights, offices, in the street etc. There is a good chance that if the first paragraph does not grab their attention, they will never get to the second one.

That progress is not always determined by the quality of the intro. Other factors play a role: a good headline will sometimes inspire people to dig beyond the intro, a strong interest in the subject matter may force them to read past the direst intro in case the story perks up, and they are also influenced by the size of the paper (one of 96 pages obviously offering more alternative articles to sample than one of 12). As a journalist you cannot influence or have fore-knowledge of these factors. (And don't say you know the size of the paper. Of course you do, but the reader may be buying several others.) The only way you can make a reader get beyond the intro is to make it a good one.

Whatever kind of intro you are writing, on whatever kind of story, there are some general points to remember.

General guidelines

The job of the intro is to capture readers' interest and set the tone for the article that follows

The intro should be direct, uncluttered and unambiguous

There should only be one question in readers' minds when they read an intro: 'Do I want to read this story?' The answer is liable to be 'no' if you give them extra questions raised by ambiguity and complication. It is also important to clear out any unwanted clutter, such as needless detail, precise titles, or attribution, that can wait until the second paragraph or later.

The intro should be self-contained

Except with certain types of features, it should not depend for its sense on what follows, only for its explanation and exposition. Neither should there be any unidentified facts, people, events, organisations or places unless strictly necessary.

Never start any story with a subsidiary clause

For instance, 'Despite the rising number of murders ...' or 'Although murders are increasing almost daily ...'. This approach is slow, delays the main point and puts questions in readers' minds. Subsidiary clause beginnings have this effect on any sentence and so should be used sparingly in even the body of the text.

Never start a story with numbers in digits

Never start stories with official names of official bodies

The first eight or so words of a story are very important. So unless you have an exceptional reason or are being ironical, long bureaucratic titles are a bad way to start a story. If you start a story, 'The Ministry of Agriculture and Fisheries Pollution Monitoring Unit yesterday announced ...', readers will turn away before they have a chance to read that all fish caught in a certain river are contaminated and should not be eaten. Begin instead with either a short form of the name, such as 'Government pollution experts', or, far better, tell people what has happened and attribute it later.

Only rarely begin with quotes

Beginning stories with quotes mystifies readers because until you tell them, they do not know who is talking. There are a few isolated occasions when a quote will be a good way to start, but, in these cases, the speaker should immediately be identified.

Do not get too obsessed with the length of intros

Some papers have rules about the maximum length of intros. If yours does, you have little choice but to conform. But otherwise, do not worry too much if an intro's length breaches some mythical 'limits'. In more than 20 years in journalism I have never read a letter from a reader complaining about the length of an intro. So long as an intro is grabbing readers, it is doing its job.

Normally when intros are written about in textbooks, the author will list various types of newspaper story (straight news, human interest etc.) and set out the intros used in each case. This is unhelpful, stupid and wrong. It gives the impression that writing is a matter of acquiring techniques, that journalists can be provided with a bag of tricks or tools which they open and use according to the circumstances: 'Ah, here is a human interest story, so out comes the delayed intro approach ...'. And it produces the formula writing which is such a disease. Far better to set out the different approaches to intros and leave it to the writer to decide how to apply them.

Hard news approach

Papers used to present hard news stories (that is, dramatic, clear-cut ones) with headlines of many lines, or decks. This gave all the main points of the story and sometimes contained as many words as today's headline and first paragraph combined. Consider this from the *Philadelphia Inquirer* of Monday 17 April 1865 reporting the news of President Lincoln's assassination on the Friday before:

The Great Tragedy!

A Nation Mourns Its Honoured President

Joy Changed To Mourning!

The Great Martyr To Liberty!

MURDER OF THE PRESIDENT

Full Details of Assassination

Account of a Distinguished Eyewitness

Mr Lincoln's Deathbed Scene

A Noble Patriot Gone To Rest

Escape of the Dastard Assassin

Mr Seward Still Alive

His Condition is Favourable

Andrew Johnson Inaugurated as President!

His Inaugural Address

Views of the New President

He Retains The Old Cabinet!

Official Gazette From Secretary Stanton

Our Special Dispatches!

No wonder that after all that there was no need to write what we would now call a hard news intro. There are 80 words in the headlines above, far more than would be in the headline and first two paragraphs of a newspaper story today.

Nearly a hundred years later in the afternoon of 23 November 1963, came the assassination of President Kennedy. Here are the headlines and intro from the following day's *Dallas Morning News*:

KENNEDY SLAIN ON DALLAS STREET

Johnson Becomes President

Pro-Communist
Charged With Act

A sniper shot and killed President John F. Kennedy on the streets of Dallas, Friday. A 24-year-old pro-communist who once tried to defect to Russia was charged with the murder shortly before midnight.

There are 48 words here for headlines and intro, only a little more than half of the headlines alone for the Lincoln story. Leaving aside the question of the loaded references to 'pro-communist', the intro is identical in form and intent to ones put on hard news stories throughout America, Britain and much of the rest of the world today.

Chronological or leisurely intros on hard news stories began to disappear at the beginning of this century. Headlines became bigger in type size but far smaller in terms of words and so the intro had to do the job that all those headlines did before. Stories shortened as mass literacy spread and so had to be written more crisply, and papers became far bigger, thus increasing competition within the paper for readers' attention. All these pressures within the newspaper industry speeded the evolution of the hard news intro.

Factors outside the press were at work, too. The pervasive impact of advertising with its snappy, catchy language and simple messages has had an enormous effect on popular culture throughout the world. Readers now have far less time to read papers than they did before social changes like mass car-ownership, radio, television and greater general affluence. And the lack of formal censorship means there is no need to write in an elliptical way for readers to read between the lines. Readers want directness and you can give it to them.

So much for the theory of the hard news intro. Now the practice. And we are talking here about reporting news *in the first instance*. Stories written on a subject several days after the event may need a different approach and certainly would if they had in the meantime been reported on radio or television.

The aim of all intros is to grab readers and arouse their interest so strongly that they will want to read on. With hard news intros, this means that the most newsworthy aspect(s) of the story should be right up there at the top. This is particularly true if the headline style in your country is for ones which are cryptic, with literary allusions which often give little detailed information about the story underneath. All the more reason to come to the point as soon as you can.

This is not normally difficult on strong or clear-cut stories. If 345 people have been killed in a plane crash in the capital city of your country, there is not much doubt about the hard news intro: 'At least 345 people were killed when a Global Airlines Boeing 747 crashed into an apartment block in the suburbs of Moscow last night.' But as we know, most stories are not as direct as that. They have several angles (aspects) and we cannot get them all into the intro without making it hopelessly cumbersome. Unless you want an intro which cannot make up its mind, you have to select which aspect is the most newsworthy by applying news value.

That makes it sound simple, but it isn't. Too many highly experienced journalists have spent too many hours writing, rejecting and then re-writing intros. And the issue of what is the best angle for the intro is probably the part of the job that causes more arguments in more newsrooms around the world than anything else. There is invariably no simple right and wrong, just conflicting opinions.

So if you are in two (or three) minds about how to write the intro for the story, is there any help available? Thankfully there is. It was some advice given to me many years ago and I think it is the single most useful tip anyone has ever given me. It is called the Parable of The Friend On The Hill and it goes like this:

> Imagine you have all the story's information in your head and you are walking in the country. Suddenly, on top of a hill, you see a friend who you know will be keen to learn about your story. You run towards him, up and up, and when you get within reach of him you only have enough breath for one sentence before collapsing. What is it that you blurt out? That is your intro.

There are variations on this theme, such as to imagine you are sending a telegram about the story, the charge is £10 a word and you are paying. Set yourself a very severe target for the number of words in the telegram: six, or even four. What that will do is force you to think of the key word or words in the story. You can then build the story around that.

I was once told by Geoffrey Murray, the Reuters correspondent who broke the Ping-Pong diplomacy story of the 1970s, an anecdote which perfectly illustrates this. It involves the Reuters correspondent in India covering Mahatma Gandhi at an engagement in 1947. The yarn conflicts with the version in the official history of the news agency, but that does not detract from its therapeutic value to the confused writer of intros.

The Reuters man was at a prayer meeting attended by the Indian leader when a man suddenly leapt forward and shot him. Gandhi was badly wounded, but not immediately dead. The reporter ran down the road to the nearest post office to send a cable to London, but found he only had money enough to transmit four words. What should they be? 'Mahatma Gandhi shot here'? – well, you can probably assume your office will know the leader's full name and be aware of his, and your, whereabouts, so 'Mahatma' and 'here' are wasteful. What he filed was: 'Gandhi shot worst feared' – thus conveying an assassination attempt, the victim, method and likely outcome, all in four words. He had also alerted the office to prepare the obituary to run – a vital thing for the agency and all its clients.

One word of warning for such circumstances: avoid ambiguity at all costs. A message from New York was received at Reuters London office in September 1901 which read 'McKinley shot Buffalo' and was spiked by a young sub-editor with the words, 'These Yanks. They seem to think we're interested in their blooming President's shooting excursion.' The story was rescued by the editor in charge who realised that Buffalo referred not to the animals but to the city in New York State. Thus did the agency first flash the news of the assassination around the world.

Other approaches

In most cases where you are reporting on news of general interest, and doing so in the first instance, the hard news intro is the best choice. Yet there are, of course, many other ways to begin a story and some of them can be applied to news stories in the right situation. Feature openings are generally a lot more free-form and, for these especially, the only criterion is what works. This point is equally true of intros to analysis, colour, comment and personality pieces.

Every writer should make intros a lifetime's study, taking every available paper or magazine as a potential text. Once you begin to study intros you soon realise that what you thought were about four or five main types soon multiply into dozens. Trying to identify all the different approaches would be a lifetime's work, and an attempt to categorise them into a finite number of types would be pointless. You would not be able to move for exceptions and conditions. The vital thing is that you are fresh and inventive. However experienced you are, there is always a better alternative to the knee-jerk intro. The following, however, are some of the main types found on news stories and features. Some of them raise the issue, dealt with more fully in the chapter on construction, that intros are often conceived not as one paragraph but as several.

Narrative

This is intro which deals with the story in a chronological way. Used commonly on features, it is sometimes used on news stories where how it happened is more interesting or important than what happened. Use, and subsequent abuse, of the chronological start in news features by the *Sunday Times* of London gave birth to a now much-derided school of intro writing. For example:

> At 12.47 p.m. two men in identical blue suits, each carrying a Samsonite attaché case, left the Ruritanian Embassy by the rear entrance.
>
> They hailed a taxi, asked the driver to take them to Victoria Station and sat back in its black leather upholstery. In the 25 minutes it took the driver to negotiate the capital's heavy lunch-time traffic, neither let go of his innocent-looking case for one second.
>
> At Victoria Station the taller man took out a brand-new £5 note and paid off the driver, 47-year-old father of three Harry Wingfield. Little could he have known their final destination ...

And so it might go on for another few paragraphs. This novel-style approach has its uses, but one warning: tantalising the reader like this means that when you finally get to the point, it had better be a strong one. If, in the example above, they were smuggling secrets or off to blow up a rival embassy, all well and good. If, however, they had been given a half-day off and were merely on their way home to spend an evening with their stamp collections, you will have a lot of disappointed readers who are likely to depart the story.

Anecdote

This is intro which relates a self-contained anecdote to illustrate an aspect of the story's subject, and is often used on lengthy news

features either to introduce main players, show features of their relationships, or relate an unknown vignette from the story's otherwise
well-known sequence of events. It is vital to ensure the anecdote
is good and makes a point.

Delayed drop

This is intro of several, sometimes many, paragraphs where the 'real'
intro is saved up, like the punch line of a joke. It is often used on
soft news stories and light-hearted articles where perfectly ordinary
everyday events and scenes are conjured up for a few paragraphs,
to be followed with the introduction of the point of the story in a
paragraph that inevitably begins, 'Now ...' or, 'And then ...'.

Somewhat stylised and hackneyed, it often produces banalities
of the 'Little did they know ...' variety, as in: 'It was a perfect flight.
The weather clear, the wine good and the meal excellent. But little
did they know as they fastened their seat belts for the landing that
two minutes later the plane would catch fire, fall to the ground in
seconds and that only two of them would survive.'

Bullet intro

This is the opposite of the story above. Here the whole story is encap-
sulated in one telling sentence. Economical, evocative and powerful
when it works but disastrous when it doesn't; it needs experience,
real talent and good judgement. Most appropriate use is on a story
which is important, not entirely unexpected and which will be run
by virtually all news media. The best I have ever come across was
on the death of Hitler in May 1945. Imagine that was your story.
What could you write on this (already reported on the radio) that
would not read as if it were too obvious and unexciting? It is a tall
order. But the British *News Chronicle* began its story with the stark
sentence: 'The most hated man in the world is dead.' Running it
a close second was an intro written by Jack London, author of *White
Fang*, for *Collier's Weekly* in April 1906. His assignment was the
earthquake and subsequent fire which destroyed most of the
buildings in San Francisco and made 225,000 people homeless.
London began his report with a paragraph of just four words: 'San
Francisco is gone.'

Summary intro

This surveys the territory into which the reader will be taken by
the writer and is used to its best advantage to distil the main
elements of a complex chain of events. For instance, a story about
a very complicated betting fraud involving horse racing could have

begun: 'A betting syndicate yesterday tried to swindle £4 from bookmakers across Britain.' But a better alternative was: 'Joe Martin was a gambler who was so keen to win on the horses that he invented a racecourse, held a "meeting" there, got his friends to bet on its fictitious results and nearly, very nearly got away with it all.'

This type of intro is used also when no one single aspect of the story is outstanding, but the main point of interest is that a number of developments have occurred. Although very useful, the danger with the summary intro is that if it is insufficiently comprehensive it only delays the problem of deciding the most important aspect until the second paragraph. Perhaps the best way to avoid this is to think of it as akin to a film trailer, giving highlights of what is to come. Then it is especially valuable on stories surveying a broad range of subjects or people, or on profiles of individuals. For example: 'Farouk is not just the King of Egypt. He is also a road hog, racketeer, womaniser, glutton, pickpocket and, now, an overweight playboy in exile. He is, in fact, the king who never grew up.'

Singular statement intro

This is an opening where the writer throws a bizarre or amazing statement at readers in the hope of tantalising them into reading on. A war reporter once began a piece with the line, 'This morning I shaved in vintage red wine ...', before going on to write that the unit he was with had just taken one of the more important vineyards from the Germans.

Jolt intro

This is where you take two pieces of information in the story, most likely the origin and the outcome, and put them together so that they provide a jolt. Deliberate understatement is often essential. For instance, this by an American writer on what might have been a fairly routine accident story: 'Billy Ray Smith lit a cigarette while soaking his feet in petrol. He may survive.'

Scene-setter intro

This is intro where the writer paints a word picture of a scene that is unusual or else vital to understanding the subject. Used most commonly on long soft features or on colour pieces, it has to be both well-written and have its significance explained soon afterwards. It is at its best when there is some 'the clock struck thirteen' peculiarity to it. As in:

Imagine the scene. It is winter and inside an unheated apartment sits an old man wearing nothing but a thin gown. He is bent over a table, examining something through a microscope. A small candle burns by his elbow. All of a sudden, he leans back, smiles, takes a $5 note from his pocket, puts it in the candle's flame and uses it to light a small cigar.

You are compelled to read on to discover what it is that he is looking at, why he has no need of heat or warm clothes and what he is doing using dollars to light cigars. He is, the story goes on to explain, a banknote forger fallen on hard times.

Question intro

This is a dangerous opening, since readers are apt to give an immediate answer and pass on. So best not ask them direct, easily solved questions. Nor ones to which there is a surprising reply, since this is an infallible indicator that the information given in the answer would be better deployed in the intro. It is often used (ill-advisedly) on soft lifestyle features, as in, 'How many times did you wash your hands today?' but is best used on features where the question has a complex solution(s), could not possibly be answered by any reader and you delay answering it completely until the end of the piece. Even then, it should be used very sparingly. Its application to news stories (which are supposed to provide answers, not questions) would be absurd.

Joke intro

This is one of the most common of all intros, but, as indicated in the previous chapter, humour is attempted more often than achieved. Despite this, it is a very effective opening when successful because readers feel they are in the company of an amusing writer and will always read on in anticipation of more humour.

The opening can be a one-liner, like this from P.J. O'Rourke of the American magazine *Rolling Stone*: 'There are probably more fact-finding tours of Nicaragua right now than there are facts.'

Or it can be a number of sentences that build to a punch-line, as in this, also by O'Rourke:

> My friend Dorothy and I spent a weekend at Heritage USA, the born-again Christian resort and amusement park created by television evangelists Jim and Tammy Bakker. Dorothy and I came to scoff – but went away converted. Unfortunately, we were converted to Satanism.

Philosophical intro

This is the feature intro most often attempted, and least often really successful. It consists of making some broad and sweeping, epigrammatical statement that is supposed to sound profound and yet rarely is. Be aware that the thought you conceived about the condition of humanity, which came to you just as the clock ticked towards your deadline, is unlikely to look so rich in meaning the following day.

A variant of this is that old college essay trick of putting up a statement in the intro solely for the purpose of demolishing it in the rest of the piece. The problem with this approach is that it often comes across as a writer's trick rather than an inventive or appropriate start springing naturally from the material.

Historical intro

This is when a story begins with a statement about the the subject's history, as in: 'In 1948, the Ruritanian government decided that hence forward their borders would be effectively sealed, thus ending their long tradition of automatic hospitality to foreigners.' With this type, either the historical fact itself must be fascinating enough to grab the reader, or the twist (usually provided in a second paragraph that begins: 'But ...') must be strong. Otherwise it can read very flat. It is nearly always better re-worked with the information in the second paragraph in the intro.

False intros

Finally there is one species of intro which is not a type at all but a widely made mistake. Called a 'false intro' it is an opening which the writer thinks is selling the story to readers but which is entirely disposable. Commonly used on features or light news stories, it has two usual forms. First is the failed joke, as in this on a story about a new sports car: 'Move over girls, here comes a curvy desirable object that's going to replace you in your man's dreams.' Second is the intro in narrative openings which starts one phase too early, as in this on the story of a couple's disastrous vacation: 'Olive and Ian Meredith were really looking forward to two weeks of fun on the sun-soaked beaches of Thailand.' The fact that they arrived to find the hotel only half built and the beach covered in untreated sewage is only revealed in the second paragraph. It should be in the first. After all, most people *do* look forward to their vacations.

Do you always write the intro first?

In both the above cases, the piece would be far better without the annoying, inane intro. Practice intros are like a dancer's warm-up routine – perhaps essential to the performance, but certainly not part of it. They are a private thing and should not reach the public. They are also a reminder that we often need to get something down on paper or screen just to get ourselves going. There is nothing wrong with that; any behind-the-scenes routine that delivers the goods in the paper is worth following. Just don't let anyone else see it, that's all.

Some feature writers, if they have the time, prefer to write in longhand and then type the result, polishing as they go. They claim to choose words more carefully and write more economically if they have to do so manually, rather than on a computer. They maintain that fast, sensitive electronic keyboards encourage verbosity and loose sentence construction, and make writers compose 'off the top of the head' rather than forming and reforming sentences before they write them down, as they would do with a pen and paper.

There are as many writing habits as there are writers (Nabakov, for instance, often wrote standing up; Victor Hugo naked). But there is one habit which is decidedly dangerous – writing the piece without a proper intro and then going back to compose the first paragraph last. The great problem with this is that the process of thinking of the intro is often what gives a clear idea of the piece, its construction and the tone you should adopt. If you draft a piece and then go back and write the intro, you often find that you then want the article to have a totally different tone and structure, which means a re-write.

The only time when this habit may be useful is if the story has a clear, probably chronological structure and you can start at the beginning of the narrative and then go back and put a summary, declaratory, or some other kind of intro on it. The most obvious instance of this is with disasters and the like when you have to start writing before the final outcome, cause or death toll is known. This is called a running story because it is still running when you have to begin writing. With these, it is always best to start at the chronological beginning of the incident and then, just before deadline, add the intro and, possibly, final two paragraphs or so.

Bad writers are those who write with reference to an inner context which the reader cannot know.

Albert Camus

11

Construction and Description

Anything that is written to please the author is worthless.

Blaise Pascal

Good story construction is a matter of clarity, organisation and efficiency. It ought to be a simple matter and generally it is, especially on straightforward hard news stories of up to about twelve paragraphs. Once you have the most interesting information in the intro, arranging the rest of it is not the most challenging of tasks. The oft-quoted model for this is the inverted pyramid, a pseudo-technical phrase for the rudimentary matter of placing the material in descending order of interest and importance. Do that, and you will be at the end of the story before you know it. And it should have the same effect on readers.

Problems of construction come with articles that are more lengthy, complex or both. This is especially true of news stories that do not have a chronological sequence of events. These helpfully impose their own structure on the story once the intro paragraph(s) have been written. Feature-style reports are also more difficult to construct because they often involve a lot of different themes and strands. Parts of the story seem to fit in several different places and others seem to fit nowhere.

The construction difficulties mostly centre on this: how do you present often diverse aspects clearly and logically in a way that presents a coherent picture at the end? What goes where and how does it hang together? These problems at their worst are like trying to solve a jigsaw puzzle where the pieces can be an almost infinite number of sizes and shapes and the picture on the box is missing.

Fortunately you are in command. And this last word is the vital one in this whole process. Good construction is about taking command of the material. That means you have to survey the information you have, decide on its essence, envisage the overall picture and effect you want to achieve, decide which pieces you need and which you don't, what size and shape they should be and how they should fit together.

If there is a secret of good construction it is in thinking of the story as being made up of building blocks. These are sections of information that make up units with which you will construct the story. When you first spread out your information and survey it, you are looking for what is essential and what is not. Then you start to see these essentials falling into several different building blocks or aspects of the story. You then start allocating the more minor information to these blocks and also begin to think of what order the sections will go in. Links between them then occur to you. In anything but the most elementary cases, some of this planning will be done on paper, even if it is only a few scribbled headings.

A lot of this process naturally becomes unconscious after a while and setting it out as above may give the impression that it has more in common with filing than composition. What cannot be reflected here is that, with experience, construction planning becomes a more intuitive business. If these are the generalities of construction, there are quite a few detailed points given below.

Construction guidelines

Deal with each aspect of the story in one place

Don't jump about from one part of the story to another and then back to the first part. This is confusing for you and the reader. Deal with each aspect separately and clearly.

Make the links between building blocks as natural as you can

You can always tell a story where the order of building blocks has not been properly worked out, by the proliferation of 'meanwhile' and 'but' and 'however'. You should be able to move logically from one block to another without a lot of these. They are used to introduce something which conflicts or contrasts with what has gone before and are a great construction trip-wire. You can easily find yourself wanting to use them every third or fourth sentence unless you are careful. Minimising them is a matter of arranging all the material that argues in one direction, and then following it with the contradictory information, where possible. If you do need a linking thought or sentence, make it a smooth one.

On longer stories, think of the intro as a building block in itself

It is often helpful to think of the intro as being not just one paragraph but a block of maybe three or four. This would contain not only the opening paragraph but also the highlights or summary of the story that follows. Typical second or third paragraphs on news stories (where the main angle is in the first paragraph) are the amplification of that angle, a quote to support it, or a summary or taster paragraph. This is a sentence or two of the story's highlights, telling the reader what is in store. If, for some reason, you are using a construction which means some of these good points will be dealt with well down the story, then give a taste of them high up in a highlights paragraph.

Beware of blind alleys

When making your plan, be on the look-out for any building block that does not lead to another. Typically these are peripheral side-issues or side-effects of the main thrust of the story. Such blind alleys should be left to the end of the story, otherwise, like the real thing, you will find yourself having to reverse out of them to go anywhere else.

If the events in the story have a chronological structure, use that

A chronological narrative is simple, easy to follow and often the best option. After your intro paragraph(s), don't be afraid to say 'It all began when ...' and then proceed from there to the end.

Make denials follow accusations as closely as possible

If there are two conflicting sides to a story, ensure where possible that the denials or challenges to points made by the first side follow closely the accusation. Separating these by several paragraphs is one of the easiest ways to confuse the reader. It is also wasteful because distance between these two parts means you may have to recap the original claim.

Never be afraid to spell things out

Some stories are highly complicated and there is a danger of readers getting lost, however good the construction. In these situations don't be shy of setting things out textbook style and telling readers what they are going to get, as in: 'There are four aspects to this complex issue. They are ...'.

Don't put background in large, indigestible chunks

Some stories need to contain a lot of background or recapping of previous stories to either make sense or be at maximum strength. In most cases, this kind of material is best woven into the main narrative and given succinctly in passing. In rare, highly complicated cases, you can however resort to the 'The story so far ...' device.

Beware the consequences construction

This is a way of writing light human interest stories that has become stylised, ritualised almost, by over-use. An example would be:

> A little Bolton schoolboy will never forget the day he got his head stuck in the school railings.
> First ... this happened.
> Then ... that happened.
> And ... something else happened.
> For ... another thing.
> But ... here comes the feeble news point.
> And now ... everything is all right (otherwise it would be written another way, see?)
> So ... here are some quotes.

It consists of starting with a short jokey characterisation of what resulted, and which does not give the final game away. Then names, time and place are introduced, followed by a chronological narrative, each step of which is governed by prepositions like 'for', 'and', 'but', 'so'. The penultimate preposition brings us the final consequence and then, at last, we have the quotes from all the main parties. It is occasionally useful, but depressingly over-used.

Use quotes to change the pace in a long section of reported speech

Just as a long section of quotes would be tedious, and also inefficient in terms of length, so prolonged reported speech can get monotonous. Insert some variety, and a human voice with a quote or two, however brief.

Statements given in reported speech in the intro should be supported by quotes later in the story

This should always be done, but applies particularly when the reported speech statement is controversial.

On follow-up stories remember to recapitulate

When constructing a follow-up story, you should take care to insert sufficient recapping of the original to make your new story intelligible. This can either be done as a glancing sentence, or as a longer background section. It is vital when recapping that, if an accusation has been denied in earlier stories, any follow-up story which repeats the accusation, also repeats the denial.

Analysing story structures

Most of us spent endless hours of our youth sitting in schoolrooms and university halls, studying and deconstructing poems, short stories and novels. But suggest to journalists, young or old, that their own writing would benefit from giving newspaper articles the same analytical treatment and they will look at you as if you had just advocated the neutering of all males over 25.

Yet there is a lot to be gained from a little time devoted to such analysis. It does not have to take long, and the objects of your attentions can be good or bad; you can learn from both. All you have to do is make some notes of the job each part of the story does. Here, by way of illustration, is an example:

Speech stories
1. Intro stating most important news point, with or without supporting quotes.
2. Any further major points, with or without quotes.
3. Elaboration of intro with direct quotes.
4. Development of speech and quotes.
5. Summary of other main points.
(Note: audience reaction, demeanour and appearance of speaker, essential background etc. given as passing remarks unless significant.)

Payoffs

American writer Ernest Hemingway once claimed he re-wrote the ending of *Farewell To Arms* 39 times before he was satisfied. Not many newspaper stories would get published if this practice was imitated (although more than a few intros could benefit from this kind of attention), but it is a reminder that endings are important as well as openings. Not as important, but still worth thinking about.

Longer articles, especially, are better when rounded off. They do not have to resolve themselves in the same way as a piece of nineteenth-century symphonic music does. And they should certainly not come to one of those dreadful phoney, forced conclusions where the writer feels he has to give a verdict or give the reader a kind of farewell wave in words. But neither should they end abruptly as if the writer just got bored, nor just meekly fade away.

Anecdotes, preferably without the writer's quasi-philosophical wrap-up remark, are a good way to close. So are short descriptions of a final scene, a telling quote, ironic fact or statistic, some twist to the main thrust of the story that you have held back; maybe even an echo from the intro or something else earlier in the story.

Anything, in fact, that gives completeness and prevents the reader concluding that the author got so far and then suddenly remembered a pressing engagement.

Here is one of the finest closing sentences in the history of the printed word. It was written by the American-born correspondent of the London *Daily News*, J.A. MacGahan, at the conclusion of one of his searing dispatches that revealed the Turkish atrocities against the Bulgarians in 1876. After a controlled account of the slaughter in Batak (the one extensively quoted from in Chapter 2), he surveyed the scene in the churchyard where thousands of bodies lay as they were felled, 'children who had died shrinking with fright and terror; young girls who had died weeping and sobbing ... mothers who had died trying to shield their little ones with their own weak bodies ... There are no tears nor cries, no weeping, no shrieks of terror, nor prayers for mercy.' And then he adds: 'The harvests are rotting in the fields, and the reapers are rotting here in the churchyard.'

Attribution

If there is one thing that American journalists can teach the world, it is how to be disciplined in sourcing stories. For some reason, attribution is an area where a lot of reporters have an attitude problem. They feel that anything other than the bare minimum of information-sourcing involves a certain loss of journalistic virility – presumably in the belief that if material in their story has no source attached to it, then readers will credit them with the original idea, or with the necessary deductions and calculations. This is, of course, nonsense.

In properly sourcing a story, all you are doing is giving readers what they need to help them judge your story, or the separate pieces of information within it. The reader should never have to ask, 'How does the paper know this?'

The degree of sourcing depends on the nature of the story and the type of publication. Controversial stories and specialised publications generally need attribution that is more detailed and prominent. Here are some other points on when, where and how to source.

Where sourcing is not needed

Attribution is obviously not needed on what you might call general knowledge, information that is in the public domain, or that which can be immediately verified by a host of other sources. No one should feel the need to write something like this: 'Budapest is the capital of Hungary, a foreign ministry official said today.' If, for instance, there is a big fire in your country's capital, there is no need to have a source for it. Thousands of people would have seen it outside their windows, and millions more on their televisions. Generally, however, the contents of most news stories will need sourcing in print. And that means every statement should have a clear derivation.

Source everything that is, or might become, contentious

In the example of the fire above, you would need a source for the casualty figures, damage and cause – all of which might be challenged by another source. Any information that is now, or might in the future be, contentious should be sourced, as should anything judgemental or which you feel might not be immediate public knowledge (for example, instead of a fire it was a bomb and you felt that the authorities would contest that a bomb had gone off).

Never use passive attribution

Do not write, 'It was said', 'It was announced', or 'It was understood'. They all beg the question, by whom? Somewhere in the world there is the person or organisation that said it, announced it or believes it. Tell us who they are. Apart from anything else, passive attribution uses the impersonal voice of the bureaucracy claiming omnipotence – and we all know how reliable that is.

Make clear how information was obtained

If it is relevant, and it usually is, make clear how your information was obtained. This need not take much explanation, just a simple phrase will do, such as 'said in a prepared press statement' or 'told reporters in answer to questions'.

Be as specific as you can

Sources carry so much more weight when they have a name, title and anything else that might establish their credibility or help the reader judge the quality of their information. 'Army spokesman Ronald Elwill' is far better than 'army spokesman'. Add any extra information that may be useful. If your source was at a meeting or on the scene of an incident, then say so. His words will carry more conviction if he is on the spot, as opposed to sitting in head-quarters, miles, or even continents, away.

Unnamed sources

When you cannot name a source (negotiating and dealing with this situation is dealt with in Chapter 5) you should give as much information about the kind of person they are, their credentials – short of anything that might reveal their identity. Don't write just 'sources' or 'analysts' or 'government sources' or, God forbid, 'this newspaper's sources'. Be as specific as you can, and use the plural only when it is justified. If it is a single source then say so. Finally, if your information comes from a variety of anonymous sources, do not attribute each item. Write, 'Interviews with senior bankers revealed differing reactions to the news. Some said ...'.

Develop ranks of unnamed sources

Readers will be helped considerably if you grade unnamed sources. Reuters uses the following categories:

- Authoritative sources exercise real authority on the issue in question. A defence minister is an authoritative source on defence matters but not on finance.
- Official sources have access to information in their official capacity, but their competence as a source is limited to this field.
- Designated sources are, for instance, diplomatic sources, conference sources, intelligence sources or sources in the mining industry. As with an official source, they must have access to reliable information on the subject in question.

One of the great troubles with no-name sources is that, unless you give such guidance, the reader does not have the first idea whether you are quoting the President or the man who cleans his shoes.

Placing of attribution

Sourcing should come high in every story, and be in the intro if the story is contentious. Intro sourcing need not be inelegant and is always better than those ugly constructions which start a story with a bald, unsourced statement and then follow with a second paragraph which opens, 'That is the opinion/view/finding etc. of ...'. This applies particularly if the story is about something being said rather than done. Intro sourcing should, however, be minimised as much as possible to avoid clutter. Full and official titles, for example, can be given lower down.

Elsewhere in the story, attribution can be given discreetly at the end of sentences. Where one source covers most of the story, it does not need to be repeated more than is strictly necessary. However, every statement in the story, unless it is covered in the exceptions above, will need sourcing. This does not mean every sentence, for it is usually possible to write the story to make it clear that clumps of information have the same source.

Starting with the source

There are two situations where a news story is better understood by readers if it starts with the source. They are both 'say stories' (that is, those where nothing has happened except that someone has said something). The first is where the statement/accusation/claim has been made by a figure of such prominence and significance that his or her identity should be known before what is said is revealed.

The second is where a highly contentious accusation or claim has been made, often of a personal nature. It would, for instance, be absurd to read a story that began, 'President Bogdorov of Ruritania has killed off many of his country's old people with his new health policies, says opposition leader Mr Yuri Snickerov.' Far better to write, 'Ruritanian opposition leader Yuri Snickerov has accused President Bogdoriv of killing off ...'. The first is an apparent statement of fact, followed by a source; the second makes it clear that this is an accusation, and, given who it is coming from, certainly a clearly motivated one.

Description

Description, or colour as it is sometimes called, should be part of most stories. It is easy to be so consumed with relating the bare facts of the story that you forget to describe someone or some place that is at the centre of it. Even if it is only a few phrases giving readers the most basic idea of what a building or person looks like, it is worthwhile. Descriptions, whether they are passing remarks or whole passages, add extra information and help readers better imagine what has happened, to whom and where.

You are the readers' ears, eyes and noses. Almost every day you are meeting people and seeing things that readers will never experience. If you don't tell them what these things are like, they will never know. If, for example, you are interviewing a well-known politician, readers will want to know what his or her office is like. Is it grand, or surprisingly modest? How is it decorated? Are there any interesting personal possessions about? Is the person nervous or calm? How do they appear to treat those who work for them?

You cannot rely on a photograph in the paper doing these things for you. Instead, you have to paint a word picture, however brief. And whether there is or is not a photograph, your words can convey things that pictures cannot. Description brings the story alive, takes readers to where you have been, and evokes atmosphere. It can put flavour in the most arid and dry news story and make the difference between a report that satisfies and one that does not. So long as you remember that description goes into a story to aid readers' understanding and not provide you with an opportunity to display your latest vocabulary, it will be an aid to clarity and not an obstacle to it. Here are a few other points.

What is familiar to you may not be to the reader

Too often journalists take for granted that readers have seen the people, places and events they are writing about. Even the reporter's most familiar surroundings may be strange and unknown to readers. How many of your readers, for instance, have been inside your country's legislature? They may have seen it fleetingly on television, but do they know whether it is overheated or cold? Are the seats comfortable? What pictures are hung there? What is the atmosphere like? This is not extra information just for the sake of it, it helps take readers there.

Avoid big chunks of description

Unless the main purpose of a piece is to be descriptive, colour is best doled out in small helpings here and there rather than in long, unbroken passages. You can tell readers an awful lot in a series of small asides, remarks made in passing and in the occasional sentence. The thing you have to watch is where you place these. The fact that the person you are quoting is red-haired and collects stamps is worth recording somewhere, but probably not in the intro or immediately after you have them calling on the government to resign.

Relevance is the key. Introduce description where it helps, not where it is incongruous. More detailed descriptions of a certain person or place are, however, best given in one part of the story and not sprinkled through it. It is irritating to read a piece where, every time someone is mentioned, you are thrown another little crumb of description about them.

Bring people alive to readers

Even the smallest piece of information about people is a help to readers. After all, a name does not tell you very much about someone, apart from their sex. Age helps, as do details of appearance, demeanour, and so forth – where relevant. The test is that anything which assists readers in better understanding should be included.

Be precise

Precision in general was dealt with in the chapter on writing, but it applies especially to description. Avoid vague, judgemental adjectives and descriptions. To say that an office is 'imposing' tells you something, but not very much. Far better to say that it is so big that you could park two cars in there, and it has plush red carpet, a new black desk with brass fittings and that the windows command a view of the capital. That gives a far better idea. Apply this thinking to people, too. Avoid words like attractive, handsome, good-looking, pretty, impressive. Instead describe their hair colour, how they are dressed, their height.

Precision is also the best motive for using adjectives – to qualify nouns in a way that adds information. Using them to try and add emphasis will degrade the impact and lead to wordiness. Descriptive writing is about finding ways of bringing something to life, not the random sprinkling of adjectives through a piece.

Take care with similes

Writing that something is 'like …' is only effective if you chose a simile that actually matches and is fresh. Phrases that exaggerate, unless you are writing humour, are immediately spotted for what they are, and anything tired and clichéd will have no impact on readers. Here, at the end of this short extract, is a near-perfect example of a fresh simile. It comes from Floyd Gibbons of the *Chicago Tribune*, the first reporter to cover the effects of the Great Famine in the Soviet Union of 1921. He is writing from Samara:

> A boy of 12 with a face of sixty was carrying a six-month-old infant wrapped in a filthy bundle of furs. He deposited the baby under a freight car, crawled after him and drew from his pocket some dried fish-heads, which he chewed ravenously and then, bringing the baby's lips to his, transferred the sticky white paste of half-masticated fish-scales and bones to the infant's mouth as a mother bird feeds her young.

(Having written his report, Gibbons still had to find some way of getting it to his paper, 6,000 miles away. The prospects of this did not look too promising when he went to the post office to find an emaciated telegrapher on duty. Naturally the man spoke no English. So Gibbons typed his story, changing each Latin character to its nearest Cyrillic equivalent and handed it to the old man. He tapped out the story, sent to Moscow, where a colleague of Gibbons's sent it to London. There it was transmitted to New York, and finally Chicago.)

Develop an eye for detail

It is the small things that are often the most telling – little details or moments in a scene that can be described and used to make a point about the whole story or event. Develop an eye for detail, and learn to focus on such things and paint a word picture of them for readers. This is especially effective when you have been sent to write a colour or atmosphere piece about a big scene or event. But detail can also be used to great effect in all reporting, when you observe a little thing that seems significant. You do not have to cast a great spotlight on it, or give the detail immense symbolic significances whose weight it will not bear. Such lines are often most powerful when delivered simply and starkly without further elaboration.

Curzio Malaparte covered the battle of Leningrad for the Italian paper *Corriere della Sera*. One of the eventual saviours of the city, after much suffering, was the 'Lagoda Life-Line', the convoys of food taken across the lake by boat in the summer and over the ice in winter. In researching his piece about the cost in lives of opening this vital channel to the starving city, Malaparte took a walk over the frozen lake, looking through the ice as if it were a window:

> Under my shoes, imprinted in the ice as in transparent crystal, was a line of beautiful human faces, a line of glass masks like a Byzantine icon. They were looking at me, staring at me. The lips were narrow and worn, the hair long, the noses sharp, the eyes large and very clear. They were the images of Soviet soldiers who had fallen in the attempt to cross the lake. Their poor bodies, imprisoned all winter by the ice, had been swept away by the first spring currents. But their faces remained printed in the pure, green-blue crystal. They watched me serenely and it even seemed as if they tried to follow me with their eyes.

That detail, that image of the faces, is imprinted on the mind of the reader just as surely as those soldiers' features were marked on the ice. (Malaparte's real name, incidentally, was Kurt Suckert, and his father was German. Nevertheless, he fought for the French and Italians in the First World War, was decorated by both countries, and, in 1933, was arrested for anti-fascist reporting and imprisoned for three years on the Lipari islands, off the coast of Sicily.)[1]

However, if you are going to use detail, make sure you get it right. A reporter covering an earthquake in Central America and wanting to make plain its effects on ordinary people, wrote about how he had even seen starving families eating rats. In fact, they were eating small guinea pigs, which are a standard local delicacy. The reporter thus earned the nickname Rat Man for ever more.

Use familiar references

In all forms of journalism you should always think hard how to tell readers information in a way they can immediately grasp. In description, that means using imagery and comparisons from their lives rather than data that means little or nothing to them. If a building is 50,000 square feet, you should say so, but then add that this area is the equivalent of five tennis courts or whatever. If someone has been on some travels covering 8,000 miles, say that this is the distance from London to Tokyo, or the same as going from London to Aberdeen ten times. Use comparisons that people can relate to.

The wastepaper basket is still the writer's best friend.

Isaac Singer

12

Comment, Intentional and Otherwise

No story is fair if reporters hide their biases or emotions behind such subtly pejorative words as 'refused', 'despite' 'admit' and 'massive'.
Ben Bradlee

Journalism is by nature a subjective process. It can no more help producing and projecting views of the world than a cow can help making milk. Be it intentional or unintentional, overt or covert, comment comes with the territory. To deny this is to deny that ink makes a mark on paper.

As far as intentional comment is concerned (columnists, leading articles) no one would want to deny it. After all, a newspaper without such opinion would be like someone who had a personality by-pass operation. The problem comes with comment that goes in disguise, dressed up as straight reporting, speaking in its voice and aping its mannerisms. The problem, too, is with comment that creeps in under cover of a paragraph in a news story and has infiltrated before either reader, and sometimes writer, knows what has happened.

Comment, then, is only a problem when it does not advertise itself; when it is not conscious. We will never eliminate this, but we can hope to minimise it by searching for it, studying it, thinking about it and trying to recognise it for what it is. This, plus the more up-front types of comment, is what this chapter is about.

Comment in news stories

There are three types of comment in news stories: overt, covert and inadvertent. Overt comment is obvious to readers, where the reporter passes judgement or states an opinion in a direct and open way. This type of comment is simply banned on news pages in many papers around the world. Indeed in Britain and the United States, it is thought to be so obviously wrong that many journalism textbooks do not even give it more than a passing mention. The authors take it for granted that none of their readers would contest the view that news pages are for information given as straight as it can be, and comment is for columnists and opinion pages.

In most circumstances (the exceptions are dealt with later) this is right. Readers know where they are and can read news stories on the assumption that what they are getting is an attempt to present facts, even if it is not always successful. As noted in the chapter on news value, everyone has a comment, relatively few have fresh information. The one is a commonplace, the other scarce. That is why news is invariably more interesting than comment and it is certainly why there is a real risk of devaluation when the two are mixed. For when they are, hard information becomes tainted and so loses its worth.

But there are exceptions. The highly experienced reporter writing on a subject which he has followed for a long time should be allowed to let his judgements inform a story, and hence the readers. The same latitude should also be given to specialists or foreign correspondents who have been resident in their posts for a long time. Their comment should not appear in the form of drum-banging opinions of the 'Well he may say that, but here's what I think ...' variety, but appear as asides, little nudging remarks which give the story, or aspects of it, context. But they should, above all, be *apparent*.

Such comment should be used sparingly but perhaps deployed more often than it is. Conventional facts-only reporting should be the mainstay of the paper's news coverage but other, broader forms should be used more often, especially in longer, overview-type pieces. They, after all, as television, computers and other media become ever more sophisticated, cheaper and better at getting hard information to people at speed, will be a more important part of newspaper content. And it is plainly hypocritical for newspapers to spurn any idea of overt comment when other forms are unavoidably part of news stories. The only stipulation is that overt comment should be honest and immediately apparent for what it is and not try to hide itself or masquerade as something else.

Surreptitiousness is what is wrong with covert and inadvertent comment. The difference between the two is that covert is intentional, inadvertent is not. But they both deliver the same thing and by the same route: papers in their presentation, the juxtaposition of items, and in the selection of stories or language chosen for the headline; reporters in the language, material and sources they use, or omit.

Matters of selection, news values and balance are dealt with elsewhere, what this section is concerned with is news writing. And in this respect the chief vehicle for covert and inadvertent comment is loaded words. These are words with pejorative meaning and there are many examples in every language. Here are two situations which produce many examples in almost every language.

Attribution of speech

The words 'said' and 'told' are neutral verbs. They merely inform us that the words quoted were spoken. Reporters often look for alternatives, but the problem is that many of those alternatives are not neutral. The words 'confessed' and 'admitted' do not merely tell us that words have been spoken, they communicate more than that. They mean that someone has either been pressured into revealing some hitherto unknown, perhaps shameful, act; or that they have decided after wrestling with their conscience to tell all. Both cases are rather different from 'said'.

'Concede' also implies an admission (or concession) of guilt, while 'alleged', 'claimed' and 'maintained' can also carry the implication that you do not believe what is being said. Meanwhile, 'emphasised', 'stressed' and 'pointed out' all infer that you support the speaker. Similarly, if someone is explaining some of their actions or decisions, do not write without reasons that they 'tried to justify' their actions or 'defended' them. That would only be appropriate if they had been criticised or were under some other pressure to explain.

Another rich source of unintentional comment is the story that begins, 'Fears that ...' or 'Hopes that ...' and omits to mention who it is that is doing the fearing and hoping. There is no harm when the fears or hopes are ones that every person would share, as in: 'Fears are growing for the safety of three children who failed to arrive home yesterday after attending an after-school party.' But when the story is: 'Hopes rose yesterday that a lower price for gold is coming ...', you really have to say whose hopes. Gold producers, and those whose economies benefit from higher gold prices, will presumably be fearing rather than hoping.

Politics

Describing briefly someone's views and political position throws up all kinds of problems. Terms like 'reformer', 'radical', 'hardliner', 'reactionary', 'moderate' and 'extremist' are used all the time as if they were fixed reference points in the same way that party labels are. But they are not. They are frequently on the move, and most depend on the position from which you are describing them. And they are all used pejoratively. Someone who disagrees with you, or the mainstream, is an 'extremist', which does carry all the implications of 'excess' that are so obviously in the word's antecedents.

Never lose sight of that old adage that one person's freedom fighter is another person's terrorist. And this saying is a reminder that there are many more loaded words where those two came from. Their use often depends on your prejudice, conscious or otherwise.

Action by the authorities against a particular group of people is, depending on your point of view, a 'crusade' or a 'witch hunt'. People you approve of make 'mistakes' or 'errors', people you don't 'bungle' or 'blunder'. Demonstrators you disapprove of are a 'mob', others constitute a 'crowd'. And people can be 'refuseniks' or 'rebels' and so on.

The moral is that you should choose words with great care and always be aware of their connotations. The most innocent choice of phrase can convey the wrong impression. In the United States and elsewhere, for example, abortion rights have been a highly contentious issue for many years. Call what is growing inside a woman an 'unborn baby', however early in its gestation, and you are unwittingly lining up with those who would restrict abortions. Call their protagonists 'pro-abortion campaigners' and you double the offence. (For the record 'aborted foetus' and 'pro-choice campaigners' are the more neutral descriptions.)

The big I

The personal pronoun is one of the most contentious words in any language. Some journalists will go to extreme lengths to avoid ever typing it, writing such variants as 'this reporter', 'your correspondent', or 'this paper's representative'. Others will use it at the slightest excuse, making almost every story they write an exercise in informative vanity. There has to be a middle way, and preferably one that is a lot closer to the modesty option.

Yet achieving this is not always easy. When President John F. Kennedy was composing his inaugural address, one of the most memorable speeches of this century, he told his advisers that the personal pronoun would be banned. Some of the best brains in America worked on successive drafts, but 'I' still crept in four times.

Reporters covering 'big stories' are particularly vulnerable to the temptations of the first person, perhaps feeling that some of the importance of the story has rubbed off on them. Then there are those journalists who believe that their reactions to a story, their emotions, their doings, are so fascinating that they should be frequently included. As a character in British dramatist Tom Stoppard's play, *Night and Day*, says, 'A foreign correspondent is someone who flies around from hotel to hotel and thinks that the most interesting thing about any story is the fact that he has arrived to cover it.'

Of course, as a reporter, you are seeing things, meeting people, having experiences that are, by definition, interesting – after all, you would not be there if they were not news. But what the reader wants to know is *what* you saw and *what* you discovered, and not *how* you saw it or found it, and certainly not what you ate, drank, or felt while finding it. In as much as anything in reporting is a rule, this is one, unless you are a big name journalist whose stock-in-trade is personal reporting.

On the assumption that you are not, you should save highly personalised writing for when you have an experience to relate which is utterly fascinating (to the readers, not to you and your family). In any normal career, such occasions will be few and far between. As an example, here is a piece George Orwell wrote while covering the Spanish Civil War. The personal approach is justified here because Orwell had an experience considerably out of the ordinary and one that many people wonder about – being shot. It is a model of understatement:

> I had been about ten days at the front when it happened. The whole experience of being hit by a bullet is very interesting and I think it is worth describing in detail.
>
> ... Roughly speaking it was the sensation of being at the centre of an explosion. There seemed to be a loud bang and a blinding flash of light all round me, and I felt a tremendous shock – no pain, only a violent shock, such as you get from an electric terminal; with it a sense of utter weakness, a feeling of being stricken and shrivelled up to nothing. The sandbags in front of me receded into immense distance. I fancy you would feel much the same if you were struck by lightning. I knew immediately that I was hit, but because of the seeming bang and flash I thought it was a rifle nearby that had gone off accidentally and shot me. All this happened in a space of time much less than a second. The next moment my knees crumpled up and I was falling, my head hitting the ground with a violent bang which, to my relief, did not hurt. I had a numb, dazed feeling, a consciousness of being very badly hurt, but no pain in the ordinary sense.

Political correctness

There have been tremendous changes recently in the way people write and think about different groups in society: women, blacks, the disabled, homosexuals. All of these have been – and often still are – patronised, and regarded and treated as second-class citizens. One of the main targets of those tackling this has been the language applied to them. A lot of changes have resulted, most of which do not translate from one language to another and one culture to another.

Although the more extreme advocates of political correctness have provided endless amusement to the mainstream with their excesses, very few of us would want to go back to the days when blacks were called 'negroes', and women 'ladies' and always with a brief note attached telling the reader whether they were 'pretty', 'vivacious' or 'attractive' and what colour dress they wore.

Political correctness is now an intense preoccupation to journalism schools in many parts of the world. One recent textbook gave more space to how to write about the disabled than it did to news values. This is silly, because for the universal journalist the matter can be resolved into three broad principles:

- Do not refer to someone's race, sex or disability unless it has a direct bearing on the story.
- Do not apply different standards to writing about one group in society from those you would apply to another. Don't, for instance, describe a woman politician's dress and hairstyle unless it has a bearing on the story or possesses news value in itself. The test is: would you describe a male politician's appearance in the same situation?
- Be precise and do not use euphemisms. The fashion in some countries is now to refer to a blind person as 'visually impaired'. They are not, they are blind. A visually impaired person is one who can partially see, and is thus better called 'partially-sighted'. Best of all, do not use any vague phrases; be precise. Instead of 'disabled', which many object to, say what the disability actually is – providing it is relevant to the story.

Analysis

Any news story or feature of substance should have some measure of analysis in it, whether it is woven in with the main fabric or written as a separate section. But often a story is of such a size or sudden importance that a piece which is nothing but analysis is called for. These dissect events, themes, issues and developments in an attempt to explain what is happening now or will happen in the future. They should also try and explain the significance of these events and their context.

Such pieces should not merely be a series of assertions. Neither should they be old news stories reheated and served up with a few opinions. They must bring fresh evidence and fresh insights to bear on the story. These can either be yours, or, preferably, those of named authorities and experts. The accent should be on interpretation and explanation. This approach can be applied to other types of stories. Profiles of prominent public figures, for instance, can often be a fairly superficial recycling of well-worn material. But they can also be a serious attempt to set their lives into a context, with some detailed research into their backgrounds and work. The views of those who have encountered them can be collected and added to present a rounded portrait.

Interpretive pieces are even more needed by readers now that they often receive the first reports of events from television and radio. As well as giving the reporting in depth that broadcast media cannot, newspapers should also explain what the events and developments mean. This need not be some quiet backwater of the paper, where commentators suck their thumbs, ruminate and, as American journalist A.J. Liebling said, 'write what they construe to be the meaning of what they have not seen.' It should be to report new understandings and insights – a new sense of what things mean. As such, it should be part of news coverage. It is what Willi Gutman, a newspaper librarian who fled Hitler's Germany, called 'scoop by interpretation'.

Nor, where they appear on pages other than news ones, do analysis pieces have to be directly tied to stories. Newspapers have an important part to play in the free exchange of ideas in society, especially the presentation of new and challenging ones. They should provide a platform to writers, inside and outside the paper, to express these ideas. Some of the most influential concepts in the modern world were born on newspapers' opinion pages. After all, if papers do not provide an incubator for these, what will?

Leaders or editorial opinion pieces

Serious comment pieces that read interestingly, and have some pace and authority, are very difficult to write. Too often seriousness comes out as solemnity, authority as pomposity, and the subject is as predictable as tomorrow's date. Such pieces have all the freshness of last week's bread.

It is a near-universal convention that each issue of a paper should have a column that gives the paper's view on some topical issue(s). In countries where basic freedoms are under threat, editorials can be a ringing voice in the defence of people's rights. They send public word to regimes that they are being watched and opposed. They bolster and inspire those who are fighting for freedom and justice.

Elsewhere, in more comfortable circumstances, the wisdom of having daily editorials is debatable. I have sat in many editorial conferences where for some considerable time the assembled minds rummaged hopefully through recent stories for a subject – any subject – that the paper could sound off about. The clock would tick steadily onwards, until at last some issue was agreed (invariably one of the ones suggested at the beginning of the meeting). With the problem solved for another day, everyone then heaved a collective sigh of relief. Except the poor devil commissioned to write the thing.

A lot of us find it very testing to write a good comment piece unless we have a genuine conviction about an issue. Fabricating one will often produce a piece that is hollow and insincere; trying to write the piece without one leads to inconclusive waffle or, worse, a succession of comments saying it is too early to pass judgement on this matter – a dead give-away that the paper has chosen the wrong subject, or the wrong writer.

Some larger papers have specialists solely employed to write nothing but editorials. This gave rise, on the *Daily News* of Chicago, to one of the better-class journalist's practical jokes. Groups of readers used to be regularly shown round the paper, which was known for the high moral tone of its editorials. Knowing that such a party was due, a reporter called Eugene Field, later a poet, got together with a member of staff who was the readers' guide and hatched a plan.

As the prim matrons of the town reached the door marked 'Editorial Writers', the guide opened it to reveal a figure seated at a desk, composing one of the paper's pious editorials. It was Field, unshaven, snarling, and dressed in the arrowed uniform of a convict, complete with ball and chain. 'He's a trusty from the state pen, up for murder, you know', explained the guide, 'Our editor Mr Stone is very economy minded, always thinking of the paper's expenses. He used his influence to get this fellow in twice a week. A free editorial writer, get it? Doesn't cost us a dime.'[1]

However, if you are a more conventional member of the paper's staff and have been commissioned to write an editorial on something about which you have no burning convictions, you have two choices. You can either speak to experts inside and outside your paper and collect strong views, or retire to a dark corner and rapidly acquire some. This is not as cynical as it sounds. It is surprising how often a few moments' contemplation suddenly focused by the approaching deadline will give birth to original opinions.

Originality, however, has its limits. Joseph Medill, the ultra-conservative owner of the *Chicago Tribune* wrote an editorial in 1884 on the problem of the city's large mobile population of homeless, jobless men. Not for him any plea for work to be found for these unfortunates. Instead, an editorial written in vindictive seriousness and which read in part:

> The simplest plan, probably where one is not a member of the Humane Society, is to put a little strychnine or arsenic in the meat and other supplies furnished to the tramp. This produces death within a comparatively short time, is a warning to other tramps to keep out of the neighbourhood ... and saves one's chickens and other portable property from constant depredation.

Passion, too, has its limits which were certainly reached and appreciably exceeded by the *Messenger*, an English-language paper in Cameroon in July 1995. A front-page opinion piece was headed 'Kill This Man', and read in part: 'Such a man is not fit to live and should be wiped out of existence. Such a treatment, however harsh, befits Oben Peter Ashu, Governor of the South West Province.'

Editorials, like all opinion pieces, should not be a series of wilful assertions laid upon each other. As well as a fresh point of view, they should contain sufficient elements of background and analysis to make them understandable to those who have not read the story(ies) they are based upon. They should be arguments constructed as tightly as a well-wound spring.

And if you wish them to have impact, concentrate your creativity on a few memorable phrases. The list of newspaper editorials that have lived beyond the paper's next issue is not long. In fact it is very short. But those that have achieved any kind of immortality owe it not to a brilliantly argued case, but to a memorable phrase. That indeed is all they are remembered for: C.P. Scott's 'Comment is free, facts are sacred' (*Guardian*, Manchester 1921), 'Communism with a human face' (*Rude Pravo*, Prague 1968), 'The smack of firm government' (*Daily Telegraph*, London 1956), 'One picture is worth a thousand words' (*Printers' Ink*, US 1927).

But there is a thin line between presence and pretentiousness. Just as politicians are only politicians, papers are only papers, not players on the world stage. There is nothing more preposterous than a squeaky voice from a newspaper, especially a small provincial one, 'calling on the United Nations to act now'. Witness the *Skibereen Eagle*, a four-page sheet published once a week in the city of Cork, Ireland in late Victorian times. Once, when the Tsar of Russia had done something to displease the Eagle's proprietor, one Frederick Peel Eldon Potter, a vehement leading article informed its 4,000 readers: 'The *Skibereen Eagle* has its eye on Russia.'

Individual classified advertisements have done more to change the world than all the billions of words of blustering newspaper editorials in history. The battle of Gettysburg, one of the bloodiest in the American Civil War, for instance, was caused by an ad for footwear. It appeared in the *Gettysburg Compiler* and had been placed by a shoe store announcing fine new boots for sale. It was seen by Confederate General James Pettigrew who at the time was marching his bedraggled army through Pennsylvania. They were in a sorry state, having worn out their boots and many were marching barefoot. Pettigrew ordered his men to change direction and head for Gettysburg. On the way they were spotted by Union forces and so began the bloody, three-day battle of Gettysburg. At the end of it, 5,662 men lay dead and 27,203 wounded.

Indeed, it is very hard to find a single case of a newspaper comment actually changing the world. The one usually cited, Emil Zola's famous 'J'Accuse' about the Dreyfus case published in the French paper *L'Aurore* in January 1898, was actually an open letter to the government and not an editorial (and had only a limited direct effect). The other case was where the comment was actually made in error.

In April 1888, Ludwig Nobel died. He was the elder brother of the moody yet idealistic inventor of dynamite, Alfred Nobel. A leading French newspaper misread the report and ran an obituary of Alfred, calling him 'a merchant of death'. Reading that obituary and being stung by the idea that he would be remembered as a 'merchant of death', was one of the main reasons why Nobel changed his will and left his fortune to establish the Nobel Prize awards for peace, literature and the sciences.

Columnists

Anyone who has reached the stage of being awarded a column either has no need for advice; or has (or will soon acquire) an ego which precludes them from taking any.

Reviews

There are three schools of reviewing and two of them should be closed down. First, there are those professional journalists who are perfectly good reporters when given a story, but when presented with a book, play, film or concert to review are stricken with a sudden desire to prove they are writers.

Then there are those amateurs, often a rival (or, worse, a friend) of those whose work is under review, who grind in-crowd axes in public, to the bewilderment or deceit of readers. In both cases what we often get is a piece where the writer omits to describe the content of the work, so anxious is he to discharge opinions, fanciful divinations of meaning, wild guesses at the artist's intent and, of course, what he hopes will be the resonating verdict.

Readers should beware these schools of reviewing. So, too, should writers. As Vladimir Nabakov observed of book reviewers: 'Criticism can be instructive in the sense that it gives readers, including the author of the book, some information about the critic's intelligence, or honesty, or both.'

The school of reviewing that deserves preservation is that whose prime aim is to give information about the work in question; to describe it as precisely and fully as possible, to scrutinise its style, content, thinking. And to liberate themselves by learning off by heart this immutable law of reviewing: it is not illegal to write a review that contains no glib opinion. If you feel tempted, just remember the *Odessa Courier*'s anonymous book reviewer who in 1887 wrote of a novel: 'Sentimental rubbish. Show me one page that contains an idea.' The book reviewed was *Anna Karenina*.

> *Of all the fantastic fog-shapes that have risen off the fog of human confusion since the big war, the most futile and at the same time the most pretentious is the deep-thinking, hair-trigger columnist or commentator who knows all the answers just off-hand and can settle great affairs with absolute finality three or even six days a week.*
>
> Westbrook Pegler

13

News Editing

A paper without murders and robberies, and rapes and incest, and bestiality and sodomy, and sacrilege, and incendiary letters and forgeries, and executions and duels is said to be devoid of news.

Anon 1783

Newspapers can get away with some poor reporters on their staff, one or two boring columnists and even, for a while, an editor who is half-asleep, drunk or always out of the office. But no newspaper can disguise for even an issue a news editor who is no good at the job. If ever there was a task that was absolutely central to producing a lively newspaper, this is it.

And central, in every respect. The news editor should obviously be directing the reporters, shaping the paper's news coverage in general and in detail. But he or she, with or without assistance, should also be at the centre in another sense. The paper's news desk should know at any one time what is happening in the world (or its circulation area if it is a provincial). It must be a place which keeps constantly up to date with events and forms a quick view of what, if anything, should be done about them (which will, of course, be revised in the light of any developments). It should also be the paper's nerve centre.

On daily papers, especially those of any size, that should mean subscribing to as many news wire services as your paper can afford. It should also mean having one journalist dedicated to the job of monitoring these services, drawing the news editor's attention to anything of interest, sounding the alarm when a big story breaks. Even quite large dailies often think that this job, called news taster in Britain because it involves tasting or sampling the incoming news, can be a part-time one. It can – but only if you want to miss stories consistently and react slowly to those you do see. Others think it can be done by the news editor in 'spare moments'. Well, if he or she is doing their job properly, there won't be any, for the news editor has an awful lot to do, as outlined below.

The news editor's role

Keep a news diary

A lot of news is made up of events that you can anticipate: court hearings, press conferences, openings, closings. These should all be entered in a diary so you can better plan your coverage and not miss anything. You should also read newspapers and magazines with this in mind and put in the news diary any future events or expected events that you read about. For instance, if the government announce an inquiry into an issue and say that the team is due to report in three weeks' time, then make an entry in three weeks so that a reporter can write a follow-up story. That is one of the ways you both keep on top of stories and get a beat on the opposition. You can also record anniversaries and any other landmarks in this diary.

Start an ideas file

The quality and range of ideas is one of the things that makes the difference between news pages that crackle with interest, and those that are so limp and wet you could not even start a fire with them. You should be getting, or collecting, more ideas than you can possibly cope with for a single issue. You should therefore have a file where you can put notes on your ideas, plus cuttings from other papers and magazines that might make a future story.

Read newspapers and magazines

This is a very obvious part of the job, so you can keep up to date with stories, know what the opposition is doing (and thus not repeat stories) and maintain your own general knowledge. Small articles in other papers can also be the starting point for some good stories for your own paper. The thing you have to be careful about is that this is a part of the job that is often squeezed out by other, apparently more pressing tasks. Do not let that happen. Otherwise you will miss things, waste reporters' time with them working on stories that have already appeared elsewhere, and look stupid when someone points out that the report that you are so excited about has already been published in another paper.

Make and remake the story list

This list, together with the diary and ideas file, is one of the basic tools of news editing. You should start each issue's life-cycle with a list of stories and the reporters who are doing them. This should be constantly revised in the light of new stories coming in or existing ones becoming less strong. You should never become so wedded to certain stories that you are not prepared to throw them off the list if they weaken or something stronger comes in.

You should always be thinking about these stories and their relative merits for two other reasons. First, you should always be able to defend your choices in a news conference. Second, on your paper the news editor's job may well involve deciding on the prominence or space given to them.

Keep the reader in mind at all times

When deciding on what stories to research, you should never lose sight of the different groups of people that make up your paper's readership. This means making sure that you have something in each issue that caters for these groups. Is there something here for women readers? For younger readers? For older ones, those interested in the environment, culture etc. News editors should constantly be concerned with achieving the right mix.

Ensure there is variety

News pages are where the paper reports on the issues it thinks important, but the mixture of these pages should be like a well-planned meal: not all the same food and with something light to go along with the heavy main course. There should not be too many stories in one area, not too many political stories or crime stories, but a variety. Lightness is important too. News pages should deal with the big issues, but that diet should not be unrelieved. Pages can be serious, but never solemn. Light, humorous, even trivial stories should be included. Here are some of the types of light stories:

- Colour stories – scenes at events and from everyday life. A good descriptive writer can make even the most mundane occurrences interesting.
- Amusing stories – news agencies are a good source of these anecdotal stories, since they draw their material from such a wide area.
- Anniversaries – big events, inventions, innovations and other social milestones are always good for a look back. Very few readers can resist indulging in a little nostalgia.
- Discoveries – researchers in archives, the sciences, archaeology and so forth are always making discoveries. Some of them are important, but others just interesting or amusing. Universities and specialist journals are a good source of such stories.
- Social observation – new trends in society and in people's behaviour make interesting, light stories.

- Strange advertisements – people are always offering the strangest goods and services for sale. Stories can either be about individual ads or themed (for example, 'get-rich-quick' offers).
- New publications – controversial books, films or television programmes are an unfailing source of light stories.

Make sure you have thinking time

With a job as pressured as news editing, where you have a staff to manage and things are happening all the time, it is very easy to be so busy that you have no time to think, or at least for any reflective thought. This is dangerous. You should always carve out a little bit of each day where you can turn over some of your decisions in your mind, especially the ones you have some doubts about. It is also important, if you have no deputy, to find someone who can act as a sounding board for your ideas and decisions. It is remarkable how often merely talking out loud about something will help you sort out your thoughts and sometimes make you realise that you have made – or might be about to make – an error.

Match the right reporters to the right stories

There is no great mystery to this process. Most of it is merely a matter of putting people on stories that they are likely to be interested in. The other part of it is making a judgement about the kind of work involved in a story and matching that to a reporter's aptitudes. After all, if the story involves a lot of aggressive research face to face with some fairly rough types, it is not much good giving it to that shy reporter who is a great writer but hates offending people. Of course, occasionally, the really inspired news editor will do just that and get wonderful results. The point is that you should be thinking of who might do the best job on each story all the time.

Brief reporters

This is one part of the job it is vital to get right. Most of the times I was disappointed with a story a reporter handed in, it was because I failed to brief the reporter properly, or did so but failed to ensure they stuck to the brief. The main thing in briefing staff is that you cannot be too detailed. It is no good having a clear idea of the story and how you want it researched and written, and then expect reporters to somehow understand this by telepathy. You have to tell them in detail, covering the sort of areas that you want researched, what you think the story is really about, how long it should be, when you want it by and whether you want it done straight, or light, or wistful or whatever.

Keep on their case

This means that you maintain full contact with reporters while they research the story and speak to them, at length if necessary, just before they write it. You soon get to know the reporters who need close attention and those who work better when left alone. But all reporters need to feel that you are interested in their story, and none are so good that they will not benefit from you discussing their enquiries and making suggestions. Keeping on their case also means letting them know what you think of their piece when they have filed it.

If they are based away from the office, out of the city or abroad, you should be scrupulous about keeping in touch with them, as it may be difficult for them to call you. Reporters often go to places where phone lines are scarce and getting through to you takes hours. If they then find at the other end of the phone someone who has no interest in their problems, they are not likely to do their best work. Make things as easy as you can for them – and that includes calling them rather than waiting for them to call you.

Re-write stories when necessary

If a reporter's story is not up to standard, get them to do it again. But if there is no time, or they have already tried again and still failed, then you will have to do the re-writing. This is better and safer with the reporter sitting beside you. If that is not possible, then you should make sure you show the finished result to the reporter and explain why you changed it. They will learn what you want and they can tell you if you have unwittingly changed the meaning or accuracy.

Know the different ways to tell a story

There are not only all kinds of ways to write a news story, but there are also ways other than a straight news report to tell a story and help readers' understanding of it. A news editor needs to know of these and be aware that using them is another way to get variety and life into news pages. You should always be thinking about whether a news story could be supplemented, or followed up by one or more of the following:

- Backgrounder – a piece explaining the recent past of the issues or themes at the centre of a story. This gives a sense of such developments being part of a continuing process, rather than unprovoked eruptions of fate.
- Analysis – a piece examining the reasons why something has happened, or not happened.

- Colour piece – an article describing a scene or event which throws light on some of the themes or people involved in the main story.
- Fly on the wall – the journalist as observer, pure and simple, asking no questions; merely watching, recording and noting the behaviour, speech and interactions of the subject(s). The published report will probably use a lot of quotes and verbatim exchanges between people. This type of piece is commonly used on some place or institution which is exotic to your readership.
- Behind the scenes – has similarities to the above but differs in being an explanatory, rather than observational, piece. It should describe how something works. This approach is often best on subjects that readers take for granted, but in reality know very little about.
- Profile – normally a study of a personality at the centre of a story, but can also be portrait of a place, organisation, religion etc. It can be a report of one encounter with the subject or can gather many views and give context.
- Interview – a report of a question and answer session with one of the main personalities, either written as a news feature or given as a verbatim, but edited, account of the interview. If the latter, the questions should be not too long, more carefully phrased than usual and any editing of questions and answers should be made clear. The subject needs to speak well and interestingly, as there is no scope for making good this deficiency with writing from the interviewer.
- Sidebars – simple lists of facts associated with the story, or previous instances of the event that is at the centre of your story, or a chronology.
- A history of … – relating the antecedents or background to a subject is most appropriate when the subject has been around for a long time and then, suddenly, events have thrown it into prominence. This will also work well on familiar subjects whose history is not broadly known.
- In disguise – the journalist assumes the role of subject to see how people react. This can be done for two reasons. First, for fun, such as dressing up as a priest to see how this affects people's behaviour (a London journalist recently did this, and in addition to just wandering around in his disguise, also went into bars and nightclubs). Second, it can be done for a serious purpose, such as taking the role of a homeless person to see what treatment is available. Several years ago a reporter roamed around the United States posing as an HIV sufferer to write about how this altered people's perceptions and treatment of him when he slipped this 'fact' into his conversation.

- Full texts – when you have a story which deals with an important speech, statement or document, it is worth thinking about running the complete text.
- My testimony – personal experience written by a journalist after interviewing the subject, or by the subject him or herself (in practice more normally spoken and recorded). The latter method always has the edge, as it provides the unmistakably rough and honest tones of a real person compared to the smoothed-out sentences of the paper's journalists.
- Vox pops – short verbatim quotes from people you have telephoned or stopped in the street for their reaction to the story.
- Experts' round-up – the same as the above, but with specialists rather than members of the public.
- Opinion poll – a poll of people's views carried out by an accredited research organisation. Having your own staff carry out the poll can be done, but the results will not be very scientific.
- Review – an appraisal of anything from a film or play, to a new car, health treatment, vacation or service. A common trap is for journalists to be so wrapped up in their own opinions of the subject that they forget to describe it adequately to readers first.

Disasters

Major accidents and catastrophes are very difficult to deal with quickly and well. With hindsight they can look very straight-forward, but that is not how they first come to you – in confusing little pieces of information which conflict and can easily mislead. Often the first reports of what turns out to be a major disaster arrive on agency wires as apparently trivial incidents, and then build into something huge. Sometimes it can be the other way round, appearing to be a calamity of vast proportions, which later reports correct to a relatively mundane event. Experience can teach you not to rush to judgement, but it cannot give you infallible ways of telling which are the big ones and which the trivia. Hopefully, it may give you instincts and a feel. But you have to make some sort of decision. You cannot just sit there, waiting for everything to become clear or, even worse, dithering. The first thing, if at all possible, is to get a reporter to the scene. You can use what they are telling you, or further wire reports, to decide whether to send any other reporters there.

Let us assume that you have established that this is a major disaster you are dealing with. In order to discuss the issues raised by managing the coverage of this sort of event, let us assume you are about to deal with a major air crash in your country. I will now describe how a national paper in London might handle the story.

The first hint would probably come in a one-line report over the wires: 'Incident at Heathrow airport at 14.26, involving EuroAir Boeing.' Now you know the domestic news agency would not bother with complete trivia, but at this stage the incident could be almost anything, from a full-scale crash to merely a small fire which leaves no one injured. So you wait, but alert one reporter and the picture desk. Then, maybe ten minutes later, the agency reports: 'EuroAir from Frankfurt crash-landed. No reports yet of fatalities.'

This is the point where you send a reporter and photographer to the scene. And you also do several other things: you tell the editor and assign a reporter to read the wires and become your anchor person. This job will involve pulling together the highlights from all the wires, reporters and freelances who may be involved in the story and, eventually, writing the main front-page piece.

Further reports will now be coming in, making clear that this is a major disaster. The plane caught fire on landing, over 100 people have died, and there are many unanswered questions. You will by now have had a brief meeting with the editor and other senior executives, assigned as many reporters as you can to the story, and got the art desk working on maps and graphics. You should be careful not to send too many reporters to the scene as much more than two tend to get in each other's way and duplicate work. Besides, the agencies and freelances will be filing a lot from the scene as well.

A lot of your job is not unlike that of an air traffic controller, if that is not a tasteless analogy in the circumstances. You should be making sure that your staff are not duplicating work and that the highlights of what they find are going to the anchor person and to anyone else who needs to know, like the person doing the graphics. They need to be kept fully up to date with developments and new information so they can incorporate it in their work. You would almost certainly have working with you at least one or two secretaries who can act as runners, carrying information to and from you and your reporters.

Another vital thing is to concentrate on discovering a detailed chronology of what happened. This means contacting all emergency services, hospitals and authorities regularly. And do not be in a rush to apportion blame. The first reaction of many papers when confronted with a disaster is to hurry to lay the fault at somebody's feet. You are liable to get it wrong that way. Concentrate on reporting the fullest picture of what happened.

Death tolls are an incessant source of confusion in the first few hours, and, in the case of substantial catastrophes, maybe even several days. There will always be conflicting figures for the numbers of dead and injured. With major disasters like earthquakes, the death tolls can only be estimates and these can later prove to be wildly inaccurate. In the Tokyo earthquake of 1923, for instance, newspaper reports of the number of dead went from 10,000 to 500,000, and then to more than one million in just three days. The real figure was about 150,000 and by the time papers had reported that, they had also stated that Mt Fuji had erupted (it hadn't), an island in Sagami Bay had disappeared beneath the tidal waves (not so), and that the Japanese Prime Minister had been assassinated by a frantic mob (also not true).

Since early estimates can also undershoot the eventual figure, it is best to quote, with attribution, the tolls that various authorities are giving. With luck, there will be sufficient common agreement for a reliable round figure to be used for your headline and intro. If not, then take the lower figure from a source that is usually reliable and say 'At least X people died when …', or take the highest figure that seems educated and say 'Up to X people are feared to have died when …'. This latter course should, however, not be used as a licence to hype the story.

And speaking of hype, be careful about the use of such words as 'disaster' or 'catastrophe' to characterise the event. Calling a train crash where three people have been killed a 'disaster' will not make the story any stronger. If you feel tempted to misuse such words, bear the following in mind. In 1918, a flu epidemic killed 15 million people worldwide. Yet when a British newspaper historian came to study global coverage of it, he could find not one single instance of any word like 'disaster' being applied to this, the biggest non-military catastrophe in the century.

In the case here, this is what happened: a EuroAir Boeing 737 had some technical troubles as the plane approached Heathrow Airport. These grew worse. A fire started in one engine, which fell off in mid-air, another engine caught fire, the plane's electrics failed and the pilot had to land manually with only two engines. On board were the German Trade Minister Dieter Boch, who died in the fire after the crash landing, and rock star Elton John, who helped in the rescue. The fire started in the cabin after the landing and within ten minutes had engulfed the plane. Only 60 of the 210 passengers are known to have survived, many of them injured. The engine that fell off landed on a school, which was fortunately unoccupied.

These are the components of the coverage that I would try and arrange. Not all of these pieces would run separately, but I would commission them and make a decision later:

- **Eye-witness reports** – From reporters at the scene, wires, freelances and office-based reporters calling people who have been on TV and radio as eye-witnesses.
- **Chronology of what happened** – This would be a minute-by-minute account of what occurred, from the moment it started to its final conclusion. It would almost certainly be written by the anchor person and be the core of their account.
- **Cause** – Both the narrow, immediate cause of mechanical failures and, perhaps, the wider cause.
- **The safety record of Boeing 737s** – How many accidents have they been involved in? What were their causes? If there was time, this could also incorporate what the Boeing company have to say about this accident.
- **Profile of EuroAir** – Full details and history of the airline involved, plus possible effects of the crash on the company, share prices etc. If the airline's headquarters was within reach, I would also send a reporter there to speak to staff and get any information about whether the company has been economising. It may be that they have recently cut back on the regular maintenance of planes in order to try to save money.
- **Profile of the pilot** – According to the information we now have, he played a heroic role in landing the plane manually and without two engines. People will want to know about his background and experience.
- **Dieter Boch obituary** – This may not be worth a separate piece, but when anyone prominent dies in a disaster, you should always put a reporter on to doing an obituary of them.
- **Casualties** – It may be that the identities of the dead will not be released until after your deadline. If you can learn who they are, then you will want a piece on them. There are nearly always stories about the person who only caught the plane at the last minute or something similar.
- **The rescue** – What happened on the ground once the plane had crashed? How did the emergency services react? Who were the heroes and heroines of the rescue? How was it carried out?
- **Elton John** – What was his role in the rescue? What was the reason for his journey etc?
- **Chronology of recent crashes** – This would be a list of the fatal crashes in Britain in the last ten years, or the major air crashes around the world in the last two years. It is the kind of material that the agencies routinely supply.
- **Description of the scene** – I would ask one of the reporters at the scene to write a description of what can be seen, the atmosphere at the airport etc.
- **The black box** – What is a black box flight recorder? Do you know how they work, what they actually record and what one

looks like? The black box is one of those objects that we always hear people talking about but very few people actually know anything about, beyond the fact that they are an important part of any crash investigation. It is, for example, not black. Some details on the black box could stand on their own or be part of a piece on the investigation that follows.

- **Pictures and graphics** – Apart from the obvious pictures of the scene and of the people involved, you may want pictures of a black box, EuroAir's headquarters, a map of the scene, a graphic on the rescue and another on the cause. In London we would be able to use one of the computer database systems, on which would be held all manner of drawings of the 737, its engines, cutaway graphics of its inside etc. You can capture these on your computer system and then adjust and adapt them as you want.
- **Expert's view** – With many disasters, especially those which are rare, you suddenly need experts to explain technical matters. Plane crashes are quite frequent events, but, even so, an expert on air safety could be interviewed at length or write a piece for the paper. There may, for instance, be a retired former crash investigator who could give some fascinating insights. If you do get hold of experts like that, try and bring them into the office. They will be invaluable for your reporters to speak to and if they are in your office, other papers cannot get to them.
- **Anchor piece** – All the best information from these above stories (and other enquiries such as the effect on flight schedules and telephone numbers for anxious relatives to ring) would be pulled into the anchor piece. This would be your page one account of the crash and would be long and comprehensive.

Some people may think that such coverage would be over the top in scale and scope. But on a story of this size you have a chance to report in depth on a matter of great public interest. Television will bring the immediate news and pictures to people first, but they cannot offer anything like the depth papers can. A half-hour news programme contains only about as many words as does the front page of the average broadsheet paper. And, although this is not the first consideration, you as a news executive will be judged by your staff and peers on the accuracy, speed and depth of your coverage of the big stories.

For papers which lack the space to give such wide-ranging immediate coverage, some of these stories would be published on subsequent days. They would be part of the follow-up to the main story. You would also be looking for aspects of the story that needed further enquiries or did not make sense and required an investigation.

Campaigns

A campaign is an orchestrated series of news stories and comment pieces in which the paper uses all the powers and resources at its disposal to fight for a cause. The subject will probably be a situation that should be altered but where officialdom is at present refusing to act, such as a much-needed change in the law, safety improvement or compensation for those harmed by official or commercial organisations.

On a provincial paper it may be something as simple as a campaign against the closure of a local school or rail service. They can also be as complex and long-running as the famous *Sunday Times* campaign for the children who were born without arms or legs or both as a result of their mothers taking the drug thalidomide when pregnant. That took many years and hundreds of stories to reach a successful conclusion.

I have been involved in campaigns against commercial companies polluting rivers, for better rail safety after a number of people were killed as a result of unsafe train doors, for better food safety laws, against the wrongful conviction and imprisonment of a man for the murder of a policeman, and for compensation for people who had been given Aids-infected blood during treatment for other unrelated diseases. All of these cases produced some good reporting, allowed the papers to show their character and beliefs and gave their readers a sense of involvement in these issues.

The best campaigns are designed to correct injustices. They can be for new laws, the repeal of bad ones, against corruption and negligence, or in favour of action on a subject of public interest. But they should be chosen with two thoughts in mind:

- Campaigns should have easily-defined targets and be specific. Set down demands and aims for the campaign in the paper and, perhaps, a deadline.
- Campaigns should be achievable, in theory at least. Ones that have aims which are too vague, or too unattainable, are not suitable. Murder and sin are wrong, but a campaign against either is liable to be ineffective.

The following sections give some general guidelines on how to run a campaign.

Readers should be told in the plainest terms what you are doing

Launch the campaign by telling them about it and its aims. Give the campaign a title or slogan and a logo which is carried on all stories.

Make sure a story related to the campaign is in every issue

If you run a campaign, have the heart for it and don't give up just because you do not win a quick victory. For the sake of the campaign you may even have to run stories that would not otherwise strictly merit inclusion in the paper. So long as those are isolated examples, that is fine. It is a greater problem when the campaign is proving difficult to win. You have then got to make a decision – to stick with it or dump it. What you cannot do is run it for a few issues, forget it for some weeks, and keep on blowing hot and cold about it.

Keep comment pieces to a minimum

Most of the campaign should comprise stories illustrating the injustice against which you are fighting. Concentrate on the victims. It is their plight, and any negligence you can prove that contributed to it, that will win the campaign. When the London *Observer* ran a campaign to win compensation for those infected with the HIV virus as a result of hospital treatment, we published many stories on all aspects of the issue. But I think the article that won the campaign for us was an interview with a young man who had entered hospital with leukaemia, was successfully treated for this terrible disease, only to be then told that he had been given blood infected with the HIV virus. Comment pieces are all very well to launch the campaign, but they should be used sparingly.

Solicit support

From politicians, experts, readers, public bodies and so forth. This will give the campaign force and may result in some stories for it. Report the support and ask politicians to raise your issue in the legislature and with the government.

Keep faith with the campaign

You can win a lot of the time. I have been involved with successful campaigns to keep schools open, for road safety, against lead in petrol, against tax laws that encouraged the destruction of the environment, for the closure of inhumane psychiatric hospitals, for the Aids victims, against crooked auctions, for action to relieve the plight of the Kurds in Iraq and famine victims in Somalia and Rwanda. There are few feelings in journalism as good as knowing that you have not merely written about an injustice, but helped correct it too.

Contributed reports

On 21 March 1975 in an English provincial newspaper called the *Romsey Advertiser* there appeared on its sports pages a report of a soccer match which read in part:

> Mick Harfield arrived late and made the eleven, despite the tragic news that his wife had passed away early the same morning. Everybody was stunned to hear this, and at half-time both teams observed two minutes' silence in respect. The idea of Mick playing was to take his mind off the matter and he was a hero indeed to stay for the duration of the match.

In the next issue of the paper, the following appeared under the heading 'Fit and Well':

> Mrs Rosina Harfield asks us to point out that reference to her in the report of the Braishfield football match last week was completely untrue. She is fit and well, and we would like to apologise to her for any upsets the report could have caused.

Nothing could better illustrate the dangers of contributed reports – a common practice with provincial papers the world over. Papers that cannot employ the huge staffs needed to cover every local organisation and event will accept reports from members of those organisations or untrained correspondents. The paper's staff will then edit (or often re-write) them for publication. While few of these correspondents will exploit their position for hoaxes like the above, they are not professionals and their copy should be treated with the greatest care. Anything that is out of the ordinary, such as the idea of a man playing soccer just hours after his young wife dies, should be passed to reporters to check out, and not put straight into the paper.

Great care should also be taken with freelance reporters you do not know. When they first call up with a story, you do not really know if they are sensationally good or pathological liars who have never received a day's training in their lives. It is a sound policy to never, if you can possibly help it, run a story from a freelance you have not met. At least if you see them face to face and talk about the job, you have a chance to make some sort of judgement.

Corrections

Thomas Jefferson once said: 'Perhaps an editor might divide his paper into four chapters; heading the first, Truths; the second, Probabilities; the third, Possibilities; and fourth, Lies.'

The fifth would be corrections. Even the smallest newspaper contains thousands of facts and the process of journalism means that however skilled the staff, whatever painstaking lengths are gone to to check before printing, some errors will creep in. They should be corrected as quickly as possible. This is not an admission of weakness, as some editors seem to think, but a simple matter of honesty and better informing the reader. Anyone who denies that would clearly sooner be known as a confident liar than a journalist.

A prompt correction can also help stave off a defamation lawsuit, or at least form part of the subsequent defence. This, presumably, was the motive for the *Irish Sunday Press* running the following: 'In the edition of the *Sunday Press* dated March 18 1990 a photograph of Proinsias De Rossa TD was published with the caption "prospective monster". This should have read "prospective minister".' Similarly the English local paper which had to correct a headline on a court story: '"Father head butts his son" should have read, "Father head butts his son's attacker".'

Corrections are often best carried in some regular place, such as the foot of news in brief or where you print readers' letters. And, unless they are being carried at the point of a lawyer's writ, they merely have to recall the mistake and amend it. No need to grovel, promise you won't do it again, apologise or launch into an explanation on how it was the regular editor's night off and his assistant got a little drunk. Nor is there any need to correct tiny scraps of misinformation. Giving the wrong temperature for some far-flung foreign capital in the weather reports does not require solemn correction. Nor would I have carried the following sentence which appeared in the American paper the *Boston Globe* the day after it had carried a review of a new cartoon film: 'In our film review yesterday, statements made by Sylvester the Cat were erroneously attributed to Daffy Duck.'

Promptness is a virtue in corrections, but on a few occasions newspapers have not been deterred by the passage of time. In 1920 the *New York Times* publicly ridiculed Professor Robert Goddard, the father of space exploration, for his claim that rockets could operate in a vacuum. In its issue of 13 January it commented: 'He seems only to lack the knowledge ladled out daily in high schools.' Some 49 years later, when Apollo 11 carried the first men to the moon, the *Times* published the following: 'It is now definitely established that a rocket can function in a vacuum. *The Times* regrets its error.' The record, however, is the 199 years that elapsed between the *Observer* of London reporting the death of Mozart as having happened on 5 December 1791 and it correcting this date to the 3rd in early 1991.

Finally, being assiduous about carrying prompt corrections does not mean that as soon as someone objects to a story, you roll over like an eager-to-please puppy. Check and see if you were right or wrong, and, if the latter, then you correct it. And find out how the mistake occurred.

> *I stand before the face*
> *– There is no emptier place –*
> *Than before the absent*
> *Face of an editor of news.*

Marina Tsvetayeva 1939

14

How to Manage Staff

In my experience a newspaper is not a well-ordered democracy.

Sir Gordon Downey 1990

One night, towards the very end of the nineteenth century, James Gordon Bennett Jnr, the owner and publisher of the *International Herald-Tribune*, rose from the soft bed of his large apartment in the Champs Elysees, Paris and ordered his carriage driver to take him to the paper's offices. He was not in a good mood. His paper, he had convinced himself, was not what it should be and he was determined to do something about it.

Sudden, nocturnal visits from their brilliant but capricious employer were something that the staff of the *Herald-Tribune* were used to. They were more prepared, in fact, than Bennett could have known. They had formed a bond with his butler and the disloyal servant had an agreement with them that he would always telephone a warning to the office that Bennett was heading their way. On this occasion, however, no call came. And so a while later, into the offices burst Bennett, still clad in the red pyjamas he been wearing when he began his bedtime brooding. He was now in a cold rage. Without pausing, he delivered a brief harangue of his startled staff, itemised their alleged shortcomings, and sacked every man sitting on the right-hand side of the room.

This was no isolated example of Bennett's eccentric and arbitrary methods. On another occasion he sacked his music critic Charles Henry Meltzer for the length of his hair, and there was also The Case of the Extraordinary Telegrams. This was when he cabled William Reick, the man who ran his New York paper, to send out to Paris a particular employee. Reick cabled back that the man was 'indispensable' in New York. Bennett then asked him for a list of all such 'indispensable' members of staff and, when Reick supplied it, cabled back: 'Fire them all. I want no indispensable men working for me.'[1]

In treating staff like personal serfs, to be used and abused according to whim, Bennett has since had many imitators. But whatever the culture in your paper and your society in general (and there are many places which still offer a lot of scope for the would-be tyrant), there is no need for you to be one. This is not entirely a matter of virtue; self-interest comes into it, too. Manage people well and you will get a lot more out of them. Contented staff work better and are more inventive than those bullied, pushed, cheated, oppressed and intimidated.

Like most things in journalism, managing staff is not a matter of learning a few tricks, but of thought and honesty. Some people have an inspired gift for it, and their journalists will be ready to crawl over broken glass for them. The rest of us have to work at it, make mistakes and try and learn from them. The following points are based on what I have learnt from mine. Regrettably I did not always put them into practice.

Good management practices

Remove barriers between you and the staff

The first thing to note when visiting a newspaper is its geography. Does it have a large open-plan office where people can interact and communicate easily? Or does it have lots of small rooms? How accessible are the editor and his or her senior colleagues? Do staff have to negotiate their way past two formidable secretaries to see them? Where do the department heads work? With their staff or shut away from them?

Such things affect the relationships in a newspaper, and the relationships affect the quality of work. Editors and heads of department should sit with their staff. They can see how people work, can hear when a story breaks and, crucially, their staff can see them and will feel they are sharing the sweat of the day's rough and tumble. If you have a private office, use it as infrequently as possible and shut its door only when you have to.

Make sure you are seen to be fair

This is especially true of pay and working conditions. I have been fortunate to always work in countries and on papers where there was a general culture of fairness. On national papers in Britain (but not in the provinces) journalists are generally comfortably officed and equipped, paid well, given six week's holiday a year and treated like adults. The atmosphere is informal but businesslike, almost no one watches the clock (except to see approaching deadlines), and the journalists' own 'code' of professionalism is as much a motivator as any supervision from their bosses. And, by and large, everyone is treated equally. There are no great discrepancies between pay for people doing the same kind of job and all have a pretty good idea of what each other earn.

All this is vital. Treat and pay staff fairly and you can demand a high standard of work and dedication. But it is crucial that the fairness is visible. Newspaper offices produce enough rumours and resentments without management being deliberately furtive about pay or calculatedly preferential with staff. Treat everyone the same where possible and do so publicly.

Talk to everyone who works for you every day

Even if it is only a greeting at the beginning or end of the day, make personal contact with all your staff. You might think you don't have time – but make time, for the bigger the staff, the more important this is. Go sit on the edge of their desks, ask them how their story is going, ask for ideas, enquire how their children are, if they had a good weekend, whether their grandmother is still in hospital. Ask them anything. You may not like some of them, but that is not the point. You are not doing this for social reasons, but to make them feel that they matter.

Encourage new ideas

Good journalism is about fresh thinking, challenging conventions, debunking myths, asking the simple question that no one else has thought of; or, if they have, are too shy to speak. The journalist's hero ought to be the little boy in the Hans Christian Anderson story of the Emperor's New Clothes. This applies just as much inside the office as outside. Staff have to feel they can voice ideas, sometimes unusual ones, without being laughed at. They should be able to say, 'I know this is a bit off-the-wall, but can't we do it this way?' Or ask the simple questions, without attracting sneers. It is your job to create an atmosphere where staff can take risks with ideas and be adventurous in their thinking.

Let staff know how they are doing

Journalists have a good idea of whether they are delivering the kind of stories you want from where – or if – they appear in the paper. But you ought to give them a verdict on each story they file. If they are doing good work, your words will encourage them to do more, and if they are failing, they should be told why. Unless you tell them they are filing the wrong kinds of stories, failing to research them properly or writing them poorly, they will not know and cannot be expected to improve. And if consistent failure means you have to dismiss them, it will be much more difficult if you have said nothing about their work. They can claim – and rightly – that they had no idea their work was lacking, or why. People should know what is expected of them and if they are delivering it.

Establish rules and see that people stick to them

Your rules and procedures should be made totally clear to all staff and then enforced. These rules should cover most common situations in the office: overtime, time off, weekend or late night working. You may decide, for instance, that anyone reporting sick should do so before 10 a.m., or that all reporters out on a story should ring the news desk every two hours. But whatever your rules are, they should be clear, the same for everyone, be they high or low, and enforced impartially.

If you have to sack someone, do it quick and straight

No one but a fool or a trainee psychopath enjoys sacking staff. It is unpleasant, even if the person concerned has been idle or incessantly stupid since the day they started. It is especially painful when they have tried their best, and failed, or when economies mean people have to be fired through no fault of their own. Whatever the circumstances, tell them the news person to person, in private and in an unequivocal way. Tell them the reasons honestly. If they are being sacked for being no good, do not tell them that this is an economy measure. Do not give them the idea that there is any chance of a reprieve (unless there is), and do not say: 'Of course, if I had my way, you would be staying. This is a decision made by others.' That gives people the false hope that they may be able to launch an appeal. And never say: 'I am just as upset as you are.' This is patently untrue. After all, you still have a job and they do not.

Firing staff is probably the one part of editing where it is not a good idea to be unconventional. James Gordon Bennett may have sacked staff by telegram, but face to face is best. Humour, too, is ill-advised. Bennett once asked an editor to make a reservation at Del Monico's, the famous New York restaurant. When the man asked why, Bennett told him it was for his own farewell party. And the editor of the London *Sun* sacked his astrologer in a letter that opened: 'As you may well have foreseen ...'. All very funny to us decades later, but not to the newly jobless journalist.[2]

Finally, unless the person is being summarily dismissed for breach of contract or serious misconduct, give them some choice about their departure date and the story about their leaving that they will tell colleagues. Losing their job will be bad enough, but if you can give them some way of minimising the humiliation, then it is better for all. But check later that some outrageous version that reflects badly on you is not circulating among the rest of the staff. Nothing can poison the atmosphere in a newspaper quicker than stories of an unfair sacking.

Give bad news straight

Some of us hate giving bad news. We like pleasing people – or being thought to do so – and so we have an alarming tendency to try to apply layer upon layer of cosmetics to try and make bad news more palatable. This is never a good plan. Plain dealing is always the best policy. If, for instance, an article is no good, say so. Do not say that it is just what you were looking for but unfortunately there is not quite enough space to run it. The reporter will know this is hogwash and that if you really liked it, you would drop another piece and run their one. This applies to all other forms of bad news. People will forgive their bosses most things, but not deceitfulness.

Never blame things on 'events beyond your control'

Another ploy for those who want to court favour with their staff is to hide behind some excuse when things go wrong. If you are a department head, you blame the deputy editor; if you are the deputy editor, you blame the editor; if you are the editor, you blame the publisher; and if you are the publisher, you blame the sponsors, owners, the government or Fate. Now all these excuses may be true in many cases, but if you always blame things on events or people beyond your control, your staff will think two things. First, that you are not telling the truth. Second, that there is not much point dealing with you because clearly nothing important is *within* your control. They may as well go direct to who is in control. And that is not good for you or them.

There is a special danger in hiding behind more senior executives when you have to tell someone their story is not being used. It is generally fatal to tell them, 'the editor did not like your story'. If it is true, you will seriously undermine their confidence and open up a debate about what representations you made on their behalf. If it is not true, they are liable to discover this when they go marching off to the editor demanding that he or she think again. Very embarrassing. Only tell them of the editor's rejection of their piece if you disagree with the editor, have argued strongly for the piece and think the journalist concerned is mature enough to accept all this as part of the normal cut-and-thrust of newspapers.

Admit mistakes

Editors and department heads may sometimes behave as if they are omnipotent, but admitting mistakes and misjudgements will impress your staff even more. That way your journalists are far more likely to tell you of their errors. Such an open atmosphere will actually mean fewer, and less serious, mistakes than one where people are afraid ever to confess the slightest hitch.

Never ask staff to work longer hours than you work

The chances are that in their more bitter moments (and journalists have been known to have these) your staff think you are paid a salary of untold riches and are the possessor of scarcely credible privileges. The fact that neither is the case will not check their fevered imaginations. All the more reason not to give them any legitimate causes for resentment by taking advantage of your position. This applies to obvious things like harassment, sexual or otherwise, but, more commonly, to the hours you keep. Nothing will put their backs up more than if you require them to start early and stay late while you swan off on lengthy lunch-breaks and premature departures.

Department heads should have a rule that in a given week or month they work hours at least as long as the most industrious journalist on their staff. That way, whatever else they can criticise you for, it will not be idleness. And remember: early mornings and later in the evenings are often the best times to chat more leisurely to staff.

Never lose your temper

This is probably asking the impossible in a job like journalism. But get angry too often and you could lose a lot more than your temper. First, control – over yourself and others – as they come to wonder if you are equal to a job that affects you so much. Second, you will lose whatever good atmosphere you have built up in your office. Both will be difficult to reclaim. Besides, too-frequent outbursts tend to have a diminishing effect and in the end become comic. The day a senior editor at the *Observer* threw a typewriter out of a (thankfully open) window was probably the day his outbursts started to lose credibility. Overall, if you think the way to get the best out of people is to shout at them, then join the army.

Praise in public, criticise in private

Journalists are more sensitive than they pretend. But even if they were not, the above is still a good rule. Your shout across a crowded room telling someone they have done a good job will mean a surprising amount to them. Everyone, whether they admit it or not, likes praise and it is valued even more if there are witnesses. Similarly, a grouchy moan at them in front of others will humiliate and is likely to provoke a public, and possibly lengthy defence of their work. The way to criticise someone is in private, where they are far more likely to listen and appreciate your sensitivity. If they do not, point it out to them.

Send notes of praise

A word of praise means a lot, but a permanent memento of the occasion will mean a lot more. It takes almost no time at all to grab a piece of paper and write: 'Thanks for that great job you did on yesterday's story. I wish we had more of that kind of thing in the paper.' The recipient will be buoyed up and is almost certain to keep it – if for no other reason than against the day when they have to defend their job or look for another one.

Make sure staff understand the decision culture

On most papers around the world, the editor's decision (or indecision) is final. He or she may take advice, talk to all the staff about major decisions, but, in the end, newspapers are a dictatorship. And within each department, the section editors, to whom the authority in most matters devolves, are also dictators. If the editor wants the story done this way or that (or upside down, for that matter), then that is how it is done. Argue with him or her, shout, cry, stamp your feet and threaten to leave if you think it will do any good, but, in the end, if you make no impression then you carry out the editor's wishes. Otherwise, there is not much point in having an editor. Whether your paper's decision culture is like that or is something different, all staff should understand how it works. This saves an awful lot of time and unnecessary rowing.

Keep secrets

If you are in charge of something, secrets will come your way – from the editor, perhaps, but more especially from colleagues. In my years running various parts of various newspapers, staff told me about their financial problems, housing problems, marital problems, child problems and even their sexual problems. Twice people told me they had been diagnosed with terminal illnesses. These things are told to you as their boss because they trust you. Tell someone else, and that trust is immediately destroyed – and with it any claim you may have had on their loyalty.

Make sure staff enjoy themselves

If staff are having a good time, it will show in the paper, and the same is true if they are not. This does not mean that every night is party night in your office, but it does mean:

- Never let too much time go by between laughs in your office.
- Be as flexible as you can with people's working hours. If you do that for them, the chances are that they will do the same in return.
- Think all the time what kinds of work suit different people and make sure they are doing the tasks they enjoy best.

It is part of the social mission of every great newspaper to provide a refuge and a home for the largest possible number of salaried eccentrics.

Lord Thomson, owner of *The Times*
and *Sunday Times* of London 1961–1981

15

Technology and the Future of Journalism

The classified ads and the stock market quotations are the bedrock of the press. Should an alternative source of easy access to such diverse daily information be found, the press will fold.

Marshall McLuhan

In 1877 the American railroad tycoon Leland Stanford accepted a bet of $25,000 on the question of whether a galloping horse has at any time all four hooves off the ground. A strange gangling photographer called Edward Muybridge was hired to try and settle the matter. A few weeks later, with the aid of 24 cameras, assorted trip-wires and several breathless horses, the bet was won. For split seconds the hooves are airborne. More importantly for posterity, in discovering this, Muybridge had invented a system for recording and reproducing movement.[1]

For the next 20-odd years, as it was developed into the technology of motion pictures, it was dismissed as a rich man's plaything, a diversion without practical purpose. But by the middle of the twentieth century's first decade, it had spawned cinema houses all over the world. Soon it was gripping the imaginations and leisure time of the people of this earth like nothing had ever done before.

Then along came a man who said that he had a practical way of making these movies speak. The wise heads of the newly built Hollywood shook their heads and said it would never catch on. It would never, they were sure, replace the silent film. It took just one picture, *The Jazz Singer*, in 1928 to prove them wrong. Suddenly studios could not get their hands on the new technology fast enough and many of the actors and actresses who had mouthed and posed mute on the silent screen were out of a job. Muscular heroes had pipsqueak voices and sultry, smouldering sex symbols spoke with whiny accents you could cut with a paper knife.

Then came a thing called radio. It can never compete with the newspapers, said the wise ones; never rival the cinema. Within a decade it was doing both. Same with television. People looked at the early sets, with their vast wooden cases and tiny eight inch screens and awkward, limited programmes and declared it would never catch on.

Thus it has been with every new form of communications technology this century. Dismissed as an expensive and irrelevant toy, only to sweep the world, affect lives in ways never thought possible and leave those who could not adapt redundant in its wake, their mouths opening and closing in disbelief like those silent film stars who thought nothing could molest their security. In 1980 there was not a personal computer anywhere in the world. Launched by IBM a year later, there were nearly 280 million of them in 1995. The moral is: when it comes to the future, there are two things we can always be certain about. First, it will not be how we think it will be. Second, it will come quicker than we think.

These terrifyingly obvious platitudes are given here because a lot of journalists either don't think of them, or, if they do, imagine that they and their industry have somehow been immunised against the future. This, for any journalist under the age of 55, is a career-threatening delusion. We do not know what kind of future newspapers will have, or even if they will have one at all. What we do know is that the pace and scale of technological change is such that enormous convulsions lie ahead, and not very far ahead, and that journalists had better get a grip on them as soon as possible. The nature and existence of newspapers is too important to be left to the gadget-freaks and boffins.

Most journalists have an automatic, and perhaps healthy, suspicion of new technology. They see themselves as words people and if the scratch of goose quill pen on paper was good enough for Pushkin, then biros, typewriters, maybe even word processors should be good enough for us. We have no need, goes the argument, for anything more fancy than that. In the sense of merely recording your writing, that is true. But when it comes to disseminating that writing to a wider audience, we need the best and most efficient system that our papers can afford to reach our audience in the way and form they want to be reached.

It is, literally, our business to know what the technologies of infor-mation gathering, dissemination, printing and distribution can do now, and will be able to do next year, the year after that and so on. This is not some side issue, wherever you work. In many countries, like Russia, the press is afflicted with huge and apparently insoluble basic problems of paper costs, monopoly printing and dis-tribution. Yet the technology exists right now – admittedly at a price – to defeat, or at least drastically minimise those headaches. You will not know what those solutions are, or when they may be affordable, unless you get on the case. This chapter is about doing that, and asserting some measure of control over our futures.

Demand and supply

The history of success in newspaper publishing is the history of adapting well to new conditions of supply and demand. As you can see from these lists of the basic factors involved on the two sides of this equation, technology has a prime role in each.

Factors affecting the supply of newspapers include:

- Governmental control – Includes not only harassing, bribing (directly or by the granting or withholding of official advertising), censoring, licensing or banning newspapers; but also laws of sedition, privacy and secrecy. Major elements also are fiscal and legal measures to raise costs of papers, and hence make them too expensive for general population, such as taxes on paper, printed papers, advertisements or ownership of press.
- Legal restraints – Laws of libel, contempt of court, privacy, right of reply and freedom of information all affect the costs of producing papers and the supply of printable information to them.
- Distribution – The cost, means, technology, speed and ownership of distribution all affect how, how fast, in what quantities and at what price papers get to readers.
- Printing technology – The speed, capacity and cost of technology for both printing and setting newspapers affects the quantity that can be produced as well as their quality and cost.
- Journalistic technology – The capacity and speed of the equipment for news and picture gathering (typewriters, telephones, wire services, telegraph, fax, computer, satellites etc.) affect the speed, quality and cost of papers. Innovations in this and printing technology force up the cost of starting a competitive newspaper.
- Advertising – Availability of, and demand for, classified and display advertisements has a major impact on the cost and price of papers, as does the technical capacity of papers to reproduce drawings and photographs in ads.
- Capital and ownership – Cost of entry into the newspaper market is both a product of and a determinant in forms of ownership. Types of ownership operating (single proprietor, company, chains, multi-nationals, trusts, political party, state and sponsorships) affect not only the quantity of papers but also the freedom of the press.
- Labour force – Availability, cost and flexibility of the workforce capable of using technology is a vital factor in setting costs.

Factors affecting the demand for newspapers include:

- Literacy and education – Literacy rates, reading levels, and the degree of 'media literacy', that is, familiarity with newspaper language and layout and the way press speaks to readers.
- Democracy – The number of people who can vote, free elections, multi-party system, number of institutions open to accountability – all these affect the depth and vigour of the concept of the public's right to know.
- Markets with disposable income – The wealth of society not only affects demand for newspapers, but also for the goods that potential advertisers sell and hence the advertising market.
- Price – Newspapers are a highly perishable product with no re-sale value. In even high-income markets, they are very price sensitive.
- Competing media – The existence, or otherwise, of alternative sources of information and entertainment like radio, television, computers, satellite and cable systems all affect the demand for newspapers.
- Disposable time – Leisure time available to readers affects time they have for reading, and so consuming newspapers. Work, or lack of it, can affect this, as can other claims on their time – household duties, competing media and development of a sophisticated leisure market giving alternative ways of spending time.
- Quality of press – A press perceived to be under government control, or otherwise lacking in quality or ethics, can diminish demand.

Technology has both an obvious and a sometimes quite unexpected impact on newspapers. Clearly it was a revolutionary event for papers in 1814 when the introduction of the steam press meant that the number of copies printed per hour quadrupled. Just as important were subsequent inventions: such as the rotary press, Linotype machine, wire machine within the industry, and railway, telephone, computer outside it.

But could anyone have foreseen that the invention of shorthand writing systems should make possible the verbatim reporting of legislatures, courts etc? Or that the telegraph should lead to not only the fast transmission of news by a paper's own reporters but also the advent of news agencies and, with them, the concept of objective news reporting? Or that when in 1906 Professor Arthur Korn transmitted a picture of the German Crown Prince via photo telegraphy, that it would lead to the fax machine and the transmission of newspaper pages for printing thousands of miles away?

The effect of new technology is not always benign. Hundreds of thousands of printers around the world lost their jobs through computer-related technology in the 1980s, and the advent of every new information or entertainment medium diminishes the demand for conventional newspapers. This is the main reason why it is impossible to think of a developed country in the world where newspaper readership is rising. Radio started the process, and television, computers and multi-media have not only hugely accelerated it, they have also altered it. They have made, and are making, available not only alternative sources of information, but alternative forms – vision, movement and inter-action.

The result of these changes in the developed world is a certain amount of panic in the newspaper industry. Publishers look over their shoulders and see these new alternative information and entertainment carriers and see circulations fall for the press as a whole. The results are threefold: a loss of faith in newspapers and the journalism they carry (one of whose upshots has been the rise of 'lifestyle journalism'), the whirring state of almost constant re-design that some papers are in, and vast sums of money being poured into researching the 'newspaper of the future'. A little clear thinking is long overdue.

The starting point for this is that in a world where competing media are proliferating at an increasing rate, newspapers have to accept that, overall, circulations will decline. Individual papers may increase readership, but for the press as a whole, the numbers will go downhill. What newspapers have to do in response (apart from marketing themselves as energetically as possible and making sure they are sold at a profitable price) is adapt themselves to accommodate the new technologies and media, adapt the new technologies for their own use, and play to their strengths.

Adapting newspapers

In the United States, Western Europe and elsewhere newspapers and agencies are now both suppliers to and part-owners of such media as television, electronic publishing, computer-based information systems, and multi-media systems. Newspapers are selling the information and thinking they gather to alternative media. That is inevitable, but it has to be done with care. The price charged for this exclusive information has to be a good one, and it should be sold in short-terms deals that do not give newspaper readers a better, more convenient or more attractive way of receiving our material. Sell the archives, sell spin-offs, but do not sell access to today's news gathering until after it has been published on paper.

There are two basic futures envisioned for the newspaper of the future. One is that its content will be delivered in a new form: electronically to the reader's screen. The other is that it will use new technologies to deliver itself faster and better but still on paper. No one, thankfully, is yet at work on delivering the newspaper's content by thought transference straight to the reader's brain.

On paper

Newspapers traditionally print centrally and then distribute to readers, often via a complex chain of carriers, shops, kiosks or home deliverers. Then came fax technology which allowed printing at regional centres. And now there is a development of this which means remote-control printing at very local sites, like shops.

It is made possible by digital presses, developed in Belgium and Israel. These presses look like large photocopiers, which is very close to what they actually are. The paper's pages are produced on computer and then stored in a digital distribution centre. Digital telecommunication is then used to transmit the pages to each local digital press, which then prints them according to customer demand. These presses produce folded and stacked newspapers. Copies can be printed at any time at the press of a button.

The potential advantages are enormous. First, physical distribution over anything but the shortest of distances is eliminated, which is crucial where this is either expensive or a state monopoly or both. Local digital presses are also the definitive answer in countries where there is a state monopoly, or shortage of conventional printing presses. And they require no film, no plates, no wet chemicals and there is virtually no paper wastage. In very large countries like Russia, they would also allow national papers to deliver up-to-the-minute news over vast distances. What is produced and read in Moscow could be transmitted and read eight time zones away in Vladivostok just moments later.

Perhaps the greatest appeal of this technology is that it allows newspapers to compete in speed with other information-delivery media. With digital presses in stores, and perhaps other places like railway and metro stations, papers can give people news in just the few seconds it takes for transmission and printing. They can also, like television and radio, be constantly updating stories. And, best of all, they can do this on paper, which has all kinds of practical and cultural advantages over the computer screen.

The second on-paper option is for some version of digital press technology to be available as a printer attached to the home computers of the future. This would allow readers to receive the newspaper electronically and then choose whether they read it on screen or print it out as a physical newspaper.

On screen

The electronic newspaper has been a reality since the early 1990s. Several papers in the United States, like the *Washington Post, Los Angeles Times* and *San Francisco Chronicle* are available to computer owners with the right connections, as are *Gazeta Wyborcza* in

Poland, the *Daily Telegraph* in London and *L'unione Sarda* in Italy. All these on-screen papers use the Internet, the so-called global information highway that can connect computers all round the world. Using it, readers see pages of headlines on screen and they can jump straight to the story they want by clicking on the relevant headline. Such on-line newspapers simply by-pass the conventional printing and distribution stages. There are not only enormous cost savings, but also the problems associated with state monopolies, or shortages, of the means to print and distribute are instantly solved.

Electronic newspapers clearly need a high level of computer ownership in a country before they are viable, and some form of security so that only paying subscribers can receive them – something that has yet to be solved. They also need advertisers prepared to use them. There are special difficulties for the electronic advertiser since readers can choose what they look at and what they avoid. Two approaches to defeat this are presently used. With classified advertising, readers are given the means to state preferences, so that a reader can only receive ads for, say, second-hand Mercedes cars, two-bed apartments, sports equipment and vacations in Germany. With display advertising, the idea is to make the ads so appealing that people will want to see them. Since the technology delivers music and moving pictures, advertisers like IBM are combining words, film and sound to make enticing ads.

In the medium to long term this technology offers some extraordinary possibilities. Electronic newspapers will be able to offer coverage of almost infinite depth by linking stories to computer cuttings libraries and the extraordinary amount of background material available on other computers. In the distant future this could even include film and virtual reality. This is the technology which, with the aid of a special viewing headset like a motorcycle helmet, allows the user to 'go inside' a three dimensional world and influence it. Thus readers of the future may be able to not just read on-screen a story like the Chechnyan conflict, but also then access the latest film and 'walk' down the streets of the wrecked city.

Work is also now being done to develop the personalised newspaper. Researchers at the Media Laboratory at the Massachusetts Institute of Technology have already found a way for a reader to give a computer their preferred interests. The technology then selects and presents the available news information as a newspaper which reflects those reader preferences.

From the viewpoint of the late twentieth century, there are lots of objections to the viability of the on-screen paper and its developments. It seems unlikely to us that sufficient numbers of readers will ever want to reject the convenience of paper. And however transportable computers become – pocket calculator size, as wristwatches etc. – they seem unlikely to us ever to achieve the flexibility of the printed word. All one can say with any certainty is that the television looked an equally implausible threat to conventional media in the mid-1930s. In 1984 virtual reality was unheard of; in 1994 toys based on its technology were being given as Christmas presents to children in Japan and the United States.

Playing to newspapers' strengths

Newspapers, individually and collectively, must constantly answer one question above all others: why should anyone read us? And the answer has to be not because we are here, or because people always have read us, but this: to get information they want but cannot get elsewhere. As a newspaper consultant, I earn my living by discovering for papers the detail behind that generality and the right way to put it on paper in an attractive form. For the press overall, the seeds of the answer are in considering what newspapers can do that other media cannot do, and what can papers do better, cheaper, more attractively or conveniently.

This can be seen by comparing newspapers to television. For the majority of readers, television is how they first learn of major stories, and is often their principal source of information about the outside world. Television has also conditioned them, especially younger ones, to receiving intelligence visually. These points should both have an impact on newspapers' content and presentation. But that certainly does not mean that papers should allow television to set the agenda; for it has its limits, too. First, it only deals with things it can *show*; it needs pictures, and stories without film do not get played. It does not like handling ideas; it prefers action. Second, it is incredibly inefficient at delivering information. The contents of a half-hour news programme would, if written and printed, cover only one page of a broadsheet paper. Newspapers can give breadth, depth and deal with detail and ideas. And, which is their great advantage as an information medium, they allow readers to take in the subject of a great range of stories almost at once and then choose which ones to invest time in reading. With all other conventional information media, the consumer has no choice but to accept the producers' selections and the order they are given in. Newspapers are the only medium which allows the consumer freedom to select and sample at a glance.

Newspapers should do everything they can to emphasise, enhance and exploit this. That is why design is important. That is why good headlines are important. That is why intros are important. And that is why challenging the conventional way of taking the readers' eyes to stories is important. If newspapers had just been invented and a campaign was devised to advertise them, this selection freedom for readers is the feature that would probably be promoted.

Computer experts the world over are hard at work inventing ways computers can give the user control and participation. They call it inter-action. Newspapers have been inter-active for three centuries.

The strengths of newspapers are this cherry-picking convenience, the ability to deliver information quickly and in far more depth than broadcast media (and, because it is delivered on paper, for it to be easily stored), mobility, and low price. It is an impressive list; if someone invented the newspaper tomorrow, they would be hailed as a genius.

The implications of these strengths ought to be obvious. Newspapers should concentrate on what they can do, rather than on what other media do better. We can and should have entertainment and froth, but we should concentrate on breadth and depth of news coverage (both of which TV and radio cannot match), investigations, backgrounders, and analysis. Journalists, contrary to what some of them think, may not be able to save the world, but we can help its inhabitants make sense of it. And we can do one more thing. We can give detailed information services that will help our readers better lead their lives. The lack of them is one of the great missed opportunities of newspaper publishing.

All too often papers confine their information services to the routine and conventional, and then they are done to the bare minimum. But there is so much more that could be done. After all, the most exciting thought in newspapers is that every page starts life as white paper. You can put anything on it that you like, so what better than information services that are of direct use to readers. The services can be any listing of intelligence that lets readers plan their work, leisure, shopping, finances, or travel; or information which simply gives them a deeper understanding of anything from the weather to sport. The only things that matter are that the services are of use to readers, are clear and readable, easy to find, and reliable.

The services can cover the weather, finance, events, night life, culture, outdoor entertainment, places to visit, TV and radio, travel schedules, road closures, shopping, new markets, health, public service announcements, planning, new laws – the list is virtually endless. Sports information, especially outside North America, is a badly neglected area. The fullest possible results service should be given, plus fixtures; but there is also a lot of scope for giving match statistics beyond the simple result. In soccer, for instance, you can give attempts on goal, shots on target, fouls, corners and offsides for each side. Such coverage would soon be the talk of soccer fans. Introducing services that are of direct benefit to readers is, it seems to me, a lot better use of time and money than attempting to ape other media. Newspapers have great strengths and unique advantages. Print journalists should insist on their emphasis.

Newspapers' faith in themselves can be restored, because it should never have been abandoned in the first place. In the future, electronic media will continue to proliferate, TV channels to grow in number, on-line video systems arrive, the Internet be made easier and easier to access, the number of media competing with print expand, with readers and advertisers having more and more alternatives to papers and magazines. All this will happen and more. According to the boffins, the new technologies offer a complete toy box full of booby traps for newspapers. There is, for instance, in the Internet a spurious information democracy created whereby readers can have an infinite amount of material from every source under the sun. Media theorists, and some of their more practical disciples in the media labs around the world, now talk of 'the death of the editor', of how the world is entering an age when everyone becomes his own hunter-gatherer at the global village's information marketplace.

In reality, none but the obsessed few will make use of even a fraction of these options. The rest will need the material pre-edited and processed in some way, not least because what is available on the Internet is information raw material, straight from the source. Indeed, the real revolutionary aspect of on-line communication is that now, for the first time in history, millions of people (those with a computer, modem and the right software) can publish to the rest of the planet. There is no absolute need for an intermediary like a print publisher or broadcast facility. We are, in theory at least, all publishers now. In theory. The reality is that the sheer volume, obvious bias and variable quality of all these messages – from commercial corporations, interest groups, political parties, do-gooders, exhibitionists etc. – means that on the Internet everyone is shouting at once. This propaganda barrage (and the more potent parts of it come from the 'presentation sophisticates' with their spin doctors and PR advisers) makes a clear case for more journalism, not less of it.

However you cast the future, good journalists have a brighter future than many of those now predicting our demise. Whether information comes on paper, over the airwaves, down a fibre optic cable, over phone lines, by satellite or by thought-transference, someone has got to filter it, research it, test it, question it, and try to reliably report on the results. And who is going to do that? The universal technologist, the universal bureaucrat, the universal media academic, the universal politician, the universal business-man? Or the universal journalist?

It is said that one machine can do the work of fifty ordinary men. No machine, however, can do the work of one extraordinary man.

Tehyi Hsieh 1948

Notes

Notes to Chapter 1

1 Figures from Reporters Sans Frontières Report, 1993.

Notes to Chapter 2

1 Hearst's career is the subject of W.A. Swanborg, *Citizen Hearst*, Scribners 1961.
2 MacGahan's career is discussed in John Gross (ed.) *The Faber Book of Reportage*, Faber.

Notes to Chapter 4

1 Mort Rosenblum, *Who Stole the News?*, Wiley 1995.
2 Ibid.
3 Jay Robert Nash, *Makers and Breakers in Chicago*, Chicago Academy 1985.

Notes to Chapter 5

1 Bob Woodward and Carl Bernstein, *All The President's Men*, Quartet 1974.
2 Ibid.
3 S.J. Taylor, *Shock, Horror!*, Corgi 1981.

Notes to Chapter 6

1 Edward Behr, *Anyone Been Raped Here and Speak English?*, Hamish Hamilton 1981.
2 Mort Rosenblum, *Who Stole the News?*, Wiley 1995.
3 Reporters Sans Frontières Report, 1993.
4 Paul Sann, *The Lawless Decade*, Arco 1958.

Notes to Chapter 7

1 Paul Sann, *The Lawless Decade*, Arco 1958.
2 Pulitzer Prize Report, 1989.
3 All cases from Reporters Sans Frontières Report, 1993.
4 *Moscow Times*, August 1994.
5 Gunter Wallraff, *The Undesirable Journalist*, Pluto Press 1978.

Notes to Chapter 9

1 Howard Kurtz, *Media Circus*, Times Books 1994.

Notes to Chapter 11

1 Phillip Knightley, *The First Casualty*, Andre Deutsch 1975.

Notes to Chapter 12

1 Jay Robert Nash, *Makers and Breakers in Chicago*, Chicago Academy 1985.

Notes to Chapter 14

1 Charles Robertson, *International Herald-Tribune – The First 100 Years*, Columbia University Press 1987.
2 Peter Chippendale and Chris Howie, *Stick It Up Your Punter*, Mandarin 1992.

Notes to Chapter 15

1 Bill Bryson, *Made in America*, Secker and Warburg 1994.

Selected Bibliography

There are very few books on journalism worth reading. Official histories of newspapers tend to be public relations, not literature; editors' memoirs seem often to be written to settle old scores, drop names or justify expenses; press critiques are invariably a thoughtless recitation of the predictable outrages of the tabloids; and 'how to' volumes are compiled mostly by those whose unfitness to be employed at the top level has given them the time to write the book. However, there are honourable exceptions. Here are some of the more readily available.

Collections of reporting

The *Bedside Guardian* series is a treasure trove of good, sharp work, as are the compilations of the year's best offerings from *Observer* writers, now, alas, no longer published. Disappointingly little good reporting ever makes it into hard covers, which is why *The Faber Book of Reportage*, edited by John Gross, is so valuable. Some of the best passages, as opposed to whole articles, ever captured are to be found in The First Casualty (Andre Deutsch, 1975), Phillip Knightley's survey of war reporting. This book also contains many thoughtful observations on the trade. More likely to be collected are the more polemical or humorous writers, and the best examples of each approach are found in *Distant Voices* by John Pilger (Vintage, 1992) and anything by P.J. O'Rourke.

Reporters' memoirs

Foreign correspondents tend to hog the limelight here, since references to Ho Chi Minh city and Dushanbe obviously make for more glamorous reading than tales from the Manchester magistrates courts. Among the best are *Anyone Here Been Raped and Speaks English ...* by Edward Behr (New English Library, 1978), and *Point of Departure* by James Cameron (Granada, 1969). The life and techniques of a top tabloid reporter are described in helpful detail in *Exposed!* by Gerry Brown (Virgin, 1995).

Press critiques

Almost all of these are written about the popular press by academics or quality newspaper editors and writers, both of which groups seem solely preoccupied with sniffily disapproving of what they find. You search in vain for anyone with a more complicated diagnosis of the accumulated lies and distortion than rampant commercialism combined with immorality.

A partial exception is *Shock, Horror!* by S.J. Taylor (Corgi, 1991). Americans do this kind of thing better. *Media Circus* by Howard Kurtz (Times Books, 1994) is a sharp survey of the values and foibles of modern US journalism, and *Who Stole the News?* by Mort Rosenblum (Wiley, 1995) is an ex-Associated Press correspondent's thoughtful reflections on news.

'How to' books

The world is still waiting for a really intelligent manual of reporting. In the meantime, *All The President's Men* (Quartet, 1974), Bob Woodward and Carl Bernstein's account of their Watergate reporting, is easily the best description of the attitudes and some of the techniques essential to the high-quality reporter. As for books on writing, these are invariably written by those who have a tin ear when it comes to a rhythmic sentence or original phrase. Turn instead to reading examples of good writing and absorbing its virtues that way. If you must have a manual by your side, choose *Waterhouse on Newspaper Style* by Keith Waterhouse (Penguin, 1993). For copy and picture editing, the best books are still *Handling Newspaper Text* and *Pictures on a Page* both by Harold Evans (Heinemann).

Index